# PHILOSOPHY
# OF ANTIFASCISM

# Living Existentialism

**Series Editors:**

T Storm Heter, East Stroudsburg University

LaRose T. Parris, Lehman College, The City University of New York

Devin Zane Shaw, Douglas College

Existentialism is a living, practical philosophy, engaged in contemporary events and responsive to other currents of philosophy across the globe. It can be instrumental to individuals' understanding of themselves as well as to examinations of political, societal, and ecological phenomena.

This series focuses on creative, generative scholarship that expands discussions of existentialism in order to foster an intellectual space for articulating the diverse lineages of existentialism—from Beauvoir's feminist philosophy, to the anticolonial, black existentialism of thinkers like Frantz Fanon and Angela Davis, who composed their views of freedom, self, and other from the lived experience of racism and colonialism.

Existentialism has often been miscategorized as a European tradition, limited by the gravitational pull of a few thinkers. Part of the work of this series is to dismantle this incorrect impression of where existentialism comes from and what its potential is. Existential thought offers a valuable vocabulary for expressing the lived perspectives of colonized, Indigenous, and othered peoples. As such, it is increasingly relevant to the ongoing struggle for human freedom the world over.

### Titles in the Series

# PHILOSOPHY OF ANTIFASCISM

## *Punching Nazis and Fighting White Supremacy*

### Devin Zane Shaw

ROWMAN & LITTLEFIELD

INTERNATIONAL

London • New York

Published by Rowman & Littlefield International, Ltd.
6 Tinworth Street, London SE11 5AL, United Kingdom
www.rowmaninternational.com

Rowman & Littlefield International, Ltd. is an affiliate of
Rowman & Littlefield
4501 Forbes Boulevard, Suite 200, Lanham, Maryland 20706, USA
With additional offices in Boulder, New York, Toronto (Canada), and
London (UK)
www.rowman.com

**British Library Cataloguing in Publication Information**
A catalogue record for this book is available from the British Library

ISBN: HB 978-1-78661-557-2
ISBN: PB 978-1-78661-558-9

**Library of Congress Cataloging-in-Publication Data**

Names: Shaw, Devin Zane, author.
Title: Philosophy of antifascism : punching Nazis and fighting white supremacy / Devin
    Shaw.
Lanham, Maryland : Rowman & Littlefield International, 2020. | Series: Living existentialism
    | Includes bibliographical references and index. | Summary: "Drawing a line of intellectu-
    al heritage between French philosophy and antifascist practice, this book provides new,
    incisive interpretations of Simone de Beauvoir's existentialism to make the case for a
    broader militant movement against fascism"— Provided by publisher.
Identifiers: LCCN 2019057204 (print) | LCCN 2019057205 (ebook) | ISBN 9781786615572
    (hb) | ISBN 9781786615589 (pb) | ISBN 9781786615596 (epub)
Subjects: LCSH: Fascism—Philosophy. | Anti-fascist movements. | Beauvoir, Simone de,
    1908–1986—Political and social views.
Classification: LCC JC481 .S476 2020 (print) | LCC JC481 (ebook) | DDC 321.9/4—dc23
LC record available at https://lccn.loc.gov/2019057204
LC ebook record available at https://lccn.loc.gov/2019057205

*The question is not about the weapon,*
*but the spirit in which you use it.*

—Henry David Thoreau,
"A Plea for Captain John Brown" (1859)

# CONTENTS

# FOREWORD

## T Storm Heter and LaRose T. Parris

The inaugural text of this series, Living Existentialism, provocatively asks, "What human being of sound moral and political conscience would *not* punch a Nazi?" Indeed, one may readily supplant white supremacist, alt-right, Ku Klux Klan member, settler-colonialist, anti-Semite, or fascist with Nazi, for Devin Zane Shaw's philosophy of antifascism cogently demonstrates the ideological, philosophical, and methodological sites of confluence among these inherently anti-egalitarian groups.

Drawing on the ideas of Simone de Beauvoir, Aimé Césaire, Glen Coulthard, W. E. B. Du Bois, Frantz Fanon, and Jacques Rancière, Shaw outlines how the existentialist thought of Beauvoir, Fanon, and Sartre—in particular—reveals their shared egalitarian vision *and* mission. He shows that with respect to antifascism, black political thought, existentialism, and Indigenous political thought intersect. The writings and activism of these diverse traditions reveal consistency in both words and deeds, attesting to the veracity of Shaw's thesis: people of conscience must match the Nazis' discursive and physical force blow by blow, never shying away from skirmishes on the page or, equally important, on the streets. In the wake of the Christchurch mosque shooting in New Zealand on March 15, 2019, and the ongoing threat of transnational, white supremacist violence, it is important that a living philosophy orient us toward the question of retaliatory violence.

Shaw reminds us that this is a heady proposition, since the majority of the Left view "violence" as simultaneously counterproductive and degenerative. To this, Shaw urges readers to consider three troublesome, oft overlooked realities: (1) civil society's role in excluding particular groups from inclusion therein, (2) that antifascist activists do not aspire to the same reformist objectives as mainstream liberal groups, and (3) that the Far Right *is* swayed by antifascist activist organizing.

Punching a Nazi, then, becomes a lived, tangible expression of existential liberation and equality. Shaw provides a strong argument for de-platforming the alt-right. Such arguments are increasingly important as we witness digital harassment, doxing, and most blatantly, ongoing physical violence against communities of color, including Indigenous communities in the United States, Canada, and globally. The punch represents the antifascist's intrinsic freedom to defend human identity from ontological negation stemming from fascist/white supremacist, racist/ableist hierarchies, all while declaring one's inalienable right to self-defense. The blow also initiates an attack on fascist ideals that distort our common humanity and destroy the real possibility of mutual understanding. As Shaw demonstrates, the blow may be physical or discursive; in either form it allows people of conscience to take a stand against the forces that are right now plotting and scheming our collective downfall.

Thus Shaw's work is both timely *and* necessary, for we are witnessing the rise of autocratic, anti-egalitarian, and antihumanist regimes in the Global North, South, East, and West. On-the-ground antifascist organizing is necessary to undermine the Far Right—that is our political reality. Against this reality, we can ask of a living philosophy that it orient us toward modern forms of violence like synagogue, church, and mosque shootings, oppression of marginalized communities, and digital harassment. The philosophy of antifascism is a dialogue among decolonial, anticapitalist, and egalitarian thinkers. Thus, as Shaw aptly demonstrates, existentialist thinking spans the psychological, ontological, and the political.

The agenda of *Philosophy of Antifascism* is clear: we are implored to work toward the defeat of fascism in North America and across the globe. In this struggle, philosophy can ask the Marxian question of whether our theorizing has merely "interpreted the world, in various ways" or sought to change it. Antifascist organizers don't need the blessing of philosophers, but philosophers need to consider why they aren't more invested in antifascist organizing. A good start is reading and reacting to Simone de Beauvoir's thoughts on oppression, which provide a bridge between Marxist, existential, feminist, and decolonial approaches. She shows how oppressive violence divides the world into those who do and do not have "the possibility of an open future." Unlike liberal gestures of neutrality, the existential approach to politics requires a basic commitment to human freedom, understood as the concrete opposition to racism, colonialism, sexism, and homophobia.

While Sartre spoke of the impossibility of ethics, Beauvoir and Fanon pursued the theoretical basis for a political and ethical opposition to fascism, racism, sexism, and colonialism. Years earlier, in the United States, Du Bois offered a critique of whiteness, colonialism, and capitalism that anticipated European existentialist thought. Shaw analyzes "The Souls of White Folk" (1910) and *Darkwater* (1920), showing the relevance of these texts to today's fight against the alt-right.

As the late, great Robert Nesta Marley sagely reminds us, "They don't want to see us live together, all they want us to do is keep on killing one another. . . . They don't want us to unite, all they want us to do is keep on fussing and fighting."[1] While Marley was describing the hegemonic desires of antiblack colonial forces, Shaw reveals to us that these settler-colonialists share the same ideologies and tactics as fascists and Nazis who aim to eliminate black, brown, red, yellow, and "othered" humanity and then crush any who remain into their own subjugated image, only dispensing and sharing power with those whites whom they deem worthy.

If there were ever a time to promote a philosophy of antifascism, that time is now. Declaring that "existentialism is an antifascism," Shaw revises Sartre's oft cited quote, "existentialism is a humanism,"[2] to underscore how Beauvoir's thought on the ambiguity of existence urges readers to consider the ways in which the meaning of existence must be continually apprehended. To do this, one must appreciate how egalitarianism allows us to grasp that human existence, in all its varied forms, must be valued and protected from antihumanist philosophies, like fascism, that seek to crush "undeserving" groups into submission and oblivion.

Here is the Left's rallying cry. Let us read Shaw's work and heed the call!

## NOTES

1. Bob Marley and the Wailers, "Top Rankin," recorded January–February 1979, track 3 on *Survival*, Tuff Gong, 33 1/3 rpm.

2. Jean Paul Sartre, *Existentialism Is a Humanism*, trans. Carol Macomber (New Haven, CT: Yale University Press, 2007).

# ACKNOWLEDGMENTS

I began this book in the summer of 2016 as a short study examining how Jacques Rancière might conceive of emancipatory violence. In my previous book, *Egalitarian Moments*, I had drawn a number of parallels between Beauvoir, Sartre, and Rancière, but I had not yet considered if there might be some way, which initially seems paradoxical, to consider emancipatory violence in Rancière's particularly egalitarian terms. At the time, I figured this would require drawing parallels to the anarchist anthropologist Pierre Clastres. As the reader will quickly discover, a certain sociohistorical conjuncture would soon give concrete reality to my conjectures, and soon the present study would take on its current form. Along the way, I presented portions or early drafts of this book to a number of audiences: parts of chapter 3 to the colloquium series at Memorial University and the Appalachian State University Philosophy Club in Fall 2016, and a much more polished draft to the Canadian Society for Continental Philosophy in Fall 2018; early drafts of chapter 2 to "Actualities," a conference organized by radical students in Ottawa, and the North American Sartre Society Meeting in 2018; the first draft of chapter 4 to the 2018 meeting of the Radical Philosophy Association; and, finally, parts of chapters 1 and 5 at the Diverse Lineages of Existentialism II and the Caribbean Philosophical Association in the summer of 2019. An earlier version of chapter 3 is, as

I write this, forthcoming in *Parrhesia: A Journal of Critical Philosophy*. I developed some of the ideas in sections 4.3 and 5.3 in two short publications: my review of Martin Breaugh et al., *Thinking Radical Democracy*, in *Symposium,* January 26, 2016, and "We Settlers Face a Choice: Decolonization or White Supremacy," in *Anthro{dendum}*, February 28, 2019.

I began this book—my third—as a precariously employed academic, and I conclude it with a permanent position. It is important to recognize how my writing and research were enabled by grants from professional development funds won through collective bargaining. Over the years, I've attended numerous conferences to present my work, and this wouldn't have been possible without funding from these associations, especially the Association of Part-Time Professors of the University of Ottawa. One of the biggest threats to academic freedom is the precariousness of work for many junior scholars—and an injury to one is an injury to all.

Unlike my other two books, this one involved many people in its development. I wouldn't have completed this manuscript without the camaraderie, criticism, and support of many dedicated academics, organizers, and, of them, a few who manage to balance being both. Naming a few of you could inadvertently dox you, so I've decided to pay my debts to you at a different time. Others I am able to thank publicly. Frankie Mace, my editor, George Ciccariello-Maher, and the still anonymous but enthusiastic Reviewer 2 helped shape this book in innumerable ways. I'd also like to acknowledge the work of my coeditors of the series Living Existentialism, of which this book is the first entry: T Storm Heter and LaRose T. Parris.

There are, of course, many others who deserve recognition: Bill Angelbeck, Kyle Boggs, Mark Brown, Jakub Burkowicz, Shane Burley, Joseph Carew, Andrew Dobbyn, Charlene Elsby, Matt Eshleman, Geraldine Finn, Wes Furlotte, Kate Kirkpatrick (for clearing up some ambiguities about translations of Beauvoir), Thomas Meagher, Sam Menefee-Libey, Peter Monet, Marie-Eve Morin, Jovian Radheshwar, Rowland "Enáēmaehkiw" Keshena Robinson, Alexander Reid Ross, Dane Sawyer, Edrie Sobstyl, Joseph Trullinger, Sarah Vitale, and Deniz, Grey, Kevin, Nyx, Stefan, and Santi. I owe a few others more specific debts: Rick Elmore, Peter Gratton, and Jake Jackson should be noted for their hospitality when I needed places to stay while traveling, as should John and Heather, who not only let me crash at their place but sent me off with a stack of records (some hard to find) from a number of remarkable North Carolina musicians. Austin Hayden invited me to discuss this material on the podcast *Owls at Dawn*. Todd May graciously commented on an earlier draft of my criticism of his work on nonviolence. I am also thankful that I had the opportunity to develop the ideas presented in chapter 5 formally and informally in discussions with my friend and sometimes coauthor Veldon Coburn and former colleague Zoe Todd. Iain Macdonald checked and corrected my translations of Rancière in chapter 4. Matthew N. Lyons was kind enough to comment on my adoption and use of the three-way fight in this work. Nick Estes pointed me toward the work of Kevin Bruyneel, and Kevin kindly shared his research with me in advance of publication. Finally, this book wouldn't be possible without the support of my family and especially my main comrade Kylie, who's been there through all kinds of major changes, especially over the last two years.

I started writing this book for self-clarification. It became part of an ongoing dialogue with Matthew McLennan and J. Moufawad-Paul. I hope that others find it useful as well—though I hope even more that someday in an antifascist, emancipated society, people would only read it as a curiosity of a bygone era.

This book was written in part on the unceded territory of the Algonquin people, and in part on unceded territories of the Musqueam, Squamish, Tsleil-Waututh, and Qayqayt peoples.

# 1

# A PHILOSOPHY OF ANTIFASCISM

On January 20, 2017, white nationalist Richard Spencer—who incidentally coined the term *alt-right*—was punched by an anonymous antifascist during an interview with the Australian Broadcasting Company on the streets of Washington, DC. The moment went viral, and almost immediately, "punching nazis" became the subject of public debate. Within academic philosophy, if not within broader academic circles, antifascism is acknowledged to be a powerful social force but one that partisans of "civility" have sought to funnel into established mechanisms and institutions of political representation. From "leading ethicists" (as *Newsweek* put it) to Noam Chomsky, academic philosophy has seemingly united toward this end:

1. "Violence begets violence. Civil society is predicated on civil discourse. This means that we use language, argument and persuasion to make our positions known—not a fist" (Aine Donovan, quoted in Schonfeld 2017).
2. "Violence will *only* hurt the Trump resistance" (Chenoweth 2017, my emphasis).
3. "As for Antifa, it's a minuscule fringe of the Left, just as its predecessors were. It's a major gift to the Right, including the militant Right, who are exuberant" (Chomsky, quoted in Nelson 2017).

Each of these judgments is debatable. The first fails to recognize the role of state power and material means in shaping who has access to so-called civil society, a process already succinctly described in Herbert Marcuse's essay "Repressive Tolerance" (Marcuse 1969); the second mistakenly assumes that antifascist organizing has similar goals to the liberal, reformist, or Democratic #resistance; the third ignores the Far Right's own publicly voiced frustration at the power and presence of antifascist street-level mobilization.

In what follows, I will outline a philosophy of antifascism. As Mark Bray argues in *Antifa: The Anti-Fascist Handbook*, "antifascism is a legitimate political tradition growing out of a century of global struggle" (Bray 2017, xiii). We can expect that such a movement would have philosophical exponents, but it is important to stress just how prevalent antifascism is in the French and German philosophical traditions. There are in this tradition, as is well known, literal card-carrying Nazis such as Martin Heidegger. But if we restrict ourselves to philosophers who lived during the rise, the seizure of power, and the collapse of fascism in Europe, from the 1920s to the 1940s, the list of antifascists is impressive: numerous Marxists, numerous anarchists, the Frankfurt School, Simone Weil, Georges Bataille (though his analyses sometimes amount to *leering* at fascism), and existentialists such as Jean-Paul Sartre, Simone de Beauvoir, and Albert Camus. When we expand our scope beyond the confines of the European philosophical canon, we must include, among others, W. E. B. Du Bois and Aimé Césaire.

I refer to *a* philosophy of antifascism because I have chosen a narrow selection of these philosophers. Other philosophies of antifascism could readily be written and ought to be. But I have chosen to look at the existentialist Simone de Beauvoir (along with, at critical junctures, Jean-Paul Sartre and Frantz Fanon) and the contemporary French radical philosopher Jacques Rancière for their shared commitment to egalitarianism. As I will discuss in chapter 3, the Far Right explicitly rejects human equality; it holds—obviously incorrectly—that there are some human beings who are naturally superior to others. Theirs is a world of stark inequality, hierarchy, and violent domination not only in terms of race but also gender and ability. A firm commitment to egalitarianism is already an antifascism.

## 1.1. THE THREE-WAY FIGHT

Yet we cannot categorize the opposition between antifascism and fascism in the terms of a binary opposition. Antifascism is involved in a "three-way fight" (see figure 1.1). The concept of the three-way fight was introduced by antifascists as a tool to analyze and critique efforts by the Far Right to recruit from antiglobalization movements or form red-brown alliances in opposition to capitalism. This reflection was occasioned by the presence and interest of Far Right factions in antiglobalization actions such as the anti-WTO "Battle in Seattle" in late 1999. As Matthew N. Lyons summarizes,

> The concept of fascism as a right-wing revolutionary force has spawned the idea that we are facing a "three-way fight" between fascism, conventional global capitalism, and (at least potentially) leftist revolution. This approach is an improvement over wide-

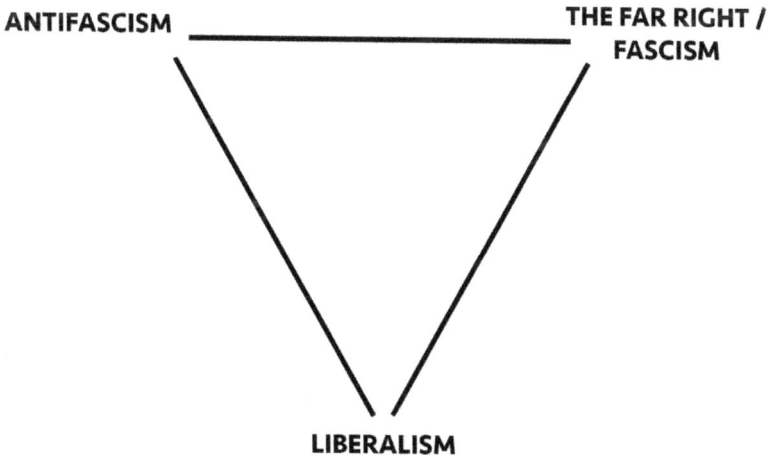

**ANTIFASCISM** —————————————— **THE FAR RIGHT / FASCISM**

**LIBERALISM**

**Figure 1.1.** **The Three-Way Fight**

spread dualistic models that try to divide all political players between the "forces of oppression" and the "forces of liberation." As some radical antifascists have pointed out for years, "my enemy's enemy" is not necessarily my friend. (Lyons 2018, 260)

Unlike some orthodox Marxist interpretations that tend to treat fascism as merely the most reactionary elements of capital, the contributors to volumes such as *My Enemy's Enemy* (Anti-Fascist Forum 2003) or *Confronting Fascism* (Hamerquist et al. [2002] 2017) contend that contemporary fascist groups must be considered as potentially revolutionary anticapitalist or, more accurately, antibourgeois movements. We will return to this point below.

## 1.1.1. Demarcating Antifascism and Liberalism

First, however, I want to demarcate a split within antifascism itself, between militant antifascism and liberal antifascism. This demarcation transforms what was previously a binary opposition between antifascism and fascism into a three-way fight between antifascism, liberalism, and the Far Right, or fascism. I will define each in turn. Let us begin by looking at figure 1.1, where I have drawn what I will call a *line of adjacency* between antifascism and liberalism: they are adjacent insofar as they share a commitment to egalitarianism. And along this line of adjacency, we will attempt to demarcate the differences between the two, while the Far Right will seek to conflate them. For example, it is fairly common to find arguments, formulated among the Far Right, that conflate and decry tepid parliamentarian liberalism as socialism or communism. The purpose of conflation is obvious: it is a "metapolitical" strategy to frame political conflict in terms that pull mainstream discourses to the right.[1] By situating the parliamentarian Left as the so-called radical limit of political possibility, this kind of conflation attempts to stifle more radical alternatives within our social and political imagination.

By contrast, we must demarcate the line between antifascism and liberalism. J. Moufawad-Paul uses the term *demarcation* to signal the militant philosophical practice of drawing clear and decisive lines between competing interpretations available in "the zones of praxis through which it cuts" (Moufawad-Paul 2019, 192). One such case of demarcation involves the concept that forms the line of adjacency between antifascism and liberalism: egalitarianism. As I will explore in chapter 3, through the work of Jacques Rancière, there is a fundamental difference between what Todd May characterizes as "active equality" and "passive equality": the former involves dynamic collective practices or direct action that combats oppression and domination, while the latter signifies "the creation, preservation, or protection of [formal or legal] equality by governmental institutions" (May 2008, 3). Accordingly, while militant antifascism demands direct action, "liberal antifascism" funnels resistance toward institutionalized forms of political representation (thus Chenoweth 2017). On the one hand, liberal antifascism defines its opposition to fascism in relation to these institutional forms. For example, the fascist's belief in white supremacy contravenes the liberal principle that in choosing principles of justice, individuals should not be granted advantage or disadvantage for circumstances beyond their control. On the other hand, the liberal antifascist opposes fascism but adheres to "a faith in the inherent power of the public sphere to filter out fascist ideas, and in the institutions of government to forestall the advancement of fascist politics" (Bray 2017, 172). As much as Chomsky identifies with anarchism, in my view, his recent remarks on antifascism fall squarely within liberal antifascism. In any case, the purpose of demarcation, in examining the adjacency between antifascism and liberalism, is twofold. First, against the slander of fascists and the Far Right, we demarcate antifascism and liberalism in order to force open the terrain of a radical, militant left beyond Left parliamentarianism. And then we demarcate the two to prepare the terrain for movement building. When the liberal antifascist is frustrated by the repeated failures of the so-called marketplace of ideas to filter out fascist ideas and of state power to curb the violence attendant to fascist mobilization, a principled and militant antifascist movement offers a sharp rebuke to the competing opportunisms of liberalism and the Far Right.

## 1.1.2. Demarcating Antifascism and Fascism

But if liberal antifascists remain reticent, we must examine their reasons. Thus we must shift our attention to the line of adjacency I have drawn, only hesitantly, between antifascism and fascism. Both movements could be considered insurrectionary insofar as they challenge the state's (de jure) monopoly on legitimate violence. I have chosen to designate this line of adjacency as *insurrectionary* rather than *revolutionary* because I do not think that any Far Right movement is truly revolutionary: they all might propagate an anti-bourgeois culture, but they are not anticapitalist—indeed, history has shown that the bourgeoisie will ally with fascism against revolutionary leftist movements.[2] Therefore we must demarcate between what are two types of insurrectionism. The liberal conflates the two. This conflation is at the basis of what is commonly called the "horseshoe theory" of politics. Recall that introductory-level discussions of politics often place different ideologies on a spectrum from left to right, with anarchism and communism on the far left and fascism on the far right; horseshoe theory merely bends the spectrum (hence the name) so that the extremes "meet" at the points of the heel. The Far Right exploits the liberal reliance on horseshoe theory when it attempts to brand "antifa as the real fascists" after physical confrontations between the Far Right and antifascists; this strategy aims to normalize Far Right viewpoints as discursively respectable while exploiting liberal antifascism's aversion to insurrectionary violence to focus condemnation on militant antifascist tactics. Ideologically the conflation between antifascism and fascism is baseless. There are, by contrast, practical considerations that merit demarcation.

The concept of the three-way fight was introduced to criticize efforts of fascists (and others on the Far Right) to recruit from and form alliances with antiglobalization movements. Antifascist theorists such as Don Hamerquist suggest that these efforts contradict the Communist International's line, developed in the mid-1930s and still maintained by some orthodox Marxists, which defines fascism "as the open terrorist dictatorship of the most reactionary, most chauvinistic and most imperialist elements of finance capital" (Dimitrov 1935). Observing the opposition of the Far Right to globalization, Hamerquist writes, "I think that fascism has the potential to become a mass movement with a substantial and genuine element of revolutionary anti-capitalism. . . . The real danger presented by the emerging fascist movements and organizations is that they might gain a mass following among potentially insurgent workers and declassed strata through an historic default of the left" (Hamerquist 2002, 28–29). Hamerquist is correct to identify how fascist movements at the time were willing to enter a leftist insurrectionary movement to recruit and form alliances. However, I do not believe that these efforts provide enough evidence to support the claim that fascism presents a threat as a reactionary but "genuine" form of anticapitalism.

To advance our point of demarcation, I contend that antifascism is anticapitalist while fascism is, as J. Sakai points out, "anti-bourgeois but not anti-capitalist" (Sakai [2002] 2017, 122). Marx satirizes and critiques bourgeois political culture in the following terms: "What is the basis of a partial and merely political revolution? It is part of civil society emancipating itself and attaining universal supremacy, a particular class by virtue of its special situation undertaking the general emancipation of society. This class emancipates the whole of society *but only on the condition that the whole of society is in the same position as this class*, for example, that is has or can easily acquire money and education" (Marx [1844b] 1967, 36, my emphasis). In other words, bourgeois political culture ("civil society") represents itself as universal emancipation of humanity *on the impossible condition*, given that capital accumulation is premised on the expropriation of surplus-value, that the whole of society could possess the material means of the bourgeoisie. Marx called this partial and political revolution of the bourgeoisie "utopian" because the scale of capital accumulation that it unleashed is unsustainable and it is "utopian" to believe that it could be sustained. But as Du Bois argues, the invention of "personal whiteness" in modern forms of white supremacy prepared the ideological grounds for the formation of a white, European, global hegemony that coalesced between the white bourgeoisie, petty bourgeoisie, and working classes that reinforced bourgeois political power. In entering this hegemonic bloc, the white middle and working classes received a "public and psychological wage" that rewarded them with some degree of class mobility and political access (Du Bois [1935] 2007, 573). The insurrectionary opposition to bourgeois society splits along two lines. The Far Right mobilizes to reentrench or protect the wages of whiteness, which are jeopardized when capitalism goes into crisis. By contrast, on the Left, antifascism is part of a broader anticapitalist movement that seeks to overthrow the conditions of capital accumulation.

### 1.1.3. Settler-State Hegemony: Liberalism and White Settlerism

In order to more fully assess the insurrectionary character of fascism, we will need to first propose working definitions of the Far Right and fascism. One might expect a philosopher to conceptually distill varieties of fascism into a succinct concept. However, I find that this philosophical procedure is often introduced in bad faith to alibi fascists who do not fetishize its German or Italian forms—not to mention that it is entirely unhelpful for understanding how Far Right and fascistic discourses shift in order to gain credibility or normalize their beliefs within broader social discourses and conflict. Thus I opt for working definitions that characterize the Far Right and fascism as social forces.

In *Dusk of Dawn*, while reflecting on how racism persists in American society, Du Bois writes that "perhaps it is wrong to speak of it [race] at all as a 'concept' rather than as a group of contradictory forces, facts and tendencies" (Du Bois [1940] 2007, 67). To interpret racism as a complex set of social practices, attitudes, and tendencies cuts against the philosophical desire for conceptual simplicity; it leaves all kinds of room for whataboutism, red herrings, and false equivocations, but then we need also understand these fallacies as ways to interfere with the opposition to complex and systematic forms of racism and oppression present *still* in our societies (see section 2.3.1). Likewise, I will consider fascism as a set of social forces, facts, and tendencies rather than attempting to define it once and for all. On the one hand, defining the Far Right or fascism in overly narrow, static terms serves to alibi forms of these forces that self-consciously attempt to reframe their goals in slightly less offensive and genocidal terms. On the other hand, defining fascism as a set of social forces allows us to consider its relations to other social forces and material conditions—in the case of the United States and Canada, settler-colonialism.

I have chosen working definitions of the terms *Far Right* and *fascism* from Lyons's recent book *Insurgent Supremacists: The U.S. Far Right's Challenge to State and Empire* (2018). I have done so for three reasons. First, the book supplies a wealth of detail on Far Right currents in the United States including neo-Nazis, Christian Identity and Christian reconstructionism, the Patriot movement, the alt-right (with some discussion of men's rights activism and the so-called alt-lite), and the LaRouche network. Second, Lyons analyzes the ideological details of these movements with a degree of "methodological empathy" (a term borrowed from a liberal historian of fascism, Roger Griffin [1991, especially 26–55]) to reconstruct how these movements articulate social critique and political vision among themselves. Far from eliminating critical distance from his account, Lyons's use of methodological empathy allows him to reconstruct the terms and arguments they use to mainstream and normalize their Far Right views—so that we can better identify them in political and ideological struggle. Then, drawing on Hamerquist and Sakai, he emphasizes how contemporary Far Right movements and fascism conflict at least potentially with capitalist—below, I will argue *bourgeois*—political and cultural power. Lyons defines

- the Far Right as "political forces that (a) regard human inequality as natural, inevitable, or desirable and (b) reject the legitimacy of the established political system" (Lyons 2018, ii); and
- fascism as "a revolutionary form of right-wing populism, inspired by a totalitarian vision of collective rebirth, that challenges capitalist political and cultural power while promoting economic and social hierarchy" (Lyons 2018, 253).

These working definitions require unpacking. First, they reiterate our thesis that the Far Right and fascism are by definition anti-egalitarian. Hence my belief that an explicit commitment to egalitarianism girds antifascist movements against fascist creep (see Ross 2017). Second, on these terms, we observe that all fascist movements are Far Right though not all Far Right movements are fascistic. Lyons admits that these boundaries are fluid, though they have analytic value. He argues that the concept of the Far Right sidesteps a number of problems that plague the concept of fascism. While "there is no more definitional consensus" with one rather than the other, the term *Far Right* is less emotionally loaded than *Fascism*. It is also less controversial to label groups that promote economic and social hierarchy on grounds other than race or nationality as Far Right than it is as fascist. Furthermore, some contemporary Far Right groups "repudiate classical fascism's goal of a strong state, which means some scholars of fascism would consider them borderline examples at best" (Lyons 2018, x). Third, we should note that some Far Right movements also display an adherence to palingenetic ideologies (ideologies of collective rebirth), though Lyons does not include this aspect in his definition of the Far Right (though this does not imply that he excludes this possibility in his definition).

Finally, drawing on the insights of Hamerquist and Sakai, Lyons differentiates between system-loyal conservatism and the Far Right, the latter of which rejects the legitimacy of established political institutions. I think, methodologically speaking, that it is important to take Far Right ideologies at their word in interpreting how they talk among themselves. However, we must also supplement the use of methodological empathy by comparing the explicit views of the Far Right against a leftist account of the political economy of the conditions that make Far Right mobilization possible. Lyons, for example, argues that "the U.S. far right emerged and developed both in conjunction with and in reaction against the rise of the neoliberal political system" from the 1970s onward.[3] Unlike system-loyal conservatives, the Far Right, as a populist movement, coalesces around opposition to neoliberal economic policies though they incorrectly ascribe the causes of economic crisis to conspiracy theories about shadowy elites (in often anti-Semitic terms), civil rights activism, and immigration. But opposition to neoliberalism does not explain how the Far Right became insurrectionary. Kathleen Belew (2018) contends that insurrectionism on the Right was driven in part by white supremacist veterans of the Vietnam War who sought to militarize the Far Right toward revolutionary—though in our terms, insurrectionary and antibourgeois—ends. These are two recent historical factors that must be accounted for. But we must also consider, for those of us who live, work, and write within the United States or Canada, how the centuries-long historical duration of settler-colonialism influences the palingenetic ideologies of the Far Right: they all desire the collective rebirth of a white homeland within a project of settler-colonialism that they perceive, incorrectly, to have failed. Lyons acknowledges the implicit acceptance of settler-colonial ideology in the Patriot movement (see Lyons 2018, 52–55), but he does not stipulate settler-colonialism in his definitions of the Far Right or fascism in the United States. Due to this omission, he overstates the antisystemic character of the Far Right.[4]

Thus we must outline an account of settler-colonialism in order to explain the recent emergence of the Far Right and fascism in the United States and Canada. I will argue that settler-colonial hegemony is constituted in a dialectic between a liberal-democratic or bourgeois project that represents the interests of capital and a project of white settlerism that helped drive the colonial seizure of Indigenous lands and, in contemporary forms such as the Far Right and fascist movements, now seeks to re-entrench whiteness within the settler-colonial project. In terms of the three-way fight, settler-state hegemony provides the line of adjacency between liberalism and the Far Right. A philosophy of antifascism must not conflate the roles of liberalism and the white supremacy of the Far Right in settler-colonialism. We must demarcate their ideological differences while excavating their common roots in the political economy of the settler-colonial project.

Liberalism legitimates state power as the realization of objective right, which means on these terms that a legitimate liberal institution must present itself as a neutral arbiter between the competing interests of individuals. But the realization of objective right has two connotations. On the one hand, given that the state attempts to uphold formal equality between individuals, some groups who have been barred access to social and political institutions have been able to demonstrate that the state has instituted barriers to their access. On the other hand, as I will examine in more detail in chapter 5, over the history of North American settler-colonialism, the institutions of liberal governance have also accepted, produced, and maintained a property interest in whiteness, where social relations of domination have been codified into law. Contemporary liberalism, for example, continues to codify white supremacy in supposedly color-blind terms. This property interest is a product of the pursuance of the two pillars of the settler-colonial and capitalist political economy: capital accumulation and the dispossession of Indigenous lands. The settler state, which is only possible on the basis of the ongoing dispossession of Indigenous lands, is an instance of what Lyons describes as white supremacist racial oppression: "The web of social, economic, political, and cultural institutions and practices whereby people identified as 'white' hold privilege and varying degrees of power over other people" (Lyons 2018, 3). The political economy of settler-colonialism undermines its avowed ideological justifications. But the liberal claim to objective right emphasizes deliberative procedures over outcomes. Therefore, formal equality focuses on equal access to deliberative procedures rather than egalitarian outcomes.

But establishing ideological legitimacy is not the same as establishing political and economic hegemony. Following Du Bois (and subsequently many others), I will contend that the political and economic hegemony of these settler-colonial societies rests on a white hegemony that coalesces around the white bourgeoisie, petty bourgeoisie, and working class. The petty bourgeoisie and working class form a labor aristocracy above other, racialized working classes. But this white hegemony is not immune to capitalist crises of accumulation. So we must add some nuance to Lyons's claim that the Far Right rejects the legitimacy of liberal political institutions. The Far Right accepts—and its interests are premised—upon the political economy of capitalist accumulation and settler-colonialism. It even accepts liberal or bourgeois institutions if they are perceived to advance white supremacy. Thus the Far Right is invested in settler-state hegemony—but it becomes insurrectionary when it perceives this hegemony as having failed to advance the interests of white supremacy. Hamerquist and Sakai both accurately perceive that Far Right mobilization is driven by the petty bourgeoisie and the declassed who are casualties of economic crisis. As Marx and Engels observe in *The Communist Manifesto*, the petty bourgeoisie typically sink into the proletariat "partly because their diminutive capital does not suffice for the scale on which Modern Industry is carried on" (Marx and Engels [1848] 1994, 172). Economic crisis threatens white hegemony when it threatens the wages of whiteness, or what Du Bois or Sakai have called the white labor aristocracy. As Menominee theorist Rowland "Enāēmaehkiw" Keshena Robinson writes,

> In general we can say that . . . in excess of the right-wing nation-al-populism of Trump and his canadian interlocutors, these forces [of white supremacy], whether they explicitly engage in the kind of German nazi fetishism associated with such individuals and organizations [as] Andrew Anglin of The Daily Stormer or the National Socialist Movement, something which many people continue to stereotype as the most publicly visible mark of fascism, they all thirst for a *new frontier*, for *recolonization*, for territories, for a *white homeland*. In other words, they thirst for the fulfilment of the settler dream—which is a project, it is

important to note, they think has failed—to be dreamt anew.
(Robinson 2019)

Though Hamerquist, Sakai, and Lyons have described the Far Right
as revolutionary or insurrectionary, it is neither emancipatory nor
completely antisystemic. It is premised on the re-entrenchment, the
*palingenesis*, of the white supremacist, settler-colonial project itself.

To summarize: settler-state hegemony is constituted by a dialectic between two predominant but sometimes conflicting social
forces, and each of these predominant forces mediates between other conflicting social forces as well. Liberal democracy is, as Marx
discerned, an instrument of bourgeois class rule. But it also relies
upon a degree of popular legitimacy that means that groups historically excluded from liberal political and cultural institutions are able
through organizing to win, at least temporarily, concessions and
fend off incursions of state power and to a degree, sometimes, economic exploitation. Liberalism mediates between these forces of
social democracy and the interests of capital. But really existing
North American liberalism is merely one component of the larger
social totality that is settler-state hegemony. This hegemony coalesces between liberalism and white supremacist settlerism, embodied in part today by the Far Right and fascism. As Robinson's
comment makes clear, the Far Right yearns for the recolonization of
the project of settler-colonialism which it perceives, *incorrectly*, to
have failed. As I will discuss again in chapter 5, white settlerism is
part of, and sometimes perceives itself within, a longer history of
acting as the paramilitary wing of the broader project of settler-
colonialism. We would then view its insurrectionary character
against its perception of settler governance. When settler hegemony
is challenged by leftist movements, the Far Right fights *for* the
reinforcement of settler-state power; when the Far Right perceives
the liberal institutions of the settler-state to have failed the white
supremacist project, it fights *against* the liberal institutions of the
state. At no point does it truly challenge the underlying political
economy of settler-colonialism: continued capital accumulation and
the dispossession of Indigenous land. Thus when the Far Right mo-

bilizes around heteropatriarchy, a masculinist ableism, antiblackness, and anti-Indigeneity, it rallies around re-entrenching the very social norms and legal structures that historically advanced the settler-colonial project itself. Though liberalism espouses a commitment to formal equality, it launders the property of whiteness in terms of objective right or, more recently, color blindness, as part of advancing the interests of capital. Thus figure 1.2.

The concept of the three-way fight, while it may be overly schematic, situates antifascism against liberalism and the Far Right. Like liberalism, antifascism is egalitarian, but of an egalitarianism of *each according to their needs; from each according to their abilities* rather than the mere formal, procedural egalitarianism of liberal governance. While this egalitarianism starkly demarcates antifascism from the Far Right, both movements are insurrectionary. However, while we might summarize the Far Right as the paramilitary wing of settler-colonialism, antifascism is—or *ought to be*—anticolonial and anticapitalist. I have deliberately used the concept of the three-way fight to situate antifascism against settler-state hegemony to anticipate my concluding argument that in settler-colonial states, the antifascist commitment to anticapitalism must also advance the causes of decolonization and Indigenous resurgence.

## 1.2. TOWARD A PHILOSOPHY OF ANTIFASCISM

For a study of a philosophy of antifascism, thus far I have said very little about militant antifascism itself. Mainstream representations tend to conflate militant antifascism with the tactics that militant antifascists use. Thus militant antifascism is reduced to images of tactics, images of anonymous, masked-up groups marching and physically confronting Far Right or fascist mobilizations. Militant antifascism *is* insurrectionary when it uses direct action to confront Far Right mobilization or push back against police power. But there are plenty of militant antifascists, philosophically speaking, who might never show up to public demonstrations. Some are at higher risk of police surveillance or intimidation. Some would face a rela-

ANTIFASCISM ————— Insurrectionism ————— **THE FAR RIGHT /
FASCISM**

Egalitarianism                                        Settler-State
                                                      Hegemony

**LIBERALISM**

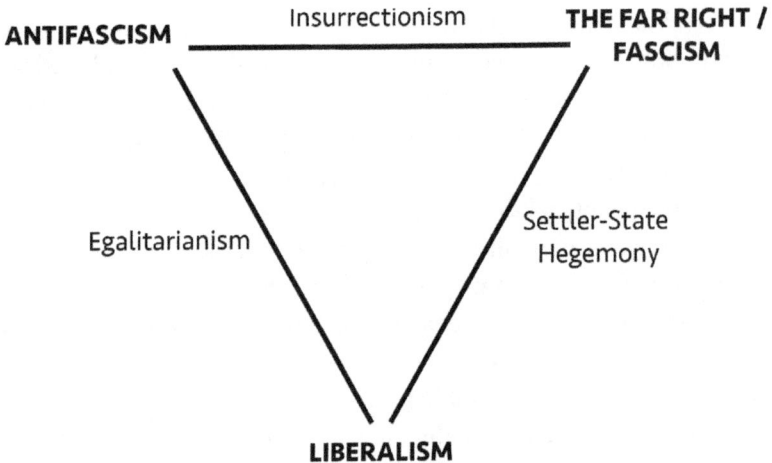

**Figure 1.2.**                    **Three-Way Fight: Lines of Adjacency**

tively greater personal risk than others in marches, protests, or physical confrontation. Some do public-facing work for the communities
that militant antifascism aids in community self-defense. In any
case, physical confrontation comes very late in antifascist organizing, though it often draws a disproportionate amount of media attention. Most antifascist work is much less spectacular, often beginning
and ending as letter-writing or educational campaigns to raise
awareness about or prevent Far Right organizing and recruitment in
public spaces. For example, most postsecondary educational institutions have diversity or inclusivity statements as well as commitments to academic freedom. An organizer involved in the Campus
Antifascist Network or a similar group might launch an educational
campaign to show that permitting Far Right groups to organize on
campus violates institutional commitments to diversity, inclusion,
academic freedom, or workplace protections. While Far Right
groups appeal—in bad faith, as we will see—to freedom of speech,
militant antifascism organizes *against* enabling or legitimating the
extension of policing over our lives. Instead, militant antifascism
aims to show that enabling fascists to organize and recruit has sig-

nificant antidemocratic and anti-egalitarian social costs in our communities, and it demands that social institutions recognize their responsibility should they aid or abet far-right organizing. Should they fail to do so, then antifascist organizing turns to political mobilization. Between here and the conclusion, I will outline a more specific philosophy of antifascism. I have chosen to focus on Beauvoir and Rancière due to their shared commitment to egalitarianism. Before doing so, two caveats are in order. First, I do not want to give the impression that antifascists typically adhere philosophically to existentialism or Rancière's egalitarianism. In fact, antifascist organizers are generally more likely to be Marxists or anarchists. In antifascist organizing, these philosophical differences are put aside to combat the immediate threat from a common enemy, the Far Right. If anything, adopting existentialism and egalitarianism from Beauvoir and Rancière allows for a philosophical approach that is both sympathetic to and, from a leftist standpoint, agnostic toward the differences between the Marxist and anarchist currents of antifascist theory, though there are limits to this agnosticism that I will be unable to avoid later.

Second, I need to clarify my methodological commitments. One might expect that I would attempt to demonstrate what given philosophers think, what their concepts are, and whether and how they relate something about the capital-$T$ Truth of our situation. For example, one might expect that I would make the case that Beauvoir's ontology—her answer to the question, "What is the being of beings?"—is *True* and that the truth of her ontology has a number of ramifications that we could apply to lived experience and social relations, politics, and ethics. Elsewhere, I have argued that philosophy too often gets embroiled in *ontosectarianism*: one proceeds from the assumption that "ontology is 'first philosophy,' that politics, or ethics, follow from ontology, and that insufficient politics or ethics follow from insufficient ontology" (Shaw 2016b).[5] We end up in debates about ontology and attempt to wedge political problems into rarified philosophical vocabularies. I could imagine a scenario where the entire enterprise of this study, on the ontosectarian assumption, founders on attempting to square the ontological commitments of the various authors considered herein, and the most pressing part, about antifascism, appears as an addendum to these philosophical considerations. In other words, one might expect that I would do bourgeois philosophy here.

Instead, I am interested in Beauvoir, Rancière, and others because they share a commitment to militant antifascism and radical politics. Though Beauvoir acknowledges that she had not taken the threat of fascism seriously until the spring of 1939, her postwar publications emphasize the crucial importance of fighting those forms of oppression that remain after the collapse of fascism while highlighting the danger that fascism poses, so that we might combat it sooner when it emerges again.[6] Rancière dates his political coming-of-age to demonstrations against the Algerian War in 1961–1962, in opposition to both the French state and the fascist *Organisation armée secrète* (Rancière [2012] 2016, 5; see also Rancière 1998a). The OAS carried out attacks against the French state in both France and Algeria as well as against leftist intellectuals. It is worth noting that "Sartre was one of the first targets of the OAS attacks. His apartment on the Rue Bonaparte was bombed twice: on July 19, 1961 and on January 7, 1962. The offices of *Les Temps modernes* were also attacked on May 13, 1961" (Cohen-Solal 2005, 440).

While their personal commitments are pertinent in a historical-biographical sense, it is more important philosophically to consider how these commitments shape their political thought. This claim does not rest on a long exegesis and a hermeneutic of authorial intent. Instead, I think this commitment can be demonstrated by showing that when we are faced with a philosophical impasse, involving rich and variegated texts such as *The Ethics of Ambiguity* and *Disagreement*, there is often space to advance through our interpretive choices a philosophy of antifascism and practices of emancipation. Thus, when we make these choices, we reveal the degree to which liberal readings have made incursions into their political thought. For example, there is a liberal (and sometimes libertarian) reading of existentialism that emphasizes individuality and individual choices. But this reading, which claims to be based on the works of the 1940s, rarely makes it explicit that it rests on interpretive choices that downplay or ignore the existentialist engagement with radical political thought—Marxism, anarchism, antifascism, and by 1948, Négritude. An antifascist reading, by contrast, emphasizes, and judges existentialism against, these militant and radical philosophies. Figuratively speaking, this antifascist reading is engaged in a three-way fight in philosophy, through theoretical struggle against liberal antifascism and in principled opposition to fascism.

In general, the discipline of philosophy handles the problem of violence poorly. The discipline, as demonstrated by the "public" philosophers I cited at the outset, is hampered by a number of prejudices that say more about the privileged place of intellectuals than it does about violence. One prejudice holds that philosophy constitutes a disinterested space for the pursuit of truth or knowledge, where people with divergent positions are able to provide reasons or justifications for their respective discourses and practices; and it is where, after some degree of debate, they disinterestedly accede to the best justifications offered and modify their discourses or actions appropriately. If this were true *within the discipline*, and it would only be *true* if those engaged in the discipline had equal access to influential platforms and material means of support, then it would still not justify an inference that our societies formulate principles of justice in a similar, disinterested manner. And yet some philosophers tend to normalize whatever violence is already present in a given social situation on the premise that, when called to account, it must have good reasons to have been instituted; others conjure social violence away altogether by acting as if we live in societies that observe a universal prohibition on violence. It is no surprise that philosophers often flounder on the rock of civility.

Philosophy's problematic approach to violence is compounded by the fact that when the discipline actually considers violence, it tends to shift the burden of justification from the oppressor to the oppressed. I place some blame for this position on the influential place Hannah Arendt continues to occupy in scholarship on Continental philosophy. Arendt argues, in *On Violence*, that political power ("the human ability to act in concert") and violence are "opposites" (Arendt 1970, 44, 56), or, in the Aristotelian terms of *On Revolution*, that humans are political beings insofar as they are endowed with speech, while violence is "incapable of speech" (Arendt [1963] 2006, 9). One might then conclude that when we are able to proffer reasons for our actions, violence recedes—and that when the oppressed turn to violence, that they bear the burden for *introducing* violence in political struggle and stifling speech. There are few more damning indictments of our discipline—although the recent efforts of some to launder transphobia as "gender-critical feminism" certainly ranks among them—than the fact that it has managed, through a number of different prejudices, to naturalize or occlude the systemic violence of oppression while denouncing in the name of civility, open inquiry, and justice, emancipatory violence.

Here I advocate for a philosophical tradition that maintains that emancipatory violence is, in the words of George Ciccariello-Maher, "a violence that speaks volumes" (2017a, 48). In other words, I will argue that a philosophical understanding of emancipatory violence requires entering into the space of reasons constructed by emancipatory practices—in this regard, my approach is not unlike Ciccariello-Maher's *Decolonizing Dialectics*. In the next two chapters, I will read Beauvoir and Rancière as philosophical antecedents to contemporary militant antifascism. The purpose, of course, is to demonstrate the antifascist character of existentialism and egalitarianism. In chapter 4, I will attempt to reconstruct a militant space of reasons to defend militant direct action and emancipatory community self-defense. Militant antifascists organize and embrace the diversity of tactics in order to fight the Far Right by undermining its recruitment efforts and challenging it when it mobilizes campaigns to harass, intimidate, and attack our communities. The reasoning is fairly straightforward: a world where fascists cannot openly organize is better than one where they can. Admittedly, militant antifascism here remains a defensive tactic. I will conclude, in chapter 5, that any meaningful attempt to extirpate fascism and white supremacy in North America must embrace anticapitalism and anti–settler-colonialism, for liberalism, in its role in settler-colonialism and as part of a class compromise between the white bourgeoisie and the white working class, has codified whiteness as a form and norm of entitlement and privilege, while the Far Right draws, more or less, from "a major social base out of the traditional settler culture" (Sakai 2003, 8).

In the often-quoted eighth thesis of "On the Concept of History," Walter Benjamin writes that "the current amazement that the things we are experiencing are 'still' possible in the twentieth century is *not* philosophical" (Benjamin [1940] 2003, 392). In a similar manner, to paraphrase Benjamin, the current amazement that the things we are experiencing are "still" possible in the twenty-first century is also *not* philosophical. This amazement is not the beginning of knowledge—unless it is the knowledge that the philosophy that gives rise to it is untenable. I advocate a philosophy of antifascism to offer an alternative.

## NOTES

1. Here the term *metapolitical* refers to strategies aimed to "gradually transform the political and intellectual culture as a precursor to transforming institutions and systems" (Lyons 2018, 58).

2. In other words, here I use *insurrectionism* to mean *a strategy that challenges the state's monopoly on legitimate violence* and not in the more technical, specific way the term is used in leftist revolutionary movements.

3. Lyons 2018, xi. He defines neoliberalism as "a set of economic policies, including minimal regulation of business, reduction or privatization of social services, low taxes for businesses and the wealthy, free trade, and relatively unrestricted immigration" (2018, xiii).

4. This is all the more significant given that Lyons specifically develops his definitions in light of Sakai, who emphasizes that settler-colonialism plays an integral role in the Far Right and fascism in North America.

5. I developed this critique of ontosectarianism through Rancière's political thought, which I discuss in section 2.3 and Shaw 2016a, especially chapter 9, 171n11.

6. See Beauvoir [1960] 1965, 359. For an overview of later criticism of Beauvoir's actions during the Occupation, see Kruks 2012, 157n15.

# 2

# THE ETHICS OF AMBIGUITY AND THE ANTINOMIES OF EMANCIPATORY VIOLENCE

## 2.1. EXISTENTIALISM IS AN ANTIFASCISM

Existentialism is an antifascism. This claim, which deliberately paraphrases Jean-Paul Sartre's *L'existentialisme est un humanisme*, is initially imprecise. In Sartre's early works, he emphasizes the absurdity of existence and the primacy of human freedom—but it is a concept of freedom that is ethically ambivalent. In her memoir *The Prime of Life*, Beauvoir admits on numerous occasions that she had failed to take the rise of fascism seriously until it was too late. Nonetheless, existentialism after the war is an antifascism. Sartre rejects the idea that the defeat of fascism in World War II singled its permanent historical defeat.[1] In *The Ethics of Ambiguity* (1947: *Pour une morale de l'ambiguïté*), Beauvoir is even more blunt: "We object to all forms of fascism" (Beauvoir [1947] 1976, 138). Her comment is not merely a bon mot; antifascism is fundamental to *The Ethics of Ambiguity*. In discussions of existentialism, though, *The Ethics of Ambiguity* is often obscured by the shadow of Sartre's *Being and Nothingness*. This is due in part to the unrecognized biases that animate the "great men, great systems" approach to philosophy, according to which the discipline progresses more or less through the supersession of great philosophical systems (Simons 1999, 101–14). On this view, one that we sometimes find Beauvoir herself espousing, *Being and Nothingness* was *the* great system of existentialism, and her own work is not *philosophy* in that sense— she suggests that *The Ethics of Ambiguity* is "not philosophy; it is an essay" (quoted in Simons 1999, 11).[2] Beauvoir's comment says more about her concept of philosophy than whether or not her own work has *philosophical value*. Beauvoir's work makes three marked advances over "early" existentialism:

1. Beauvoir maintains first, against Albert Camus and the early Sartre, that existence is ambiguous but not absurd. She writes that the "notion of ambiguity must not be confused with that of absurdity. To declare the existence is absurd is to deny that it can ever be given a meaning; to say that it is ambiguous is to assert that its meaning is never fixed and that it must be constantly won" (Beauvoir [1947] 1976, 129). One can only prioritize absurdity over ambiguity if one believes that existence *should have* had a transcendent meaning that it in fact lacks. I associate this kind of metaphysical nostalgia especially with Camus.

2. Second, she chooses to emphasize that the being whose being is in question is a "freedom" (*une liberté*) rather than Sartre's "for-itself" or Heidegger's *Dasein* (e.g., Beauvoir [1947] 1976, 29, 31). To refer to this being whose being is in question as a freedom affirms, given that freedom constitutes meaning and vice versa, how human existence is ambiguous rather than absurd. In addition, to emphasize that human being is "a freedom" circumvents the conservatism of Heidegger's hermeneutic of *Dasein* and the implied individualism of Sartre's "being-for-itself." Though Sartre maintains that "there is no difference between the being of man and his *being-free*," his analysis remains focused on the meaning of the "for-itself" (Sartre [1943] 1956, 60).

3. And third, Beauvoir situates bad faith as a practical and discursive attitude that takes on a *value* in relation to one's moral
freedom and the moral freedom of others. This view is not
unique to Beauvoir, as it also guides Sartre's discussion of the
bad faith of anti-Semitism in *Anti-Semite and Jew*, but it
marks an important shift from *Being and Nothingness*: whereas in *Being and Nothingness*, Sartre focuses on how bad faith
functions as self-deception, in subsequent writings both writ-
ers describe bad faith as a refusal of one's responsibilities or
the denial of the freedom of others.

Although these are important developments, on their own they do
not necessarily constitute a fundamental *revaluation* of existentialism. Looking back in *Force of Circumstance*, Beauvoir criticizes
the essay for "wasting time rebutting absurd objections," especially
in the early part of the book (Beauvoir [1963] 1968, 75–76). Many
of the advances I have just described happen during those rebuttals.
Yet *The Ethics of Ambiguity* does indeed bury the lede. In my view,
it is unique because it begins from a fundamentally different orientation than Sartre's *Being and Nothingness*, which *was* in part written and intended as a contribution to the history of great systems of
philosophy. Beauvoir, however, proceeds from a much more concrete and political starting point. Beauvoir's defense of Sartre's system is to existentialism what Marx's critical reading of Hegel's
*Philosophy of Right* is to historical materialism. Commenting on
Marx's method, Miguel Abensour writes, "The task of the critic is
to interpret every political question so as to translate the particular
language of politics in the more 'general' language of emancipation" (Abensour 2011, 36). This "hermeneutics of emancipation"
judges the interpretive choices that guide political thought according to whether they further the praxis of emancipation or stultify it.
Abensour's reference to "emancipation," in my view, draws from
Rancière's use of the term. In *The Ignorant Schoolmaster*,
Rancière—using an indirect style to recount the pedagogy of Joseph
Jacotot—opposes emancipation to stultification. Stultification is defined as the subordination of one intelligence to another, leading to

the differentiation between mastery and ignorance, between those whose task it is to think and those whose task it is to obey. Emancipation is put into practice when we suppose, like Rancière/Jacotot, that all intelligences are equal and that all forms of hierarchy and stratification are historically contingent. A practice of equality—such as politics—then, involves enacting the supposition of equality to combat material and intellectual inequality. The hermeneutics of emancipation does not aim to *demonstrate* or *prove* equality; as Rancière writes, "Our problem isn't proving that all intelligence is equal. It's seeing what can be done under that supposition" (Rancière [1987] 1991, 46). From our point of view, political theory and politics are evaluated as to *how* they enable us to think—as we read, interpret, and argue—emancipation, and *how* they enable us to translate this hermeneutics into practice.

Here I will argue that Beauvoir reads the problems and conclusions of existentialism through the lens of emancipatory politics. To paraphrase Abensour, *the task is to interpret every philosophical question so as to translate the particular language of existentialism into the more general language of emancipation.* However, it is not until late in *The Ethics of Ambiguity* that this standpoint becomes explicit. In chapter 3.2, she asserts that we must "reject oppression at any cost" (Beauvoir [1947] 1976, 96). Then she contends that the "concrete consequences of existentialist ethics" demand that we reject "every [a priori] principle of authority" (Beauvoir [1947] 1976, 142). We could view these passages as impossible demands on our praxis, as merely radicalized Kantian maxims. It is entirely possible that Beauvoir subsequently saw them this way (see Beauvoir [1963] 1968, 76). However, to close the book merely on the basis of her own later self-interpretations commits the intentional fallacy. Instead, I think we should treat her assertions about existentialist ethics as the lens for a hermeneutics of emancipation. We should ask, How does existentialism guide our actions if our goal is political emancipation or liberation? What normative commitments further these ends? What possible pitfalls await us if we reject oppression at any cost? These are radically different questions than those of Western political philosophy, which so often seeks to justify and naturalize oppression and inequality. By contrast, Beauvoir asks, "What are the consequences if we act *as if* we must reject oppression at any cost?" As we will see, pursuing liberation leads to a number of "antinomies of action" that show that emancipatory political praxis is not unambiguous. However, Beauvoir contends that all praxis bears a degree of ambiguity and failure, and these are not reasons for quietism—for "without failure, [there is] no ethics" (Beauvoir [1947] 1976, 10).

In what follows, I argue that Beauvoir's *Ethics of Ambiguity* demands of us to reorient our interpretation of the key tenets of existentialism; we should be able to appreciate how it summarizes existentialism's theoretical trajectory through 1947 while anticipating and suggesting future lines of research carried out by Beauvoir herself, Sartre, and Fanon. In "2.2. Ambiguity and Solidarity," I examine the normative underpinnings of Beauvoir's existentialist ethics and conclude that her position is both egalitarian (similar though not identical to the egalitarianism of Rancière) and emancipatory. The very idea of an existentialist ethics is to reject oppression, of course, but toward egalitarian and emancipatory ends. In "2.3. The Antinomies of Action," I outline how Beauvoir handles what she calls antinomies of action, focusing primarily on the antinomy of emancipatory violence. Initially it would appear that when the oppressed use violence as a means, this immediately negates emancipatory ends. Beauvoir, however, argues that evaluating the violence of the oppressed requires situating it against the violence of the oppressor. In a situation that is oppressive, oppression itself is already violent. Thus emancipatory violence must be gauged against the emancipatory goals of the oppressed and the violence of oppression. In "2.4. Vengeance, Violence, and the State," I turn from *The Ethics of Ambiguity* to Beauvoir's essay "An Eye for an Eye" (1946). There she addresses violence in the context of vengeance. She argues that the victim of existential violence is justified, to a degree, in taking revenge against the perpetrator. In this discussion, I will focus on two features salient to my argument. First, in this essay, Beauvoir specifically situates the state as an agent in social conflict rather than as an institution of objective right. Second, she outlines a theory of political agency that affirms direct action as a form of political subjectivation. Though, as I will suggest, her account anticipates that of the Fanon of *Black Skin, White Masks*, his account allows us to correct Beauvoir's overreliance on a particular form of reciprocity or recognition. Finally, in "2.5. The Three-Way Fight and No-Platforming the Far Right," I apply Beauvoir's existentialist ethics to militant antifascist praxis today. I consider Beauvoir's critique of the state in light of the concept of the "three-way fight," and then I argue that antistatism, broadly conceived, underlies antifascist practices, such as no-platforming.

## 2.2. AMBIGUITY AND SOLIDARITY

In *The Ethics of Ambiguity*, Beauvoir defends an existential ethics that assumes "our fundamental ambiguity" (Beauvoir [1947] 1976, 9). Until then, the existentialism of Sartre and Camus—and often existentialism as it is currently received—had been closely identified with absurdity. To say that existence is absurd results in two major philosophical problems. First, one can only conclude that existence is tragic and absurd if it is assumed that existence *should have had* some meaning that it in fact lacks. And, in practical terms, this position is morally equivocal, suggesting that there are no reasons to prefer one project to another. As Sartre states in *Existentialism Is a Humanism*, though later in the text he seemingly contradicts this point, "One can choose anything, so long as it involves free commitment" (Sartre [1946b] 2007, 51). Thus Beauvoir's introduction of the concept of ambiguity marks a pronounced shift in perspective. She writes that the "notion of ambiguity must not be confused with that of absurdity. To declare the existence is absurd is to deny that it can ever be given a meaning; to say that it is ambiguous is to assert that its meaning is never fixed and that it must be constantly won" (Beauvoir [1947] 1976, 129). In contrast to the paucity or lack of meaning suggested by the concept of absurdity, Beauvoir maintains that there is a surfeit of meaning that arises from the concrete practices of a multiplicity of individuals. Our freedom is the basis of all values, but all values are *ambiguous*: given to equivocal meanings within social conflict. When she contends that the "fundamental ambiguity of the human condition will always open up to men the possibility of opposing choices," this claim itself has a double significance: first, all individuals face decisive choices between fidelity to what they have chosen to be their values or negating these choices and affirming different values (this is what existentialists call *conversion*); and second, our values always both affirm and deny—meaning that there is always the possibility that our actions, aimed even at social solidarity with some other individuals or groups, will come into conflict with the actions of others (Beauvoir [1947] 1976, 118).

For Beauvoir then, the concept of ambiguity politicizes the existentialist problematic of human finitude. At the outset of *The Ethics of Ambiguity*, her initial description of finitude, as human mortality, fits within the milieu of Sartre, Camus, Heidegger, and the post-Heideggerian Continental tradition. In the first sentence, she quotes Montaigne, who writes, "The continuous work of our life is to build death" (quoted in Beauvoir [1947] 1976, 7). And whenever humans have felt this "tragic ambiguity," there have been philosophers who have attempted to mask it. They have attempted to either merge consciousness and matter in a single substance or explain finitude through dualism. The monist solution, at least in vitalist terms, minimizes *a* life as the expression of life itself. The dualist solution either denies death by promising human immortality or denies life as a veiled illusion (Beauvoir [1947] 1976, 7–8). By contrast, she argues, existentialism demands that we "assume our fundamental ambiguity" (Beauvoir [1947] 1976, 9). Whereas the post-Heideggerian Continental tradition has focused on finitude as mortality, Beauvoir emphasizes how finitude is part of our political and practical engagements—each individual is but one freedom, one being-as-freedom (*une liberté*) among other beings-as-freedom. Thus the horizon of my projects, for Beauvoir, is not primarily my mortality but the intersubjective relationality of meaning. Indeed, she writes, the "paradox" of the human situation is that humans "know themselves to be the supreme end to which all action should be subordinated, but the exigencies of action force them to treat one another as instruments or obstacles, as means" (Beauvoir [1947] 1976, 9). While Beauvoir at points describes our mortality as "tragic," she chooses to describe "fundamental ambiguity" in intersubjective terms—our practical engagements are ambiguous because in opportune circumstances they are able to disclose our projects within the horizon of an indefinite, open future.[3] However, these horizons and our sense of futurity are suppressed by situations of oppression.

When we generally talk about ethics, our goal is to discern rules, laws, or guidelines for our actions. *The Ethics of Ambiguity* does not provide an ethics of this sort. Instead, Beauvoir focuses on how our freedom involves the creation of values, while suggesting provisional "methods" and norms to evaluate these values. I would suggest, both conceptually and on the basis of the French title, *Pour une morale de l'ambiguïté*, that Beauvoir is responding in part to Nietzsche's *On the Genealogy of Morality*, which had been translated into French as *La généalogie de la morale*. "Under which conditions," Nietzsche asks, "did humanity invent the value-judgments good and evil? *and what value do they have themselves?*" (Nietzsche 2014, 209). Nietzsche's genealogy of the value of values rejects the assumption that takes "the *value* of these 'values' as given, as factual, as beyond all questioning" (Nietzsche 2014, 212). Likewise, Beauvoir rejects the assumption—which she associates, like Sartre, with the spirit of seriousness—that the values that give a meaning to existence are transcendent or objective. But she also rejects the conclusion that, lacking transcendent meaning, existence is absurd. Instead, existence is ambiguous; it must be given meaning, and it is by deciding the meaning of ambiguity that we establish the *values* which provide "our strength to live and our reasons for acting" (Beauvoir [1947] 1976, 9tm). We could then read chapter 2 of *The Ethics of Ambiguity* as a kind of genealogy of bad faith. But when it comes to concluding which values are worth valuing, there fortunately there the similarities with Nietzsche end. While Nietzsche traces a genealogy of the values of good and evil, good and bad, guilt, *ressentiment*, and asceticism in an attempt to recover a sense of the individualistic master morality that he thinks was submerged and devalued within the slave morality of the Judeo-Christian tradition, Beauvoir argues that our own freedom creates values *in relation to*—and normatively, she claims, in expanding—the freedom of others. Indeed, our valuation of the struggle of the most oppressed in our societies, whether we affirm and support or refuse their struggle, provides the most authentic picture of how we value freedom. By focusing on the social character of our free projects, Beauvoir requires us to distinguish, in our discussion of ambiguity, ontological freedom and moral freedom. She demarcates between the two to dispense with the following criticism of the existentialist concept of freedom: if, as Sartre claims, we *are* free, how is it possible to *will* oneself free? According to Beauvoir, this objection rests on a category mistake. She thus distinguishes between "a natural freedom, so to speak" and "moral freedom" (Beauvoir [1947] 1976, 24, 26). Kristana Arp argues that the phrase "natural freedom" is potentially misleading, since "there is no freedom in nature . . . and no such thing as human nature for existentialism," so in its place I follow Arp's choice, "ontological freedom" (Arp 2001, 55). Ontological freedom, for Beauvoir, describes our being-as-freedom, while moral freedom involves a normative account of *which* values are worth valuing.

While Beauvoir distinguishes between ontological and moral freedom, there are numerous passages in *The Ethics of Ambiguity* where we must disentangle the two. In the first programmatic passages about the freedom of others, she argues that freedom "regards as privileged situations those which permit it to realize itself as [an] indefinite movement" able to transcend limitations toward the future; furthermore, "freedom always appears as a movement of liberation. It is only by prolonging itself through the freedom of others that it manages to surpass death itself and to realize itself as an indefinite unity" (Beauvoir [1947] 1976, 32). These passages are both descriptive and normative. On the one hand, they describe how an individual's own projects could be carried forward by others: she argues that only the freedom of others can extend our ends beyond our life (Beauvoir [1947] 1976, 71). Beauvoir, for example, fought and advocated for women's liberation; and by working with others, her projects have been extended—though the terms and tactics might have, though not necessarily, changed—to the present day. Of course, our projects can also be extended, as it were, by negation: most of us know economist David Ricardo through Marx's criticism, anti-Semite Eugen Dühring through *Anti-Dühring*. In either case, at the level of description, we see that an individual's freedom and projects are extended beyond their finite life span, that these projects affect others, and these others have the option to continue these projects or relegate them to the past, just as our freedom is affected by our predecessors and—barring our extinction as a species—will someday be judged by our descendants. In other words, Beauvoir situates each individual's concrete freedom against their facticity, insofar as we choose in situations that are not of our choosing but that are nevertheless historically and contextually situated.

I have chosen this phrasing, to say that we must choose in situations that are not of our own choosing, deliberately, to suggest parallels to Marx. Indeed, by 1947 Beauvoir and Sartre are attempting to forge a class-conscious, if not Marxist, existentialism. In *The Ethics of Ambiguity*, Beauvoir's account of moral freedom provides the grounds for her advocacy of social solidarity, whereas at that point, Sartre's own work had remained seemingly contradictory. In *Existentialism Is a Humanism*, he maintains both that "one can choose anything, so long as it involves free commitment" and that in "willing freedom, we discover that it depends entirely on the freedom of others, and that the freedom of others depends on our own. . . . I am obliged to will the freedom of others at the same time as I will my own" (Sartre [1946b] 2007, 51, 48–49). On Beauvoir's terms, the former claim could be considered ontological, meaning that existentialists view all actions as a matter of choice, meaning that evil is a choice rather than a result of ignorance or error. She remarks that existentialism, in contrast to the Western philosophical tradition from at least Plato to Kant, gives "a real role to evil" (Beauvoir [1947] 1976, 34). Sartre's latter claim—that willing freedom for myself involves willing the freedom of others—is normative, though it marks a significant departure from the conclusions of

*Being and Nothingness*. There, as Thomas Flynn has noted, Sartre defines intersubjective relations as *ontologically*, rather than *historically*, conflictual (Flynn 1984, 20). And, Flynn continues, to define social existence as ontologically conflictual preempts the possibility of solidarity. While we find this distinction between ontological freedom and moral freedom in Sartre, Beauvoir draws a line of demarcation that provides both descriptive and normative grounds for social solidarity.

## 2.2.1. Beauvoir's Cartesian Egalitarianism

Having examined the descriptive, ontological grounds for Beauvoir's claim that our freedom prolongs itself through the freedom of others, we must now examine the moral or normative grounds. For Beauvoir also asserts that as "a freedom," I ought to engage in projects that expand both my own freedom and the freedom of others. Indeed, Beauvoir's stance involves not only a commitment toward projects that expand freedom but those that are egalitarian. Elsewhere I have argued that Beauvoir is a Cartesian egalitarian (Shaw 2016a). The self-ascribed Cartesianism of existentialism is one of its more philosophically controversial positions. Many critics follow Heidegger and allege that Sartre and Beauvoir, by appropriating the cogito, fail to dismantle the metaphysics of presence. This critique, in my view, fails to address why they may have *chosen* to frame the cogito as freedom. Beauvoir writes, "Being a subject is a universal fact and . . . the Cartesian *cogito* expresses both the most individual experience and the most objective truth" (Beauvoir [1947] 1976, 17). If we consider Cartesianism as metaphysics, Beauvoir has little warrant to appeal to Descartes. First, at the outset of *The Ethics of Ambiguity*, Beauvoir rejects dualism for masking ambiguity. And then her entire critique of transcendent values and the spirit of seriousness is incompatible with Descartes's project of reconstructing the experience of an "autonomous thought which, by its own power, discovers intelligible relationships between already existing essences" (Sartre [1947] 2010, 499tm). Beauvoir, however,

does evince the "good sense" of Cartesian egalitarianism posited at
the outset of *Discourse on Method*:

> The power of judging well and of distinguishing the true from
> the false—which is what we properly call "good sense" or "rea-
> son"—is naturally equal in all men, and consequently . . . the
> diversity of our opinions does not arise because some of us are
> more reasonable than others but solely because we direct our
> thoughts along different paths. (Descartes 1985, 111)

Thus Beauvoir, following Descartes, supposes the intellectual
equality, in terms of freedom and authority, of any possible reader.
But Descartes was not necessarily a Cartesian egalitarian in the
sense that subsequent philosophers, such as François Poulain de la
Barre, Joseph Jacotot, and Jacques Rancière are. Cartesian egalitarianism, I argue, entails, first, conceptualizing political agency as a
dynamic of subjectivation; second, positing the equality of intelligences; and third, defining politics as dissensus (Shaw 2016a,
25–49). Descartes only does the second. We can draw a further
comparison when we consider that Descartes considers intellectual
equality in epistemological terms, while for Beauvoir it is also ethical. Whereas Descartes then sets out to discover the *truth* of already
existing essences (God, thinking substance, extended substance),
Beauvoir focuses on the creation of values—the point of contention,
for which we need good sense or reason, is not truth or falsity but
good and evil or good and bad. Beauvoir's cogito supposes the
intellectual equality of all beings for whom being is in question.
Having referred to the cogito, she writes, "It is not impersonal universal man who is the source of values, but the plurality of concrete,
singular men projecting themselves toward their ends on the basis of
situations whose particularity is as radical and as irreducible as subjectivity itself" (Beauvoir [1947] 1976, 17–18tm). Thus we might
gloss Beauvoir's cogito in the following terms: as a being for whom
being is in question, I have the intelligence and the freedom to posit
the values of my actions.

## 2.2.2. Beauvoir's Critique of Marxism

But, for Beauvoir, the meaning of my actions emerges through intersubjective praxis, and the value of meaning takes on *value* in relation to how praxis or discourse relates to freedom and equality. While *The Ethics of Ambiguity* begins by appealing to the individuality of the reader, its conclusions regarding the formation of value anticipate what she calls, in *The Second Sex* (and in dialogue with Maurice Merleau-Ponty), *l'expérience vécue*: socially lived experience as the basis of value. We must consider this *socially* lived experience according to three criteria: first, as it is constituted by an individual's ability to act as a political agent or subject as one subject among a plurality of individuals; second, the fundamental attitude the individual takes toward this ability (or lack thereof); and, finally, the discourses and systematic structures of a given society that either enable this subjectivity or oppress it.

Given these three criteria, the values we choose must be situated within the socially lived practices that shape our actions and our consciousness of our respective situation(s) and in relation to the material conditions on which these practices arise. On this basis, Beauvoir outlines an interpretation of Marx that emphasizes free practice instead of economism and historical determinism. Given the lack of explicit citations, it is somewhat difficult to discern who in particular she is criticizing. We might adduce from references to Lenin and Trotsky that she is both criticizing and situating herself to the left of the Stalinism of the French Communist Party (Beauvoir [1947] 1976, 22–23; 119). In any case, she levels two criticisms at determinism. First, historical determinism postulates historical Progress as a transcendent value, a kind of archetype of an ideal and unambiguous human society. Her critique, indeed, echoes Marx and Engels's polemic against utopian socialism found in *The Communist Manifesto*:

> Unlike the old utopian socialisms which confronted the earthly order with the archetypes of Justice, Order, and the Good, Marx does not consider that certain human situations are, in them-

selves and absolutely, preferable to others. It is the needs of people, the revolt of a class, which define goals and ends. It is from within a rejected situation, in light of this rejection, that a new state appears as desirable; only the will of men decides; and it is on the basis of taking root in the historical and economic world in a certain and singular way that this will throws itself toward the future, choosing then a perspective where such words as goal, progress, efficacy, success, failure, action, adversaries, instruments, and obstacles have a meaning. Then certain acts can be regarded as good and others as bad. (Beauvoir [1947] 1976, 18–19tm)

More importantly, next, she contends, like Sartre in "Materialism and Revolution" (1946), that economic reductionism is both conceptually and practically reductive—class consciousness is reduced to external causes or becomes merely a "reflection of objective conditions by which the situation of the class or the people under consideration is defined" (Beauvoir [1947] 1976, 19). Thus, in the passage above, Beauvoir situates the existentialist emphasis on freedom and agency *with* Marx in opposition to economic reductionism.

But left at this point, her critique of reductionism is neither unique to existentialism nor focused on how this theoretical problem contributes to practical failures. Thus I think it is important to highlight how this point could translate into problems in practice and the fundamental normative question of value: Does this practice contribute to a movement of emancipation or does it stultify it? Beauvoir suggests that treating class consciousness as a reflection of objective conditions undermines the agency of the proletariat as willing, choosing individuals. While economistic interpretations reduce the political agency of the working class to reactive expressions of economic and then class interests, Beauvoir emphasizes that we must understand the political choices that guide proletarian struggle.

In other words, Beauvoir rejects economic determinism because she wants to examine how collective free praxis shapes and is shaped by political struggle. She suggests that the proletariat can come to consciousness in ways that contradict or prevent *class* consciousness, but her argument is initially hindered by the weak reasons she gives for her position. For example, she avers that economic reductionism could not explain the existence of an American proletariat that sleeps "in dull comfort" (Beauvoir [1947] 1976, 20). Beauvoir is on shaky ground here, for rhetorical flourishes about comfort are no substitute for a concrete analysis of racism and segregation in the United States. Her claims are sharper later in *The Ethics of Ambiguity*, where she suggests that the proletariat comes to consciousness in ways that are more complicated than a single-axis analysis of class could account for: "Oppression has more than one aspect"; for example, "the interests of the French proletariat are not the same as those of the natives in the colonies" (Beauvoir [1947] 1976, 89). She notes working-class struggle does not necessarily lead to *class* consciousness; hence, in her example, the working class and the parties that represent it could come to political consciousness as a labor aristocracy interested in perpetuating French colonialism.

If we widen our scope for a moment to consider *The Second Sex*, we find that Beauvoir's attempt to situate individual political agency in both socially lived experience and a gender-inflected critique of historical materialism suggests what we now would call an intersectional analysis of multiple axes of oppression (following Crenshaw 1989)—though Penelope Deutscher notes that Beauvoir often treats race, cultural differences, and gender as if they are "abstractable from all the different kinds of relevant others and alterities" while "in particular, sex remains autonomous [abstractable from] of race."[4] These criticisms notwithstanding, Beauvoir maintains that women's oppression cannot be reduced *merely* to class oppression. Summarizing Beauvoir's argument, Margaret A. Simons writes, "Practice in the Soviet Union reveals the limits of such a reductionist theory, which fails to recognize the patriarchal power of the state as oppressive to women" (Simons 1999, 153).[5] But discussions of class must be present in analyzing intersectional analysis, for two reasons. First, one's place in a given economic system functions as a material constraint for action. Second, some individuals are able to choose identifiers of privilege over status subordination in intersecting axes of race, gender, and class. Interestingly, when Beauvoir is able to implicate herself and her privilege as a cis, white, bourgeois woman (characteristics that resembled her presumed reader), she does not abstract class and race. Beauvoir writes, "As bourgeois women, they are in solidarity with bourgeois men and not with women proletarians; as white women, they are in solidarity with white men and not with black women" (Beauvoir [1949] 2011, 8). Women, as Beauvoir contends, choose themselves in a world where they are treated as others rather than subjects, and yet some will identify with the limited privileges offered them as others rather than combat patriarchy. In *The Ethics of Ambiguity*, she avers that "once the structure which shelters them seems to be in danger . . . women show themselves harder, more bitter, and even more furious or cruel than their masters" (Beauvoir [1947] 1976, 38). Critics often point to these passages when they allege that Beauvoir is antifeminist, but this criticism necessitates dismissing or deflecting Beauvoir's critique of privilege: responsibility or complicity must be measured against how individuals situate themselves not only in terms of gender but also race, class, and other distinctions that enable privilege for some and status and material subordination for others—and as I have mentioned, her own failures can be identified on these terms too.

There remains one more theoretical and practical flaw that is sometimes shared between ethics and Left critique when it lapses into moralism: bad choices are reduced, by this moralism, to error or ignorance (Beauvoir [1947] 1976, 32–34). Some Marxist theorists readily treat "mystification" as if it were a synonym for ignorance. In my view, building on Beauvoir's, using ignorance to explain ethical and political failures obviates the responsibility for these failures and interferes with explaining how there may be comprehensible but reprehensible motives behind them. Beauvoir herself sometimes appeals to mystification as a factor in determining how individuals' respective positions affect their agency when she could have opted to interpret mitigating factors in terms of the constraint of means to make choices. She proposes a case of a teenage Nazi who would be, in her view, responsible (able to be called to account) for his Nazism, but who would not be culpable, having lacked the social means necessary to choose an alternative (Beauvoir [1947] 1976, 98). There are other cases, though, where she suggests that there are people (women in "many" societies or slaves in the antebellum United States) who, by remaining in a situation of oppression, choose that situation (Beauvoir [1947] 1976, 37). Contra Beauvoir, on her terms, I would contend that the supposed lack of resistance in the latter cases does not necessarily indicate a situation where these individuals are ignorant or willing; rather, they could indicate a lack of discursive and material means to combat such systems of oppression or merely the lack of visibility of political struggle within the discourses of the oppressor classes.[6] That she accords sympathy to her hypothetical teenage Nazi but disdain for hypothetical women and hypothetical slaves is a glaring failure.

These criticisms aside, Beauvoir demands of us a rigorous analysis of free political choices. If we self-ascribe as egalitarian, for example, we are accountable and responsible for creating and applying egalitarian practices and spaces against the inegalitarian stratification of social or political institutions of a given society. Antifascists, for example, must utilize egalitarian means in organizing in political struggle—which is why fighting fascism entails a three-way fight: crushing fascism but while acting in such a way that also combats the coercive institutions of state power and contemporary capitalism. But for the moment, I want to focus on how existentialism, as Beauvoir contends, gives "a real role to evil": when the means to choose are available, and individuals choose to be fascists, then we must oppose them and hold them accountable for their actions and beliefs (Beauvoir [1947] 1976, 34). When faced with the rise of the Far Right and fascism in the United States and Canada, there are many pundits who incorrectly dismiss the racism and misogyny of the Far Right as atavistic attitudes. There is plenty of evidence that the alt-right (like the European New Right) recruits university-educated, predominantly middle-class, and sometimes social-media-savvy individuals.[7] Academia itself is not immune. Ostensibly academic leftist circles and outlets have sometimes moved toward the Right—as China Miéville once joked, *Telos* thought it had appropriated Carl Schmitt when Schmitt had appropriated *Telos* (see also Lowndes 2017). Richard Spencer holds a master's degree from the University of Chicago. With a decline in job prospects, fewer permanent positions, and a rapid increase in precarious and underpaid adjunct work, academia is also affected by economic conditions that have contributed to fascist creep among other classes. And yet many mainstream so-called analysts continue to ascribe said racism or misogyny to ignorance, poor habituation, or pathology. I want it to be clear that from an existentialist standpoint we must contend that the fascists at issue here are those who, when given the means to choose, have made a deliberate choice to re-entrench the public and psychological wages of whiteness, heteropatriarchy, ableism, and settler-colonialism, and that to do so entails the harassment, intimidation, and oppression of others. This is the only way to give the danger attendant to the recent appearance of the Far Right in public spaces the gravity it warrants.

## 2.3. THE ANTINOMIES OF ACTION

We have examined Beauvoir's philosophical and normative commitments as found in the first chapter of *The Ethics of Ambiguity*. We have seen how she outlines an egalitarian and emancipatory existentialism. In chapter 3, Beauvoir's hermeneutics of emancipation translates the problems of existentialism into the language of political struggle. It is not until this point that we can speak meaningfully of an existentialist ethics committed to political emancipation. However, Beauvoir's ethics is neither utopian nor messianic; instead, she maintains that we must conceptualize the path to political emancipation in order to identify the ambiguities and failures that our actions risk, ambiguities and failures that she calls "antinomies of action." When we focus on these antinomies of action, it becomes clear how Beauvoir transforms philosophical concepts into practical and political categories. For example, in chapter 3 of *The Ethics of Ambiguity*, she politicizes the difference between ontological and moral freedom. This distinction does not merely resolve interpretive issues present in Sartre's early work; it also places our own responsibilities within a concrete ethical horizon. Without the difference between ontological and moral freedom, it is possible to construct an individualist existentialism that views the plight of others with diffidence (though this kind of project reinvents the adventurer's attitude criticized in chapter 2 of *The Ethics of Ambiguity*). One could argue, on the pattern of a previous objection noted by Beauvoir, that "if every man *is* free, he cannot *will* himself free. Likewise the objection that he can will nothing for the other since the other is free in all circumstances" (Beauvoir [1947] 1976, 74). This objection fails when ontological and moral freedom are differentiated. Others are ontologically free, but ontological freedom does not mean that they are able to avail themselves of the social or material means to realize their moral freedom. In other words, Beauvoir establishes that ontological freedom does not necessarily entail the means to moral freedom. Freedom, to be materially realized, requires both the means and the possibility of defining oneself within the temporality of an "open future," which itself depends materially on social interdependence.

Beauvoir argues that the fact of our social interdependence "explains why oppression is possible and why it is odious" (Beauvoir [1947] 1976, 82). There are many aspects of our lives that rely on the labor and commitment of others. Throughout our lives, for example, we often rely on networks of kinship and friendship to provide material and emotional support as we engage in our respective projects. And yet in the midst of an ecologically unstable global capitalist system, the material means that we have at our disposal are produced through a system that continuously intensifies capital accumulation, exploitation, and resource extraction. Beauvoir's existentialist ethics requires us to situate our responsibilities within these systems of oppression. Our choices are never neutral: we can work with others toward common goals, we can work against others to accomplish our own, but all actions admit of a degree of ambiguity because "no action can be generated for man without its being immediately generated against men" (Beauvoir [1947] 1976, 99).

Between solidarity and oppression, our choices and actions become meaningful.

Beauvoir defines oppression as the division of one world into two groups, oppressor and oppressed:

> those who edify humanity by thrusting it ahead of itself and those who are condemned to mark time hopelessly in order to merely support the collectivity; their life is a pure repetition of mechanical gestures; their leisure is just about sufficient for them to regain their strength; the oppressor feeds himself on their transcendence and refuses to extend it [their transcendence] by a free recognition. (Beauvoir [1947] 1976, 83)

She defines oppression as a structure that involves the reduction of some humans to things or instruments for the material benefit of the oppressor; that is, oppression suppresses the possibility for the oppressed of transcendence toward an open future that makes the present meaningful, while depriving them of the material means to realize their moral freedom. These forms of oppression are intertwined, for the oppressor feeds on both the material means produced by the oppressed *and* on their futurity.

Thus, in a situation of oppression, some violence will always be present, though it will typically be represented as social harmony. Beauvoir contends that "the oppressed has only one solution: to deny the harmony of that humanity from which an attempt is made to exclude him, to prove that he is a man and that he is free by revolting against the tyrants" (Beauvoir [1947] 1976, 83). Here we arrive at her existentialist ethics. Below we will analyze the antinomies of action. At first, though, we will follow Beauvoir in attempting to situate the epistemological space in which we ought to understand the antinomies of action. She asserts that "the oppressed is more totally engaged in the struggle than those who, though at one with him in rejecting his servitude, do not experience it; but also that, on the other hand every man is affected by this struggle in so essential a way that he cannot fulfill himself morally without taking part in it" (Beauvoir [1947] 1976, 88–89). In this passage, there are two salient points. First, she contends that those who are most directly affected by oppression and social conflict have a stronger socially lived experience of oppression than those less affected. I think here of Du Bois's descriptions of double-consciousness, in which black Americans must be able to practically engage both white America and black America, or Anna Julia Cooper, who outlined how race cut across gender norms in the late nineteenth century.[8] Beauvoir believes that emancipation *must* be universal, so she would not maintain that those who do not experience could not understand these experiences to a degree, but she would rightly note that the stakes are more existential and urgent for those for whom oppression must be rejected at any cost. Then Beauvoir also introduces what I would call the "dilemma of complicity." It is one of those brief moments where Beauvoir directly addresses an audience of those who are neither the oppressors who directly suppress the oppressed (such as the bourgeoisie, the state, the police, etc.) nor the oppressed. Those who are neither oppressor nor oppressed face the dilemma of complicity when the oppressed revolt: "The ill-will of the oppressor imposes upon each one [of us] the alternative of being the enemy of the oppressed if he is not that of their tyrant" (Beauvoir [1947] 1976, 97). I interpret this passage to suggest that the dilemma is not "either tyrant or oppressed" but rather "solidarity or complicity": those who are neither directly oppressor nor oppressed also face a politically and morally definitive choice: we can fight for the oppressed or accept complicity as their enemy. We must, on her account, accept that this dilemma places a great weight on the privileges we accrue within a system of oppression so that we can examine their cost.

### 2.3.1. Discourse and Disagreement

Beauvoir maintains that the imperative to reject oppression at any cost justifies the use of emancipatory violence. Her discussion of violence applies her general method of moral inquiry: after identifying an ideal (but impossible) situation, she proceeds to map the moral coordinates of failure—where indeed some failures are better than others. Hence she first identifies the ideal situation: "For a liberating action to be a thoroughly moral action, it would have to be achieved through a conversion of the oppressors: there would then be a reconciliation of all freedoms" (Beauvoir [1947] 1976, 96–97). Presumably this conversion would be achieved through civil discourse, but Beauvoir calls it a utopian reverie. The oppressor "refuses to give up his privileges" (Beauvoir [1947] 1976, 96). Nonetheless, the oppressor provides reasons to justify oppression. Beauvoir, before addressing justifications of violence, analyzes the oppressor's justifications of oppression through the lens of political conflict. Practically speaking, the oppressor and the oppressed are not merely two sides of a debate, because the oppressor class also sets the terms of the debate (Marcuse 1969). Nonetheless, Beauvoir's analysis serves a double purpose. First, it shows how these justifications are in bad faith. Second, and more importantly, it tests the political commitments of the reader by identifying the tropes of the oppressor's discourse so that readers who might otherwise view themselves as committed to political emancipation, but who also feel an investment in these arguments, might be able to reflect upon and have done with them.

Thus we must situate the exchange of reasons within a situation of oppression, which divides the world into oppressor and oppressed. I doubt that Beauvoir believes that these reasons are offered to persuade the oppressed, for that would acknowledge an intellectual equality between addressor and addressee denied by the oppressor. Hence these justifications or reasons need only "persuade" others: oppressors and their ideological accomplices, those with privilege, access, or advantage within the situation. Beauvoir situates these reasons as individual moments of a continuous order of justifications. In the first instance, then, justifications for the status quo could be categorized together insofar as they minimize the wrongs committed by oppression. At the most extreme, the oppressor offers reasons as to why either oppression is natural or why the oppressed desires oppression (Beauvoir [1947] 1976, 83–87). If oppression is natural, then it is inevitable and impossible to fight—in this case the oppressed are attempting to overthrow the natural order of things. However, from an existentialist standpoint, where "existence precedes essence," all situations of oppression are contingent but shaped historically by material conditions—thus no oppression is natural. The second argument is a variation on the first; it maintains that the oppressed desires oppression, with the implication that those who resist have illicit desires. We know that claims of this type were common tropes in the antebellum United States (and after), where the master "interrogates" his slaves about their condition and they express their consent. Of course, this trope is in bad faith. Were it meant otherwise, it would entail the intellectual reciprocity between master and slave that is denied by the master. In a system where they could be killed but not murdered, slaves opt for duplicity; when the moral and material means for revolt are available, the answer is entirely different.

The foregoing arguments are illiberal. The remaining arguments are not illiberal. In the first, the oppressor appeals to universal, objective values. These values are then presented as unequivocally good in themselves:[9] "It is not in his own name that he is fighting, but rather in the name of civilization, of institutions, of monuments, of virtues which realize objectively the situation which he intends to maintain" (Beauvoir [1947] 1976, 91). This argument justifies the means (oppression) by appeal to lofty ideals, such as Progress. When appeals to universal, objective values like Progress are raised, Beauvoir contends that such terms cannot be posited as transcendent, existing outside of human projects. We cannot then use these values to determine the meaning of concrete projects or a particular situation; instead, our concrete projects give meaning to our ideals relative to social struggle. When these values are treated as transcendent and absolute, when one treats their societies or institutions as the embodiment of Progress, this legitimates oppression under the guise of paternalism (or worse). The ruling classes identify their institutions with Progress or Enlightenment, and when faced with opposition, they adduce, under "the pretext of ignorance" of the other, "the incompetence of the masses, of women, of the natives in the colonies," in order to maintain their rule, the status quo of oppression, capital accumulation, and resource extraction (Beauvoir [1947] 1976, 138–39). Proponents of "Western civiliza-tion," for example, have for centuries exploited native populations in the colonized world in the name of historical Progress.

The final trope frames oppression as merely one kind of *interest* in competition with other interests. As we have seen, oppression is a social structure that divides society into two, *producing* social con-flict. To frame oppression as interest reduces political conflict to what Rancière has called *parapolitics*: all political claims are mere-ly expressions of conflicting interests (see "3.1. Demarcating Egali-tarianism"). This trope appeals broadly to abstract right: when the oppressed confronts the oppressor and seeks to correct a wrong, the oppressor objects that "under the pretext of freedom, there you go oppressing me in turn; you deprive me of *my* freedom" (Beauvoir [1947] 1976, 90). Though Beauvoir quickly dismisses this argu-ment, it demands further analysis. In one variant of the argument, these freedoms are also framed in zero-sum terms: "Respect for freedom is never without difficulty, and perhaps he may assert that one can never respect all freedoms at the same time" (Beauvoir [1947] 1976, 96). In other words, granting rights to marginalized groups comes at the cost of those who already have rights. These arguments sometimes gain traction in well-meaning liberal dis-courses because they are framed in terms of a liberal understanding of rights. Sometimes these claims are specific: when we no-platform nazis, they often complain that their rights have been violated. Sometimes, these claims are broad: white nationalists and white supremacists, for example, present their views as if they represent white *interests* against other competing interests; that is, "It's not 'white supremacy,' it's a European-Canadian majority in a nation with European roots, which includes our history, our customs, our laws, our languages, our monuments, our faith, and our people."[10] In general, these claims frame white supremacy as *merely* the ex-pression of one ethnic group among others while asserting that other ethnic groups are permitted a degree of social cohesion and social mobility *now denied* to whites.

These claims, however, are made in bad faith. Leading figure-heads of the alt-right and Far Right, such as Richard Spencer, have readily admitted that they appeal to rights such as free speech only in order to advance their agenda (Ami du Radical 2018). As Matthew Lyons points out, the European New Right has long rehearsed the rhetorical devices of—and provided an intellectual veneer to—the ethnonationalism and separatism to which these groups often appeal: they "championed 'biocultural diversity' against the homogenization supposedly brought by liberalism and globalization. They argued that true antiracism requires separating racial and ethnic groups to protect their unique cultures" (Lyons 2018, 58). These claims do not have to make a positive or convincing case; they must merely be effective in shifting the frame of the debate away from the idea that oppression is a social structure; they must merely undermine the legitimate political claims of the oppressed. Here Sartre's analysis of the rhetorical strategies of anti-Semites is apropos:

> They know that their remarks are frivolous, open to challenge. But they are amusing themselves, for it is their adversary who is obliged to use words responsibly, since he believes in words. The anti-Semites have the right to play. They even like to play with discourse for, by giving ridiculous reasons, they discredit the seriousness of their interlocutors. They delight in acting in bad faith, since they seek not to persuade by sound argument but to intimidate and disconcert. . . . They fear only to appear ridiculous or to prejudice by their embarrassment their hope of winning over some third person to their side. (Sartre [1946a] 1995, 20)

In my view, when Sartre says *anti-Semite*, he means *fascist*. His book *Anti-Semite and Jew* was published after the defeat of fascism in Europe, and I believe that the terminological choice reflects this defeat: analyzing anti-Semitism points to forms of oppression that remain present in postwar Europe, whereas his readers might have dismissed his argument had he discussed the continued existence of fascist attitudes after the war. Thus, in contemporary parlance, Sartre contends that debating fascists either normalizes their views as worthy of debate or discredits the seriousness of their interlocutor. When the Far Right frames its agenda in terms of rights, this strategy aims to normalize their racist agenda, but it also treats all demands of political conflict as if they were merely competing interests. This parapolitical strategy appeals to those invested in the status quo because it presents all grievances in general as merely competing interests—occluding the possibility that political oppression is imbricated in the status quo itself. For Beauvoir, as for Sartre or Rancière, political and social conflict is not about competing interests that can be settled in the established terms of rights within a given institutional framework. Political struggle puts the very concept of freedom into question. Liberal democratic systems of consensus rest on some variation of a concept of freedom based on the harm principle.[11] By contrast, Beauvoir defines freedom as having the moral and material ability "to surpass the given toward an open future" (Beauvoir [1947] 1976, 91). In Rancière's terms, Beauvoir's analysis of discourse shows how the demands of the oppressed are a demonstration of *disagreement*.

## 2.3.2. The Antinomies of Emancipatory Violence

We have just examined a number of discourses and tropes, both liberal and illiberal, that aim to justify oppression. Despite their differences, they all place the onus of violence on the actions of the oppressed—that is, in revolting the oppressed are presumed responsible for introducing violence into a situation of social peace. By contrast, following Beauvoir, we assert that oppression is systemic and that oppression divides humanity into two groups (those who have an open future and those who do not), and that this division itself, as it is produced and reproduced in society, necessarily involves violence. When the oppressed must work outside of these established discourses and institutions, we must situate their actions against this systemic violence. Beauvoir affirms the right of the oppressed to revolt, including the use of emancipatory violence. She contends that an existentialist ethics provides a method for the oppressed to evaluate the use of this emancipatory violence: those who use violence for emancipatory purposes must—and when they maintain an emancipatory practice, do—continuously evaluate the means against the ends of emancipation. In "4.4. Militant Antifascism Is Community Self-Defense," I argue that militant antifascism follows a similar organizing principle when evaluating the use of the diversity of tactics. Here I will focus on outlining Beauvoir's account of violence, while answering objections that have been raised in Beauvoir studies.

The general consensus in Beauvoir scholarship concerning her account of violence in *The Ethics of Ambiguity* is expressed by Kristana Arp, who writes that Beauvoir offers "a conditional defence of the use of political violence . . . where it is used as a last resort against an oppressor in order to overcome oppression" (Arp 2001, 125; see also Marso 2017, 107; Murphy 2006, 264). Arp's formulation attempts to clarify a point that for Beauvoir resists absolute clarity. There is no stable point, on her terms, upon which we could establish a "last resort" that unambiguously legitimates violence. All violence against oppression will be presented within a discourse of oppression as having *introduced* violence. And then we are always presented with the problem of asking, "Last resort" *for whom*? While a violent action might be legitimated as the last resort for the wretched of the earth, would it be for those who are faced with the dilemma of complicity? Emancipatory violence, on Beauvoir's terms, remains ambiguous. All practical engagement, though, must be lived in ambiguity and failure, conscious "of the antinomies which it involves" (Beauvoir [1947] 1976, 129). These antinomies of action, for Beauvoir, do not warrant renouncing praxis. Instead, they demand that we be ever more conscientious in our actions. When we fight for the emancipation of ourselves and others, we "must not conceal the antinomies between means and end, present and future; they must be lived in permanent tension; one must retreat neither from the outrage of violence nor deny it, or, which amounts to the same thing, assume it lightly" (Beauvoir [1947] 1976, 133).

In the case of emancipatory violence, the means appear to contradict the ends, and thus we must untangle the antinomies of this violence. Part of the violence of oppression, as we have seen, is that the oppressors treat the oppressed as mere instruments for their will; they feed not only on the material goods that the oppressed produce but also on their transcendence and futurity. Ideally, she acknowledges, oppressors would recognize this injustice and renounce their privileges. However, this recognition is a "utopian reverie." In the concrete case of oppression,

> by virtue of the fact that the oppressors refuse to co-operate in the affirmation of freedom, they embody, in the eyes of all men of good will, the absurdity of facticity; by calling for the triumph of freedom over facticity, ethics also demands that they be suppressed; and since their subjectivity, by definition, escapes our control, it will be possible to act only on their objective presence; others will here have to be treated like things, with violence. (Beauvoir [1947] 1976, 97)

In other words, when oppressors cannot be persuaded to renounce their privileges, the oppressed must suppress the oppressors; the oppressed are forced to reduce oppressors to things, to an objective presence as obstacles to emancipation. It appears, then, that emancipatory violence falls into an antinomy of means and ends that is morally or ethically self-defeating. Beauvoir, however, rejects this conclusion. She argues, in certain concrete cases, that emancipatory violence is legitimate *despite* its failures.

To evaluate the use of emancipatory violence, we must place it back in a concrete context within the social relations of oppression. First, Beauvoir argues that in a situation of oppression, "no action can be generated for man without its being immediately generated against men" (Beauvoir [1947] 1976, 99). In other words, oppression divides the world into two, the oppressor and the oppressed, and any action could potentially impose violence on the oppressed or subvert the structures of oppression. If the oppressed choose to use violence to advance their emancipatory goals, this violence is already surrounded by the violence of a system of oppression. Nonetheless, the violence of the oppressor and the oppressed differs in significance, though they are meanings that can never escape the ambiguity of being constituted within the struggle of two groups with opposing values and ends. The oppressor uses violence to enforce a state of oppression—the end of violence is the reproduction of a situation of oppression itself. The oppressed are forced, by contrast, to constrain the use of violence only to further liberation. As Beauvoir writes, this emancipatory violence "is only justified if it opens concrete possibilities to the freedom which I am trying to save" (Beauvoir [1947] 1976, 137). Hence the extensive discussion above of the normative dimensions of Beauvoir's ethics: *if* forced to use violent means, the oppressed must nonetheless measure these means against egalitarian and emancipatory ends.

Arp, who provides perhaps the most in-depth and nuanced analysis of Beauvoir's justification for violence, nonetheless concludes that Beauvoir's arguments are "somewhat unconvincing" (Arp 2001, 125). By contrast, I think that the interpretation of violence has been unsatisfactorily handled in the literature. We must confront Arp's critique, because our own discussion of violence hinges on Beauvoir's. Arp contends that Beauvoir's justification for physical violence against the oppressor neglects to consider alternatives to outright physical violence or warfare. In other words, Beauvoir "does not explore how targeting the oppressor's power [his material means], not his freedom, might be sufficient to overcome oppression" (Arp 2001, 126–27). On this point, we agree, but for different reasons. In both *The Ethics of Ambiguity* and "An Eye for an Eye," Beauvoir seeks to make sense of the political aftermath of fascism: in the former, interpreting and affirming the actions of the Resistance; and in the latter, justifying the punishment of fascists and collaborators. Though I believe that Beauvoir's purpose is to demonstrate, for the antifascists of the future, the real threat of fascism when it reemerges, in both cases, again, her reasoning is retrospective—which means that it cannot be entirely useful (on its own terms) in prospectively evaluating diversity of tactics. Beauvoir's account of violence, focusing on the French Resistance, is cast al-

most entirely in outright military terms.[12] Obviously our own discussions of no-platforming and punching nazis examine much lesser
degrees of violence.

Arp, however, provides an alternative that rests on a questionable assumption about the social means available to the oppressed.
She suggests imprisonment as a form of depriving material means
as an alternative to killing the oppressor. For the prison abolitionist,
this option would entail legitimating carceral power. But one need
not adhere to prison abolitionism to see the flaw in this argument; it
assumes that the judicial system has an interest in mitigating oppression rather than policing oppressed classes. We could conclude, on
Beauvoir's terms, that a justice system that exists in a system of
oppression will be limited in mitigating it—if indeed the latter is
even its purpose (q.v. Alexander 2012). As Beauvoir maintains in
"An Eye for an Eye," the state and its judicial institutions are themselves agents in social struggle. But it is also important to note that
if emancipatory violence is justified *as a last resort*, on Arp's own
terms, the judicial option must have been already exhausted. We
could nonetheless approach Arp's objection from a different angle;
we could consider how boycotts, blockades, or strikes might serve
to deprive the oppressor of the material means of oppression. This
consideration turns on reasons of tactics or strategies, but we might
conclude on this basis that boycotts, blockades, or strikes are means
that typically have geographical or temporal limits; even depriving
some oppressors of their particular means does not necessarily overthrow the systemic legal and material conditions (such as ownership
of the means of production) that make particular accumulation or
particular, concrete inequalities possible. Thus Arp can only conclude that Beauvoir's account is unconvincing by assuming that
there are reformist options available to the oppressed that are not
necessarily available. Beauvoir is not merely describing what Lori
Jo Marso has called "varieties of *dissent*" (Marso 2017, 99, my
emphasis). In my view, Beauvoir's justification of violence requires
both an examination of the antinomies of action and a fuller, more
nuanced account of the situations in which emancipatory violence is
used, that is, situations of systemic violence and oppression. The

latter is lacking in *The Ethics of Ambiguity* and the other texts from the period. Next we must examine Beauvoir's own limited attempt to consider systemic oppression and violence.

## 2.4. VENGEANCE, VIOLENCE, AND THE STATE

### 2.4.1. An Eye for an Eye

A crucial premise of Beauvoir's argument is missing. In *The Ethics of Ambiguity*, she does not explicitly address the role of the state in her antinomies of action. This oversight is perhaps a consequence of her focus on the political subjectivity of the oppressed; perhaps she expects her audience to recall the injustice of the toppled Vichy regime; perhaps, in embracing Marxism (to some degree) she presumes that the state as an instrument of class domination is already implicated in the antinomies of action. Despite a few brief remarks about the police, in which she contends that the police are merely an instrument to shore up political power, Beauvoir does not explicitly analyze state power in relation to these antinomies. [13] The absence of a critique of state power blunts the radicality of Beauvoir's ethics of ambiguity. As I have already noted, the first principles of existential ethics—to reject all a priori authority and to reject oppression at any cost—upend the deeply rooted assumptions of Western political philosophy. However, without an explicit analysis of state power as a force of oppression, we cannot use Beauvoir's work to rebut what Mark Bray has called "liberal antifascism": "By 'liberal anti-fascism' I mean a faith in the inherent power of the public sphere to filter out fascist ideas, and in the institutions of government to forestall the advancement of fascist politics" (Bray 2017, 172). This liberal antifascism, first of all, rests on the problematic assumption that a public discourse largely mediated by corporations following the exigencies of capital accumulation will filter out ideas that work against the public good. But even if this assumption is jettisoned (as it ought to be), the liberal antifascist could still assert that the state can protect us from fascism by asserting its monopoly on violence. To overcome this objection, we must demonstrate how the state itself is imbricated in social and political conflict. Though such a demonstration is lacking in *The Ethics of Ambiguity*, Beauvoir addresses state power in her essay "An Eye for an Eye" (1946). Her critique of state power is situated in and specific to her analysis of the relationships between vengeance, punishment, and what I will characterize as "existential violence." After outlining her analysis, we will be able to sketch a general critique of state power.

I use the term *existential violence* to mean violence that reduces human beings to mere material objects, suppressing their freedoms, and cutting off their futurity. Not all violence has the gravity of existential violence. In the opening paragraph of "An Eye for an Eye," Beauvoir argues that individual criminal acts do not rise to the level of existential violence because they are products of social inequality, and while they may warrant judicial sanctions, these acts will not be eliminated until their root causes in an unjust social order are extirpated. This kind of violence is not "existential" because these crimes do "not compromise any of the values that we [are] attached to."[14] Existential violence must attack the values and norms that orient our existence as practical subjects; it must attack the values we have chosen or the social reciprocity that makes our freedom morally and materially possible. Beauvoir argues that this kind of violence "arises only at the moment that a human treats fellow humans like objects, when by torture, humiliation, servitude, assassination, one denies them their existence as humans"; she characterizes "the degradation of a human into a thing" as "absolute evil" (Beauvoir [1946] 2004, 248). Beauvoir rarely evokes evil or absolute evil, and I believe these few references serve to emphasize the depravity of certain kinds of violence. In *The Ethics of Ambiguity*, for example, Beauvoir calls lynching an "absolute evil" (Beauvoir [1947] 1976, 146). Individuals are the targets of existential violence; but as I interpret Beauvoir's argument, an act is existential violence when it attacks either the very sense of subjectivity or bodily integrity of an individual or the existence and futurity of an oppressed society or community acting as political agents and living in a world of their chosen values. A lynching in the United States signifies that the only future is one in which black communities are subject to the terror of white supremacy. The genocide of Indigenous peoples during the more than five centuries of European colonization is existential violence and—because, as Patrick Wolfe writes, settler-colonial "invasion is a structure, not an event" buried in the distant past—ongoing settler-colonial projects are contemporary instances of existential violence and dispossession.[15] Vengeance on the part of the oppressed has a fundamentally different ethical meaning than this existential violence; it aims, she argues, to establish the social reciprocity extinguished by the oppressor.

The immediate occasion of "An Eye for an Eye" was the trial and execution of Robert Brasillach, a French right-wing author and critic who collaborated with the Nazis. As Sonia Kruks summarizes it, "During the Occupation he had been editor in chief for more than two years of the fascist weekly newspaper *Je suis partout* [I Am Everywhere]. Among other unsavory practices, the paper would list the names and whereabouts of Jews and members of the Resistance, who could then face Nazi deportation, torture, or execution. . . . Brasillach was not tried on charges related to any specific deportation or death or for his anti-Semitism but for 'complicity' with an enemy power" (Kruks 2012, 156). In modern parlance, Brasillach made a career of doxing people. He was executed on February 6, 1945.

As an occasional text, "An Eye for an Eye" provides Beauvoir's justifications for her refusal to sign a petition urging a pardon for Brasillach. As a philosophical essay, it opens an examination into the ambiguity of vengeance and punishment. Beauvoir writes,

> Every attempt to compensate for this absolute event that is the crime manifests the ambiguity of man's condition, that he is at the same time a freedom and a thing, both unified and scattered, isolated by his subjectivity and nevertheless coexisting at the heart of the world with other men. This is why all punishment is partially a failure. In the same way that hatred and revenge do, love and action always imply a failure, but this failure must not

keep us from loving and acting. For we have not only to establish what our situation is, we have to choose it in the very heart
of its ambiguity. (Beauvoir [1946] 2004, 258–59)

All vengeance (and thus punishment) is ambiguous because its
meaning cannot be unequivocally established: it paradoxically attempts to compel the oppressor to freely accept retribution and guilt;
it attempts to establish social reciprocity that could still be refused
by the guilty party; it affirms our subjectivity at the same time it
punishes another subject. And yet Beauvoir believes that we should
not renounce vengeance—similarly, as we have seen, she believes
that political violence is in some cases a necessary means to liberation—rather "we must stop seeing vengeance as the serene recovery
of a reasonable and just order" (Beauvoir [1946] 2004, 259). Despite its failures, for Beauvoir vengeance nonetheless "answers to
one of the metaphysical requirements of man": the affirmation of
reciprocity in social, intersubjective relationships (Beauvoir [1946]
2004, 247).

Vengeance answers a human need, though not unambiguously.
As Sonia Kruks argues, for Beauvoir revenge "is almost always a
failure *on its own terms*. For it cannot actually restore the prior
situation or cancel the prior suffering. Nor can it provide full moral
satisfaction by establishing actual reciprocity" (Kruks 2012, 160).
As Beauvoir outlines the problem, vengeance demands a situation
of a nearly impossible recognition. Existential violence is an "absolute evil" because it reduces a human being to a thing, or, in other
words, it negates intersubjective reciprocity between human beings.
In addition, given that Beauvoir is considering vengeance in relation
to fascist or collaborator crimes against Jewish peoples, other marginalized groups, and partisans of the Resistance, we should conclude that such violence aims to eliminate the very possibility of the
political agency and existence of these oppressed groups. Vengeance, on her account, is one way that the victim attempts to reestablish reciprocity with the perpetrator.[16] Like Beauvoir, I think that
vengeance is ambiguous because it cannot unequivocally establish
reciprocity between oppressed and oppressor. However, I will argue

that her account here neglects a possibility outlined later by Fanon: insofar as vengeance is a form of political agency seized by the oppressed, it could allow the oppressed to affirm bonds of solidarity between *themselves* that were destroyed by the actions of the oppressor. This form of political subjectivation does not necessitate violence or vengeance; it attempts to explain what violence potentially means to the oppressed who revolt. Thus, while the oppressor may not recognize the oppressed in being punished, the oppressed themselves form bonds of solidarity and, to paraphrase Walter Benjamin, rescue their martyrs and histories from a history written by the oppressor. These are possibilities suggested by Beauvoir herself in works contemporaneous with "An Eye for an Eye." In "Moral Idealism and Political Realism," she castigates "prudent people" who could not see why the French Resistance continued to fight once it was clear that the Allies would soon liberate Paris: "The goal was not a liberated Paris, it was the liberation itself; for the combatants having Paris liberated was not enough, they wanted to liberate it themselves" (Beauvoir [1945] 2004, 183–84). And in *The Ethics of Ambiguity*, she contends, "We must try, through our living projects, to turn to our own account that freedom which was undertaken in the past and to integrate it into the present world" (Beauvoir [1947] 1976, 93). Beauvoir also suggests this concept of self-affirmative reciprocity in the third volume of her memoirs, *Force of Circumstance* (1963).

In "An Eye for an Eye," Beauvoir analyzes three types of vengeance. In the "privileged case," the direct victims of violence avenge themselves against the perpetrator(s). The other two cases are indirect, whereby a third party acts indirectly on behalf of the victim: Beauvoir considers both "private acts of revenge," or extralegal vengeance in their name, and "official justice," legal prosecution and state-sanctioned punishment. We will examine the indirect cases first. First, Beauvoir rejects "private acts of revenge" where individuals carry out vengeance against the perpetrators or their accomplices.[17] Private revenge is fallible (meaning that it may carry out revenge on mistaken grounds) and arbitrary, and it risks being tyrannical, as, she contends, "popular revenge expresses the pas-

sions of the moment instead of manifesting a reflective act of will"
(Beauvoir [1946] 2004, 251, 258). It is unfortunate that Beauvoir
does not elaborate further on the faults of private revenge. I would
like to suggest that her reference to the "barberings" (when women
were publicly humiliated for being involved with Germans or collaborators during the Occupation) could give a concrete character to
the kinds of arbitrary and tyrannical actions she had in mind. Barberings punished women for being involved in social situations and
relationships that were the *symptom* of the Occupation and did not
punish those people who were *responsible* for the Occupation. Since
it did not punish the subjects responsible for the Occupation, the
vengeance of barbering lacked the possibility of reestablishing reciprocity between oppressed and oppressor.

Beauvoir then contends that the legal system also fails to establish reciprocity between victim and perpetrator. Since private acts of
revenge are arbitrary and verge on tyranny, ideally we ought to
prefer a legal system that reduces these risks. However, she argues
that even if the legal system does so, "official tribunals claim to take
refuge behind an objectivity that is the worst part of the Kantian
heritage. They want to be only an expression of impersonal right
and deliver verdicts that would be nothing more than the subsump-
tion of a particular case under a universal law" (Beauvoir [1946]
2004, 258). In other words, official trials produce a separation between "principles and reality" (Beauvoir [1946] 2004, 258). To assess the failures of official justice, we must contrast its separation of
"principles and reality" with the situation of the privileged case of
vengeance. In the privileged case, she writes, "The victim takes
revenge on his own account. When at the hour of liberation the
concentration camp inmates massacred their S.S. jailers, revenge
existed for them in the most concrete and obvious way possible. The
victims and their torturers had really exchanged situations" (Beauvoir [1946] 2004, 250–51). First, direct vengeance occurs within the
immediate milieu of social conflict, where there is a concrete reversal of victim and perpetrator. By contrast, official justice separates
the temporal sequence between crime and punishment. Beauvoir
suggests that by placing Brasillach's crimes in the past, the official

tribunal humanizes him: "We desired the death of the editor of *Je suis partout*, not that of this man completely occupied in dying well" with dignity.[18] This temporal distance is exacerbated by the transformation of the situation in which these crimes occur; between crime and trial, she writes, "between these two universes[,] no passage seemed conceivable" (Beauvoir [1946] 2004, 254). Thus, second, in social conflict marked by existential violence, this conflict also occurs where there is no common normative ground between parties. Instead, part of this social, even existential conflict is marked by the concrete opposition between different normative and social values. In official trials, the state and the court represent themselves as objective, neutral deliberative procedures for rendering justice. Here the state's motives contradict the victims' motives for revenge. Recall that Beauvoir maintains that "it is *our* values, *our* reasons to live that are affirmed by their punishment"—and by contrast the state evokes objective right (Beauvoir [1946] 2004, 246, my emphasis). By evoking universal, objective right, the state situates its decisions *above* social conflict, thus neutralizing its own agency in social conflicts. Drawing on Beauvoir's claims from *The Ethics of Ambiguity*, we conclude that the state must choose, implement, and/or enforce some values and not others. Whether the state's appeal to universal right contradicts the concrete will of direct vengeance, as Beauvoir argues in "An Eye for an Eye," or whether the state's interests as an agent in social conflict differ from the concrete will of the oppressed, as I have noted, official justice fails because it cannot assert the concrete will that direct vengeance does, and thus it cannot reestablish reciprocity.

In the "privileged case" of direct vengeance, the oppressed takes direct, immediate revenge against the oppressor. Beauvoir contends that vengeance is justified against those who commit the "evil" or "fundamental injustice" of degrading and treating other human beings as mere objects. As I have already argued, this degradation and violence puts the future of the community in jeopardy—and vengeance aims to destroy the source of this existential violence. She cites two clear cases of this immediate vengeance: the execution of Mussolini, and those few incidents where captives of concentration camps carried out revenge against S.S. prison guards. In both cases, the oppressed carry out revenge directly—the revenge carried out by the victim is the expression of concrete will (as a form of justified "hatred"), and this concrete will establishes an immediate relationship between crime and punishment.

Beauvoir provides two criteria of direct vengeance. First, it must strive "to destroy that evil [of treating other humans as if they were objects] at its source by reaching the freedom of the evildoer" (Beauvoir [1946] 2004, 248). Second, she writes, it must reestablish the "reciprocity between human consciousnesses the negation of which constitutes the most fundamental form of injustice" (Beauvoir [1946] 2004, 249). Vengeance accomplishes the first criterion but not necessarily the second. To reestablish reciprocity, punishment or vengeance must compel the perpetrator to recognize the agency of the victim. This agency had been previously denied when the victim was reduced to a thing—but the converse is that by reducing others to mere things, the perpetrator had assumed the position of sovereign consciousness: "The torturer believes himself to be sovereign consciousness and pure freedom in the face of the miserable thing he tortures" (Beauvoir [1946] 2004, 248). Vengeance destroys that sovereignty, by positing both perpetrator and victim as subjects of social conflict. Revenge, though, requires "compelling" a "freedom" (Beauvoir [1946] 2004, 249). If the perpetrator willingly assumed his guilt without compulsion, he potentially retains sovereign mastery over his choices; "even in the suffering he might voluntarily inflict upon himself, he would continue to mock his victims in spite of himself" (Beauvoir [1946] 2004, 249). By willingly assuming his punishment before suffering vengeance at the hands of the victims, the perpetrator forestalls acknowledging their agency. Thus, for Beauvoir, there must be a reversal of agency whereby the victims affirm their agency and the perpetrator suffers or endures violence as a victim of revenge. However, while some degree of coercion is necessary for vengeance, it is not sufficient. Revenge also must compel an admission of responsibility, be it guilt or remorse—but this requires *compelling* a free choice. The meaning of any such admission is ambiguous, and hence vengeance always risks failure. The consciousness of the per-petrator remains free to admit responsibility without accepting guilt or remorse: "One can also undergo it [punishment] with a sense of irony, with resistance, with arrogance, with a resignation lacking remorse. Here again punishment suffers a defeat" (Beauvoir [1946] 2004, 250). These attitudes refuse to accept the reciprocity of the freedom of victim and perpetrator. Thus, for Beauvoir, vengeance risks failure—and it almost always fails.

### 2.4.2. "I Had My Own Martyrs"

Like Beauvoir, Sartre, and Fanon, I believe that political agency is forged and shaped through conflict. However, from a critical stand-point, I also think that Beauvoir's model of reciprocity here remains too Hegelian. It is well known that existentialism, from Sartre to Fanon, incorporates features of Hegel's master-slave dialectic as a paradigm for social struggle. Beauvoir famously chose the passage "each consciousness seeks the death of the other" as the epigraph to her novel *She Came to Stay*. And there are numerous references to Hegel's account of struggle in her works throughout the 1940s. But in *Force of Circumstance*, Beauvoir admits that even in the much more materialist *Second Sex*, her conception of "woman as *other* and the Manichean argument it entails," was based on "an idealistic and *a priori* struggle of consciousnesses" (Beauvoir 1963, 202tm). To isolate how Beauvoir's argument is too Hegelian, I will contrast her model of political agency (as it is outlined in her account of vengeance) to Fanon's in *Black Skin, White Masks*. Though he does not cite Beauvoir, Fanon's book is notably influenced by *The Ethics of Ambiguity* (see Gordon 2015, 30–33). Fanon, too, develops a concept of political subjectivation through a critique of Hegel; he places the following passage as an epigraph to the final section of his chapter 7, "The Black Man and Hegel": "Self-consciousness exists *in itself* and *for itself*, in that and by the fact that it exists for another self-consciousness; that is to say, it *is* only by being ac-knowledged or recognized" (Hegel quoted in Fanon [1952] 2008,

191). Like Beauvoir, Fanon argues that social struggle is central to political subjectivation. However, Fanon suggests a different circuit of subjectivation. For Beauvoir, vengeance aims to reestablish reciprocity between oppressed and oppressor. For Fanon, there is struggle between the oppressor and oppressed, but this struggle aims to establish solidarity or reciprocity between the oppressed themselves—indeed, their struggle is one of *self-affirmation*. Interestingly, when Beauvoir revisits the Brasillach trial and "An Eye for an Eye" in *Force of Circumstance*, she provides quasi-Fanonist justifications for her refusal to ask for clemency.

As discussed above, for Beauvoir, vengeance has two goals: first, revenge aims to destroy the source of oppression; and second, it aims to reestablish reciprocity between victim and perpetrator or oppressor and oppressed, a reciprocity negated by the perpetrator dehumanizing the victim. Here, we will focus her concept of the circuit of reciprocity between oppressor and oppressed. At the outset, it is questionable to what degree reciprocity was established before conflict and whether or not it is a desideratum of either party. In Fanon's account of the master-slave dialectic, he notes that for Hegel, the master desires recognition from the slave, but for Fanon, the "master scorns the consciousness of the slave. What he wants from the slave is not recognition but work" (Fanon [1952] 2008, 195n10). Thus, for Fanon, reciprocal recognition does not necessarily preexist social conflict. He is, of course, analyzing colonialism while Beauvoir presumably is considering Occupied France. But even if we grant that there had been reciprocity before the introduction of oppression in the latter case, it is questionable whether the oppressed ought to have the recognition of their former oppressor as one of their political goals.

Let us return to that ambiguous moment where revenge, for Beauvoir, could fail. As she notes, revenge must compel a freedom to acknowledge responsibility. Compulsion is necessary, because were the perpetrator to acknowledge culpability without compulsion, the perpetrator could do so on terms that do not satisfy the victim. However, when compulsion is present, it is also possible that the perpetrator could admit culpability without *meaning it*. We are faced with a problematic dilemma of reciprocity: were we to respect the perpetrator without impinging on the perpetrator's freedom, the moment of reciprocity is likely to occur on the terms that privilege or favor the oppressor; or, in using compulsion, we would be always faced with a refusal of the perpetrator to authentically recognize the perpetrator's culpability (indeed, it is possible for the perpetrator to acknowledge culpability on terms conducive to the perpetrator even under compulsion). In either case, on Beauvoir's account, vengeance would fail. By introducing Fanon's account of political subjectivation, we introduce an alternative model of reciprocity: the circuit of struggle between oppressed and oppressor is a means to the self-affirmation of the oppressed, a dynamic where reciprocity among *others* becomes reciprocity between political *subjects*.

Again, contrasting Beauvoir to Fanon requires shifting between situations—she discusses vengeance, and Fanon discusses anticolonial political subjectivation. The analogy is, of course, imprecise. However, I think that Fanon raises an important critique of recognition in examining the emancipation of slaves in France and French territories. He argues that when in any circumstance where the masters freed the slaves, the "upheaval reached the black man from the outside. The black man was acted upon"; these values "were not engendered by his actions." Because these values were not engendered through self-emancipatory struggle, if the black individual accepts the values underpinning the system, when "he fights for liberty and justice . . . it's always for a white liberty and white justice, in other words, for values secreted by his masters" (Fanon [1952] 2008, 195). That is, emancipation preserved the inequalities already present in colonialism—the basic values (that is, white supremacy) and material relations remain; what the colonizer wants from the colonized is work.[19] Thus, for Fanon, the oppressed's social struggle is the dialectic that forges and affirms new values. As Glen Sean Coulthard writes, "If Fanon did not see freedom as naturally emanating from the slave being granted recognition from his or her master, where, if at all, did it originate? In effect, Fanon claimed that the pathway to self-determination instead lay in a quasi-Nietzschean form of personal and collective *self*-affirmation" (Coulthard

2014, 43). If we reiterate Beauvoir's claims in Fanon's terms, we could hold that vengeance indeed fails to establish reciprocity between oppressor and oppressed; furthermore, given the kinds of existential violence that Beauvoir describes, it is questionable whether there ever was full reciprocity between them. Beauvoir rightly sees failure because she is analyzing the wrong circuit of struggle. Insofar as vengeance can be a form of political subjectivation, it forms bonds of reciprocity between *others* as they emerge as political *subjects*. The victim need not seek the recognition of the perpetrator, for vengeance makes it possible for the oppressed to form bonds of solidarity between themselves, through the affirmation of *their* values, wresting *their* history and *their* martyrs from history as it is written by the oppressors.

In *Force of Circumstance*, Beauvoir reflects on the meaning of the Resistance, the Brasillach trial, and her writings from that period. Concerning "An Eye for an Eye," she writes, "I justified the purges after the Liberation without ever using the one solid argument: these mercenaries, these murderers, these torturers must be killed, not to prove that man is free, but to make sure they don't do it again"; in effect, she claims, her analysis subordinated "the will to live [on the part of the victims] to a search for the meaning of life" (Beauvoir [1963] 1968, 77). Similar to other self-criticisms, Beauvoir exaggerates the faults of her work. As we have seen, in "An Eye for an Eye," she argues that one requirement of vengeance is to destroy the cause of existential violence—but I disagree that other concerns reduced the will to live to an abstract philosophical question of "the meaning of life." I believe that if her earlier account of vengeance and violence fails, it is because she mistakenly limited the problem to the wrong circuit of reciprocity. Beauvoir's later recollections in *Force of Circumstance* provide quasi-Fanonist justifications for her refusal to petition for clemency for Brasillach. Her reasons are based on concern for the *values* that her intervention would affirm. Beauvoir contrasts his treatment with the fates of those members of the Resistance or Jews within her own social circles—to request clemency would be to betray the values of these people either to the interests of the French state (which, of course, would also be affirmed through its use of indirect revenge) or to the fascist Brasillach. This contrast *personalizes* the violence. *Je suis partout* had "demanded the death of Feldman, Cavaillès, Politzer, Bourla, the deportation of Yvonne Picard, Péron, Kaan, Desnos. It was with these friends, dead or alive, that I felt solidarity; if I lifted a finger to help Brasillach, then it would have been their right to spit in my face" (Beauvoir [1963] 1968, 28–29). To help Brasillach would be to betray the values of the Resistance and antifascism. As Beauvoir states, "I had my own martyrs" (Beauvoir [1963] 1968, 163). Revenge can never reestablish the situation prior to the crime, but it can help us form bonds of solidarity that give these martyrs and their struggles a meaning that is authentic to their actions—their struggles and sacrifices tell us more about the dangers and the violence of fascism than our triumphalist histories could.

The limit of vengeance as political action, however, is its negativity. While we could conceive of vengeance as forging bonds of solidarity between those who are oppressed, political subjectivation, to be sustained, must open toward the future. The other meaning of self-affirmation is futurity. Thus I believe that Beauvoir wrote *The Blood of Others*, "Moral Idealism and Political Realism," "An Eye for an Eye," and *The Ethics of Ambiguity* not to evaluate what fascism *was* but rather to demonstrate the gravity of danger when fascism emerged again. While we might find in vengeance a model of political subjectivation, it is better to confront the threat of fascism before it completely roots itself in our social and political institutions.

## 2.5. THE THREE-WAY FIGHT AND NO-PLATFORMING THE FAR RIGHT

I have outlined, in this chapter, Beauvoir's account of emancipatory violence. We have examined the egalitarian norms that justify but constrain the degree of violence warranted as means for emancipatory ends. I then examined how Beauvoir politicizes the state in social relations, namely, to show how the state has its own ends in social struggle despite representing itself as the institution of universal right. To conclude, I would like to synthesize Beauvoir's analyses through a discussion of the practices of contemporary antifascism—specifically de-platforming or no-platforming ideologues of the Far Right.

Beauvoir's analyses are contemporary with the rise of modern antifascist movements, though her writings do not suggest that she had an interest in their emergence. Nonetheless, her analyses are similar to arguments that antifascists have developed independently of existentialist currents of philosophy. For example, we could readily imagine Beauvoir making the case to no-platform the Far Right. The first modern (that is, postwar) militant antifascist groups, such as the 43 Group, used direct action to shut down fascist events. They had numerous techniques, but one involved tipping the speaker's platform to disrupt the event—so de-platforming or no-platforming was once quite literal. Other techniques included provoking arguments and fights to force the police to intervene or occupying event spaces before fascists arrived to organize (Bray 2017, 39–44). As we have seen, Brasillach published the information of Jews and Resistance members so that they could be arrested and/or deported by the Vichy regime. Beauvoir refused to petition for clemency in his case, and we could readily imagine her endorsing contemporary antifascist tactics that could *prevent* similar actions, for example, doxing undocumented students at public events at universities.

It is not my goal here to examine the particular justifications for the tactics used when no-platforming occurs. Instead, I would like to apply Beauvoir's analyses to building the case against what Mark Bray calls "liberal antifascism," and more specifically the idea that reinforcing the state's monopoly on violence protects us from fascist violence better than antifascist organizing. Recall that in "An Eye for an Eye," Beauvoir makes the case for the execution of Brasillach—and for her, it is "our values, our reasons to live" that are affirmed in his punishment (Beauvoir [1946] 2004, 246). There is no passage between the values of fascists and collaborators and those of—whom? The evocation of "our" values is ambiguous. It could be the French; it could be antifascists; it could be the voice of

*Les Temps Modernes*, the review founded by Beauvoir, Sartre, and a number of other French intellectuals. It is at least Beauvoir's, making the case that *our* values are at stake, whoever *we* are. By the end of the essay, though, we know that our values are not the state's. In fact, as she argues, the state and its official tribunals act under the pretense of universal, objective right. Though Beauvoir does not outline a theory of the state, it is clear that she concludes that the state's interests in executing a collaborator are in "our name" but do not necessarily affirm our *values*. She evokes, in these passages, a commitment to both antifascism and antistatism.

We could say, in more contemporary terms, that Beauvoir's analyses anticipate the later antifascist concept of the three-way fight. Though this requires some degree of conceptual reconstruction, it is worth noting that she describes Sartre's anticolonial standpoint during the Algerian War in similar terms. In *Force of Circumstance*, Beauvoir relates that in late 1961 the Communist Party allied with parts of the non-Party Left to form an antifascist organization opposed to the OAS (*Organisation armée secrète* [Secret Army Organization]) (Beauvoir [1963] 1968, 617–33; and see "1.2. Toward a Philosophy of Antifascism" on the OAS, in this volume). Sartre played an important role as a high-profile intellectual—and target of OAS terror—in the short-lived group. As Beauvoir reports their meetings, a tactical difference split the organization; Sartre argued that the struggle was, in our terms, a three-way fight: "Sartre and our friends wanted to express their solidarity with the Algerian revolution in acts; to destroy the O.A.S. it was imperative . . . to attack the government which was the organization's objective accomplice" (Beauvoir [1963] 1968, 617). By contrast, the Communists maintained that only the immediate threat of the OAS should be fought. Due to this split, the organization accomplished very little.

The concept of the three-way fight has a particular bearing on understanding Beauvoir's account of political agency. Though in *The Ethics of Ambiguity* she largely collapses this tripartite schema in the opposition of oppressor-oppressed, we are able to synthesize her arguments about political agency into a coherent whole. Though her account is abstract, Beauvoir maintains that the state is involved in, rather than above, social struggle. We should conclude, on her terms, that a state that holds power in a situation of oppression has a part in implementing this oppression. By consequence, a state cannot act as an impartial institution of universal right. Hence our rejoinder to the liberal antifascist: liberal antifascism defers responsibility for community self-defense—forestalling the advancement of fascist mobilization—to the state. This position assumes, first, that the state of contemporary capitalism (and in our North American context, settler-colonialism) has common interests with antifascist movements. Despite our ideological differences, militant antifascists are anticapitalist, meaning that our goal is not to defeat fascism for the status quo. The goal of militant antifascism is to transform the political terrain to mobilize against fascism and the Far Right *and* capital.

Liberal antifascists, in my view, additionally retreat into bad faith. They posit a state or situation in which it is possible to legislate and struggle in the name of all humanity. In a situation where oppression is present, however, our actions are politically decisive; as Beauvoir writes, our actions cannot affirm our values without negating others. To treat fascist mobilization as if it were merely an exercise of free speech—maintaining that no-platforming is interfering with the rights of others to free expression—requires affirming some values and negating others (not to mention that these rights are protections against state censorship, not critique and countermobilization). Liberal antifascism is in bad faith, in my view, because it neutralizes the stakes of social struggle; it treats the state *as if* it were the neutral arbiter between fascist speech and the rights of marginalized communities. The liberal antifascist approaches conflict with the attitude of what Beauvoir describes ironically as "critical thought." This presumptive legislator "understands, dominates, and rejects, in the name of total truth, the necessarily partial truths which every human engagement discloses," believing that rights can only compete if we maintain on principle a universal and objective approach to rights—to quash the rights of the fascist harms the very basis of rights themselves (Beauvoir [1947] 1976, 68). This legislator forgets that we cannot merely describe or consider both sides, that the attitude of "considering both sides" is itself *taking a side*. As Beauvoir concludes, "Instead of the independent mind he claims to be, he is only the shameful servant of a cause to which he has not chosen to rally" (Beauvoir [1947] 1976, 69). Liberal antifascists are in bad faith because they refuse to see their complicity in enabling the fascist who opportunistically evokes free speech to further a Far Right agenda. A different antifascist has described this opportunism in detail. In *Anti-Semite and Jew*, Sartre argues that anti-Semitic discourse "plays" with discourse in bad faith, for "it is their adversary who is obliged to use words responsibly" (Sartre [1946a] 1995, 20). Nonetheless, the liberal takes the fascist's rhetorical ploy in the spirit of seriousness. When asked by one of his associates, "Are we even, pro-free speech?" Richard Spencer answers, "No. Of course not" (quoted in Ami du Radical 2018). But by situating fascist organizing in terms of rights, the fascist effectively neutralizes liberal opposition by demanding that liberals take their own discourses seriously.

Beauvoir and Sartre, after the war, both published numerous works attacking fascism and anti-Semitism. However, they themselves could have debated the role of the state in fighting these forms of racist oppression. In *Anti-Semite and Jew*, Sartre writes, "I refuse to characterize as opinion a doctrine that is aimed directly at particular persons and that seeks to suppress their rights or exterminate them. . . . Anti-Semitism does not fall within the category of ideas protected by the right of free opinion" (Sartre [1946a] 1995, 10–11).

In a similar fashion, Beauvoir contends that "we have to respect freedom only when it is intended for freedom, not when it strays, flees itself, and resigns itself. *A freedom which is interested only in denying freedom must be denied* " (Beauvoir [1947] 1976, 90–91tm, my emphasis). Sartre is correct that anti-Semitism is unworthy of respect. We are under no obligation to treat racists as if their racist beliefs have any warrant. But in that brief window between 1945 and 1947, there are pronounced differences between Sartre and Beauvoir about what to *do* about racism and oppression. Sartre argues that modern racism emerges as a social category that fractures working-class solidarities, and thus race will exist (at least) as long as class divisions do. But Sartre divides his antiracist program into two pragmatic steps: first, a "concrete liberalism" that provides an antiracist education campaign that intervenes until, second, the broader class struggle can overthrow the conditions that make racism possible. While Sartre is right that anti-Semitism should not be protected and does not warrant our respect, and he identifies the kinds of bad faith used in fascist rhetoric, he seems nonetheless to accept that, for the time being, the state, which ought not protect anti-Semitism as free expression, is ultimately the arbiter over these protections.

Beauvoir builds the case that we cannot pragmatically separate our struggles against the Far Right. If my reading of Beauvoir is correct, our only chance at community self-defense is direct action, and, as I will argue later, the diversity of tactics in fighting the Far Right. The Far Right mobilizes through harassment, intimidation, and violence, to re-entrench the social hierarchies of heteropatriarchy (especially misogyny and transphobia), ableism, antiblackness, and anti-Indigeneity. When fascists show up, their goal, beyond the recruitment of a sympathetic audience, is to harass and intimidate those already oppressed and marginalized in our communities. When they choose universities as a venue for mobilization and recruitment, they do so for the appearance of a tacit endorsement by the institutional platform. But they also do so because places like universities and colleges are often communities where marginalized groups have won, through struggle, forms of respect, solidarity, inclusion, and acceptance that are broader than those of society in general. Fascists aim to break those forms of community solidarity. Their mobilization must be met *now* with better, stronger, and broader antifascist mobilization—and no-platforming is one way to stop the process of recruitment, legitimation, and normalization that abet their attempts to take root in our communities.

## NOTES

1. Sartre writes, "[I cannot] be certain that comrades-in-arms will carry on my work after my death and bring it to completion, seeing that those men are free and will freely choose, tomorrow, what man is to become. Tomorrow, after my death, men may choose to impose fascism, while others may be cowardly or distraught enough to let them get away with it. Fascism will then become humanity's truth, and so much the worse for us" (Sartre [1946b] 2007, 36).

2. But then what about Montaigne's essays?

3. Therefore, ontologically speaking, ambiguity could only be tragic if existence could have been otherwise (infinite rather than finite). For Beauvoir, by contrast, the description of ambiguity as tragic arises on the basis of our projects and attitudes. Otherwise, existence cannot be evaluated: "The fact of existence cannot be evaluated since it is the fact on the basis of which all evaluation is defined" (Beauvoir [1947] 1976, 15tm).

4. Deutscher 2008, 134. She continues: "Yet neither in *The Ethics of Ambiguity*, nor in *The Second Sex* does Beauvoir use ambiguity as a means of thinking about what it means to be simultaneously both sexed and raced . . . the conflicting realities of race and sex offer the possibility of further, and highly nuanced senses in which one might be simultaneously subject and object, being-for-itself and being-for-others, subordinate and subordinating" (135).

5. Beauvoir writes, "There is no way to directly oblige a woman to give birth: all that can be done is to enclose her in situations where motherhood is her only option: laws or customs impose marriage on her, anticonception measures and abortion are banned, divorce is forbidden. These old patriarchal constraints are exactly the ones the U.S.S.R. has brought back to life today; it has revived paternalistic theories about marriage; and in doing so, it has asked woman to become an erotic object again. . . . Examples like this prove how impossible it is to consider the woman as a solely productive force: for man she is a sexual partner, a reproducer, an erotic object, an Other through whom he seeks himself" ([1949] 2011, 67).

6. Consider, for example, Butch Lee's account: "The Underground Railroad when Harriet [Tubman] found it had already been in existence over fifty years. Not only as the largest radical conspiracy in u.s. history, involving many thousands, but as a *major front* of the New Afrikan liberation war. . . . The Underground Railroad that Harriet joined in 1849 and

came to help lead, wasn't civilian, but a military activity. In fact, it was the *main* Black military activity in their protracted war against the Slave System. It was a mass form of guerrilla warfare" (Lee 2015, 20, 25).

7. As one analyst notes, "The 'alt right' now often means an internet focused string of commentators, blogs, Twitter accounts, podcasters, and Reddit trolls, all of which combine scientific racism, romantic nationalism, and deconstructionist neo-fascist ideas to create a white nationalist movement that has almost no backwards connection with neo-Nazis and the KKK" (Antifascist Front 2015). Like the European New Right, they might champion Julius Evola, Ernst Jünger, Schmitt, Corneliu Codreanu, or Aleksandr Dugin before or rather than Mussolini or Hitler.

8. See Du Bois 1903, Cooper 1892; Zackodnik 2010. We will discuss Du Bois in more depth in chapter 5.

9. Though Beauvoir also addresses a variant on this argument that appeals to utility ([1947] 1976, 95–96), this argument is easily dispensed with by asking "Useful, for whom?"

10. This tweet was posted by Faith Goldy on April 28, 2018 (https://twitter.com/FaithGoldy/status/990367785820807169). She has since deleted her account.

11. This principle is typically associated with Mill, who argues that "the sole end for which mankind are warranted, individually or collectively, in interfering with the liberty of action of any of their number, is self-protection. That the only purpose for which power can be rightly exercised over any member of a civilized community, against his will, is to prevent harm to others" (Mill 2015, 12–13).

12. For example, she argues that the French Resistance sought "to create such a state of violence that collaboration would be impossible; in one sense the burning of a whole French village was too high a price to pay for the elimination of three enemy officers; but those fires and the massacring of hostages were themselves parts of the plan; they created an abyss between the occupiers and the occupied" (Beauvoir [1947] 1976, 150).

13. She writes, "All politics [i.e. political power] makes use of the police, which officially flaunts its radical contempt for the individual and which loves violence for its own sake. The thing that goes by the name of the political necessity is in part the laziness and brutality of the police" ([1947] 1976, 154).

14. Beauvoir [1946] 2004, 245. She argues that insofar as they are following orders and their situations involve reciprocity (that is, recogni-

tion of their common situation as soldiers in opposing armies), soldiers' actions during warfare do not constitute existential violence either.

15. Wolfe 2016, 33; he elaborates: "[The] core feature of settler colonialism . . . is first and foremost a project of replacement. . . . In destroying to replace, this logic encompasses more than the summary liquidation of Indigenous people. In common with genocide as Raphaël Lemkin characterized it, settler colonialism has both negative and positive dimensions. Negatively, it strives for the dissolution of Native societies. Positively, the ongoing requirement to eliminate the Native alternative continues to shape the colonial society that settlers construct on their expropriated land base."

16. I will here treat victim/oppressed and perpetrator/oppressor as synonyms. Specific word choices follow context.

17. See also Kruks's reading of *The Mandarins* from this standpoint (2012, 171n32).

18. Beauvoir [1946] 2004, 253. Cf. Kruks (2012, 173), who interprets Beauvoir to mean that the official process *dehumanizes* Brasillach.

19. In the case of settler-colonialism, though, what the settler typically wants from Indigenous peoples is land. See Coulthard 2014, especially chapter 2.

# 3

# POLITICS THAT DOES NOT COMMAND

## 3.1. DEMARCATING EGALITARIANISM

In the previous chapter, I outlined the core tenets of Beauvoir's antifascist philosophy. I argued that Beauvoir's work from the late 1940s can be reconstructed around a theory of political action that anticipates what is now called the three-way fight. In this chapter, I will use this concept of the three-way fight to consider the line of adjacency between antifascism and liberalism through the work of Jacques Rancière. As noted already, the Far Right rejects egalitarianism. Evoking *The Declaration of Independence*, Richard Spencer states, "We hold these truths to be self-evident, that all men were created unequal" (quoted in Burley 2017, 50). "If we consider the left's embrace of equality as its defining characteristic," Alexander Reid Ross writes, "fascism remains decisively on the right" (Ross 2017, 1). In a recent interview, Shane Burley notes that "fascism is, in and of itself, the process of making implicit inequality [that is, the social inequality already institutionalized in society] explicit" (Burley 2018a).

By contrast, antifascism and liberalism share a common commitment to egalitarianism. The purpose of this chapter, though, is to demarcate between what amounts to two distinct concepts of equality through an engagement with the political thought of Rancière. Programmatically speaking, in works such as *Disagreement: Politics and Philosophy* (1995) and his "Ten Theses on Politics" (1998b), Rancière conceives of politics as a practice of dissensus enacted in the name of equality.[1] In his work on Rancière, Todd May has previous demarcated Rancière's egalitarianism from mainstream Anglo-American theories of distributive justice: the latter focuses on "passive equality," which involves "the creation, preservation, or protection of equality by governmental institutions," while the former is a practice of "active equality" or dissensus premised on the equality of intelligences—that each individual is capable of participating in collective political agency which "declassifies" the presumed organization of roles and occupations within society (May 2008, 3, 57). Subsequent to May's reading of an anarchist, direct-action-focused Rancière, authors such as Samuel Chambers, Jean-Philippe Deranty, and Katia Genel have sought to place Rancière's work within a broadly liberal political tradition. Elsewhere, I have criticized Deranty and Genel for reframing dissensus as a variation on Axel Honneth's theory of recognition, which blunts the radicality of Rancière's methodological commitments (Shaw 2017). I will not revisit these claims here. Instead, I would like to dispel the assumption that makes this "recognition" reading—as one variant of a generally liberal reading of Rancière—possible. On this assumption, Rancière holds that dissensual speech *is* political action. As Deranty writes, "Politics in *Disagreement* is a battle of justifications, mainly a battle about what counts as justification and who is entitled to proffer and expect justifications" (Deranty 2016, 54). But there is more to Rancière than discourse. I will argue that for Rancière, speech functions as a metonymy for a broader praxis of egalitarian, dissensual politics. More specifically, I will contend that Rancière's egalitarian politics entails two forms of praxis: the symbolization of equality through dissensus *and* the subversion or elimination of relationships of command and coercion, or violence (latent or otherwise) implemented by regimes of policing.[2]

Were it merely an issue concerning interpretations of Rancière, I would not argue in the somewhat polemical terms that follow. However, I reject the recognition reading because it depoliticizes forms of policing—capital accumulation and the state—that have a stake in political conflict, a stake in maintaining inequalities that abet accumulation and control. This criticism applies to both, in Nancy Fraser's terms, "affirmative" models of recognition and "transformative" models. On her definition, affirmative models "aim to correct inequitable outcomes of social arrangement without disturbing the underlying social structures that generate them" (Fraser 2003, 74). Honneth's theory is on this definition an affirmative form of recognition. In his debate with Rancière, Honneth—unwilling, metaphorically speaking, to leave the sphere of circulation and commodity exchange—concedes that the "freedom of contract in the labor market" is integral to his model of recognition, thus depoliticizing capital accumulation (Honneth 2016, 157). Moreover, when Rancière argues that Honneth's theory of recognition emphasizes a relationship between already existing entities and identities, this not only echoes Rancière's earlier critique of Habermas (discussed in "3.3. Disagreement and Command") but it also bears a striking resemblance to Fraser's critique of affirmative remedies for misrecognition: according to Fraser, affirmative remedies propose "to redress disrespect by revaluing unjustly devalued group identities, while leaving intact both the contents of those identities and the group differentiations that underlie them" (Fraser 2003, 75; cf. Rancière 2016, 83).

Perhaps, then, Rancière's politics would be closer to what Fraser calls a transformative politics, which aims "to correct unjust outcomes precisely by restructuring the underlying generative framework" (Fraser 2003, 74). In what follows, I will argue that Rancière's account of dissensus involves both practices of symbolizing new names of equality and practices of combatting and eliminating the forms of command that implement apparatuses of inequality that are similar to what Fraser calls "status subordination." For example, Fraser argues that the status subordination of women encompasses both maldistribution (the division between so-called productive and reproductive labor and between higher-paid, male-dominated manufacturing and professional occupations and lower-paying, lower-prestige domestic service occupations) and misrecognition (the androcentrism that is "an institutionalized pattern of cultural value that privileges traits associated with masculinity, while devaluing everything coded as 'feminine,' paradigmatically—but not only—women") (Fraser 2003, 20–21). Redressing status subordination, for Fraser, would entail both redistribution (she proposes, as one possibility, a universal basic income) and a form of recognition (in the case of gender inequalities) that would deconstruct the "symbolic oppositions that underlie currently institutionalized patterns of cultural value," such as those codings that differentiate between men's and women's work (Fraser 2003, 75).

Despite the similarities between them, Rancière's politics differs in important ways from Fraser's transformative paradigm of redistribution/recognition. In his landmark *Red Skin, White Masks*, Yellowknives Dene scholar Glen Sean Coulthard criticizes the recognition paradigm vis-à-vis Indigenous struggles for self-determination, concluding that Fraser's own transformative theory of recognition depoliticizes the settler state. He writes, "Fraser's status model rests on the problematic background assumption that the settler state constitutes a legitimate framework within which Indigenous peoples might be more justly included" (Coulthard 2014, 36). Indeed, the full recognition of Indigenous nationhoods would encompass the full recognition of Indigenous title *against* settler sovereignty and throw into question the normative status of settler-state governance. Thus, he argues, when Fraser claims that her status model seeks to address political demands in "polyethnic" polities like the United States, her contention is "premised on a misrecognition of its own . . . as a state founded on the dispossessed territories of previously self-determining but now colonized Indigenous nations" (Coulthard 2014, 37).

There is an important parallel between Coulthard's and Rancière's respective criticisms of recognition. Coulthard attacks the normative status of the state as a mediator of competing claims, while Rancière's politics explicitly frames the state as a form of policing. Hence, for Rancière, the state—among the other institutions of policing—cannot play the role of neutral arbiter of political, even democratic, consensus. This point is especially salient for the analysis of settler-colonialism in chapter 5. For the moment, I will note that Rancière's concept of policing shows the coercive and latent violence in apparatuses of policing such as the state (manifest for example in the legal system, the penal system, and police enforcement), institutional political representation, and work under capitalism. I would argue, given more space, that the way that these apparatuses of command impinge on our lives varies according to social norms that, whether or not they are also to a degree latently coercive, guide, direct, or legitimate how policing impinges more frequently and/or more intensively on some individuals rather than others. Thus I will assume that the reader takes it for granted that in the United States or Canada (among other settler-colonial states, obviously) we cannot provide a complete analysis—and more importantly, we cannot organize effectively against oppression and domination—of a legal system, political representation, or work, without addressing how the norms of heteropatriarchy, antiblack racism, settlerism, and ableism privilege some people and marginalize others.

I will restrict my focus here, though, to Rancière's analysis of the problem of command and coercion. I intend this analysis to provide textual evidence from *Disagreement* and "Ten Theses on Politics" to establish that command and coercion are important problems for Rancière. Rancière, in fact, argues that command and coercion need not be legitimated by prior forms of oppression but rather that the very form of command or an order *produces* or *institutes* relations of inequality where they may not already be present.

I have divided my argument into three parts. Before proceeding, though, I would like to address how we might understand the relationship between command and coercion (which I discuss here), and violence (which I discuss in "4.3. Punching Nazis Is Not Anti-Egalitarian"). A liberal reading of Rancière might suggest, as we reconstruct a theory of political violence in his work, that Rancière's opposition of politics and policing is analogous to Hannah Arendt's opposition of political power and violence. I consider such an analogy to be superficial. On the one hand, Arendt defines power broadly as "the human ability . . . to act in concert," whereas for Rancière politics is strictly egalitarian, a dynamic of subjectivation that begins from the supposition of the equality (Arendt 1970, 44). His politics is much more narrow, relegating much of what Arendt would consider political power to policing. On the other hand, as I will show in "4.3. Punching Nazis Is Not Anti-Egalitarian," Rancière rejects the strict opposition of politics and violence when he argues that political insurrection (or the threat thereof) gives force to egalitarian demands.

Having made these interpretive decisions explicit, we can now proceed. In "3.2. Politics against the Police," I outline Rancière's opposition between politics and the police. While doing so, I propose that we can interpret Samuel Chambers's and Todd May's differences concerning Rancière—aside from the obvious fact that May is an anarchist and Chambers isn't—as rooted in the respective weight each gives to the role of symbolization and the role of combating command in Rancière's politics. In "3.3. Disagreement and Command," I show how the problem of command is outlined in Rancière's *Disagreement* within what other critics have analyzed as his polemic with Habermas. Finally, in "3.4. Why Fascism Isn't Politics," I argue that by emphasizing the way that egalitarian politics combats reified structures of command and coercion, we can have done with the objection—raised by Jodi Dean—that Rancière's politics is, at best, *merely symbolic*, that is, *merely* dissensual speech. I have titled the section as I did because I conclude by showing how Rancière's work demonstrates that Far Right social movements are not *political* but rather both *parapolitical* and insurrectionary.

In fact, we can phrase this more precisely: the Far Right is an insurrectionary movement that involves two strategies—parapolitical social mobilization and (typically) white supremacist insurrectionism. The former functions to frame the latter. Here, I will focus on the parapolitics of the Far Right; in chapters 4 and 5, I will focus on it as a form of insurrectionism. We should be precise when describing the Far Right as a form of parapolitics. For Rancière, parapolitics was "basically invented" by Aristotle and given its modern formulation in terms of the social contract by Hobbes (Rancière [1995] 1999, 70, 75). Broadly speaking, parapolitics is a form of political philosophy that identifies politics with the police order, "transforming the actors and forms of action of the political conflict into the parts and forms of distribution of the policing apparatus" (Rancière [1995] 1999, 72). In other words, the parapolitical schema acknowledges that politics is conflictual, but it reduces the conflict between the part of those who have no part and the police to concerns about *access* to institutions of governance and the distribution of rights and goods. Thus conflict is merely that of competing interests.[3] When I say that the Far Right has embraced parapolitics, I mean that when the Far Right coalesces as a movement or begins to root within a given political system, it will normalize its demands in the discursive language of that system. Or, to simplify further, the Far Right is opportunistic. Therefore, we can expect to see fascistic arguments phrased in terms that take advantage of the abstraction present in liberal enumerations of rights. But when they talk among themselves, members of the Far Right explicitly reject equality.

I have already stated that policing in North America serves to enforce capital accumulation, white supremacy, heteropatriarchy, ableism, and settler-colonialism, and thus we should expect—*and we find*—that the Far Right coalesces around perceived failures of the state to enable white social mobility, heteropatriarchy, and ableism, while enforcing patriarchal gender norms, antiblackness, and anti-Indigeneity. Therefore the Far Right, as a rule, maintains that the state has failed to uphold the privileges that it ought to, and thus *the Far Right mobilizes through harassment, intimidation, and violence, to re-entrench these social hierarchies.*

## 3.2. POLITICS AGAINST THE POLICE

Rancière draws a sharp distinction between politics and the police. For those of us involved in political organizing, his terminology vividly evokes the opposition in the streets between demonstrators and cops. But just as we acknowledge that cops enforce order when the broader forms and institutions of domination and exploitation are challenged by mass movements, Rancière argues policing is not just what uniformed cops do but also includes much of what passes as politics in our discourses (including the features of parliamentarianism such as elections, representative government, or governance). All of these practices and institutions share a common assumption: that society necessitates an inegalitarian and stratified distribution of roles and places in society. By contrast, Rancière contends that politics is the enactment of the supposition of the intellectual equality of any and all human beings.

Thus, while we might begin with the vivid image of people in the street resisting cops, there's also a degree of abstraction in Rancière's conceptual distinction between politics and the police. He refers, for example, to the subject of politics as "the part of those who have no part" rather than specific sociological groups. Such abstraction, in this case, is deliberate on Rancière's part, for it forestalls delimiting a priori conditions of political agency concerning who this part *is*, since this ontologizing move risks excluding political subjects who have yet to emerge (or have yet to enter into sociological description) and who we political theorists cannot foresee.[4] However, in drawing the opposition between politics and police, there remains a degree of ambiguity in their relation. At some points, Rancière highlights their heterogeneity: "Politics stands in distinct opposition to the police" ([1998b] 2010, 36), or "politics occurs when there is a place and a way for two heterogeneous processes [i.e., policing and equality] to meet" ([1995] 1999, 30). At other points, as already indicated in the latter quotation, he underlines that despite their heterogeneity, politics takes place when practices of equality confront policing; at various points, he defines dissensus as two worlds—one where the part of those who have no part are visible or counted by virtue of their self-empowerment, and one where they remain invisible or uncounted—in a single world (Rancière [1995] 1999, 27, 42; [1998b] 2010, 37).

This paradoxical politics has been a point of contention in Rancière scholarship. Slavoj Žižek and Jodi Dean, for example, accuse Rancière of proposing a "pure"—and thus always already impractical—politics, a form of politics that is absolutely heterogenous to policing and thus ineffective (Žižek 1999, 232–33; Dean 2011, 87). We will address Dean's critique below. But a similar line of critique has been advanced by Samuel Chambers against Todd May. According to Chambers, May advocates an "pure" anarchistic politics that departs from what Chambers sees to be a crucial feature of Rancière's thought: that politics is by definition impure, that is, politics is always a supplement to the distribution of a given order of policing. While I will grant Chambers's criticisms in part, I will also emphasize how May remains attentive to the antiauthoritarian features of Rancière's politics that are overlooked by Chambers's loosely liberal interpretation of Rancière. May is correct to point out that politics and policing must be heterogenous practices of organizing social relations, for these practices can be either egalitarian or inegalitarian but cannot be both. Maintaining this point is hardly purist.

At this point, I will begin mustering textual evidence for my reading of Rancière. In *Disagreement*, he defines the police as

> an order of bodies that defines the allocation of ways of doing, ways of being, and ways of saying, and sees that those bodies are assigned by name to a particular place and task; it is an order of the visible and the sayable that sees that a particular activity is visible and that another is not, that this speech is understood as discourse and another as noise. (Rancière [1995] 1999, 29)

Policing is a stratified form of organizing what Rancière calls a "distribution of the sensible" (*partage du sensible*). As Rancière notes, distribution or partition (*partage*) is to be understood, first, as both sharing and division of the sensible (*aisthesis*), and then, second, as an account or count of how this *aisthesis* is shared or divided. A distribution of the sensible orients socially lived experience; it defines the roles, actions, places, and meanings of those within a given community. Policing involves distributing bodies and roles, but it also symbolizes these relations in a specific manner; as an apparatus of symbolization, policing allots ways of speaking, acting, and being and delimits speech and noise, visibility and invisibility, existence and nonexistence. Rancière characterizes a policed symbolization of social order in two ways. He holds that it naturalizes distinctions so they are understood as immediate and objective rather than historically mediated (Rancière [1995] 1999, 16–17). And then he also characterizes policing as a form of symbolizing social space as saturated space. In the seventh thesis of "Ten Theses on Politics," Rancière argues that policing symbolizes the community without remainder or supplement:

> *Politics stands in distinct opposition to the police. The police is a distribution of the sensible whose principle is the absence of void and supplement.* The police is not a social function but a symbolic constitution of the social. The essence of the police lies neither in repression nor even control over the living. Its essence lies in a certain way of dividing up the sensible. . . . Political dispute brings politics into being by separating it from the police, which causes it to disappear continually either by purely and simply denying it or claiming political logic as its own. (Rancière [1998b] 2010, 36–37)

According to the logic of policing, all parts of the community are accounted for; this count precludes—via symbolization—the possibility that there is part of the community that is not counted, what Rancière calls a "part of those who have no part" or the "part with no part" (*part des sans-part*). In, for example, contemporary systems of consensus, demonstrations against the wrongs produced by that system are often symbolized as pathology, delinquency, criminality, or terror (Rancière [2012] 2016, 152).

For our purposes, thesis 7 appears to undermine my claim that policing entails both symbolization *and* coercion. As Rancière notes, policing is neither repression nor control over the living; it is a "symbolic constitution of the social." However, there are two ways to respond to this problem. First, I take such a remark to mean, as Chambers argues, that when we're talking about policing, "there can be no clear-cut difference between distribution and its enforcement" (Chambers 2013, 71). By conceptualizing the police as a regime of distributing the sensible, Rancière seeks to avoid two unilateral models of police power: The first, which he associates with the concept of an ideological state apparatus, is that a given distribution of the social order is imposed from above by the powers that be and *then* subsequently enforced by the police order (Rancière [1995] 1999, 29). The second is that of Lacanian political critique—as we will see with Dean—in which policing is *first* a repressive force and *then* a force that subsequently distorts all attempts to symbolize the social order.

There is additional evidence that Rancière does not view the police as merely an apparatus of symbolizing the distribution of social space. On this point, we can return to the differences between Chambers and May on Rancière's politics. We have thus far said little about what his politics involves, because that is the point at issue in our discussion. However, there are two programmatic claims we can begin with:

1. "Political activity is whatever shifts a body from the place assigned to it or changes a place's destination; it makes visible what had no business being seen, and makes heard [*entendre*] a discourse where once there was only place for noise; it makes understood [*entendre*] as discourse what was once only heard [*entendu*] as noise" (Rancière [1995] 1999, 30).
2. Politics involves an "open set of practices driven by the assumption of equality and by the concern to test this equality" (Rancière [1995] 1999, 30).

At issue is *how* politics relates to policing, and I have deliberately chosen two passages that leave this question open. Nevertheless, we can glean that politics involves enacting the supposition of equality and that it involves some form of distributing bodies that subverts the distribution within a given regime of policing. I will argue, in more detail below, that for Rancière, politics (*la politique*) is egalitarian insofar as it symbolizes equality by introducing new ways of relating subjects, places, and objects; and it resists, disrupts, and subverts social relations of command.

Now, Chambers argues that May effects a kind of "Manichean transformation" of Rancière, introducing a pure politics untainted by policing: "May 'elevates' politics to a pure form of action, while reducing police to an *anti*-political and implicitly repressive order of domination and injustice" (Chambers 2013, 83, 76). Certainly, there are points where Chambers's critique is warranted. For example, May, at points, too readily identifies "distribution" with "policing," arguing that "distributions are what governments do. But they are not what people do" (May 2008, 47; Chambers 2013, 79). By contrast, as we see in the first passage on politics above, if we embody egalitarian practices, that, too, is a mode of distributing the sensible. Nevertheless, I do not think that the distinction between "pure" and "impure" politics isolates the central point of contention between Chambers and May. To situate, as Chambers does, May's reading against an exegesis of Rancière's texts neutralizes how Chambers proceeds, like May, to do things with Rancière's work rather than to merely interpret it. Chambers treats speech and "literarity"—an "excess of words" to defined places—as the emblematic paradigm of Rancière's politics (Chambers 2013, 88–122). By contrast, May notes that while speech is often privileged in Rancière's account of politics, it need not be the metonymy for politics tout court—we could also conceptualize politics through metaphors of place, embodiment, and direct action (May 2008, 58–59). Their difference, then, could be that Chambers emphasizes how politics is symbolized while May emphasizes how relations of egalitarian praxis are by definition opposed—heterogenous—to the inegalitarian distributions of the police order. Thus, when Rancière argues that political conflict "forms an opposition between logics that count the parties and parts of the community in different ways," May emphasizes how these "logics" are embodied through political subjectivation or techniques of policing (Rancière [1998b] 2010, 35). And, as I will argue below, if in *Disagreement*, command is one of the central problems of policing, then we need to take seriously Rancière's other claim, in "Ten Theses on Politics," that an egalitarian or democratic politics is, according to the supposition of equality, a practice of "command that does not command (*commandment de ce qui ne commande pas*)" (Rancière [1998b] 2010, 31tm). May takes politics and policing to be heterogenous because egalitarian praxis must carve new spaces where inequality—command and coercion—are no longer instituted. This is especially evident in his essay, "Rancière and Anarchism," where May argues that Rancière's work indicates the possibility of forms of governance that embody the idea that everyone is equally entitled to govern: "At certain points, some might be entitled to give orders to others, who might be obliged to obey them. On the other hand, it would not be a form of governance that presupposes that those giving the orders would be entitled to those orders in the sense of being justified by any quality they possessed" (May 2012b, 121). While May strives to consider how relations of equality might be institutionalized—which for Rancière is not possible[5]—this hardly constitutes a kind of "Manichean transformation" of Rancière, introducing a pure politics untainted by policing (Chambers 2013, 83). If the problem is whether, when politics takes place, our politics reifies relations of command *or not*, and relations of coercion *or not*, of violence *or not*, then May's point is hardly Manichean; it's a self-reflexive question about how our practices prefigure the demands we're fighting for *or not*. This politics divides the common world in two, but it must also, to some degree, always come into conflict with policing in the common space of the community, combatting both relations of command and coercion and forms of symbolizing, legitimating, and naturalizing the arguments for inequality.

## 3.3. DISAGREEMENT AND COMMAND

So far I have argued that Rancière's claim that the police is a symbolic constitution of the social order does not preclude the further claim that policing institutes relations of command and coercion. If policing entails both the stratification of roles and occupations in a given society and the symbolization and normalization of these forms of inequality, then politics must involve resisting and combatting both. Rancière makes this explicit in the third of his "Ten Theses on Politics" during a brief analysis of Plato's *Laws*, where he focuses on how, for Plato, democracy is equivalent to drawing lots to govern; what both share is "the complete absence of any entitlement to govern" (Rancière [1998b] 2010, 31). In contrast to Plato's attempt to ground social inequality in a foundational principle, title, or *arkhê*, Rancière contends that politics is "a specific break with the logic of the *arkhê*," a form of "command that does not command (*commandment de ce qui ne commande pas*)" (Rancière [1998b] 2010, 31tm). It might be possible to consign such a remark to its circumstances, namely, his reading of Plato. However, he weaves together the threads of theses 3 and 7 in thesis 8. There he frames policing, as a symbolic constitution of social space, in the form of an order or command: when these modes of constituting social space are disrupted in a scene such as a demonstration, the police instruct the bodies in a given space to "Move along! There's nothing to see here!" (Rancière [1998b] 2010, 37). Indeed, kettling protesters or cordoning off demonstrations is not just a form of containing political action but also an attempt to control the visibility of contested social spaces.

In this section, I argue that political mobilization against command and coercion plays an important role in Rancière's account of politics in *Disagreement*—when politics is enacted, it is not merely symbolic but it also undermines or combats relations of command and coercion. By focusing on how politics is always "doubled" (cf. Chambers 2013, 57–74), confronting relations of command and forms of symbolization, we can also demonstrate the coherence of Rancière's claim that politics is heterogeneous to policing even though it possesses "no objects or issues of its own"; indeed, that "its sole principle, equality, is not peculiar to it and is in no way in itself political" (Rancière [1995] 1999, 31). Politics is heterogenous to policing insofar as it combats relations of command and coercion. But politics also has no objects or issues of its own because it enacts the supposition of equality in such a way that raises a dissensus about common objects or issues; it takes terms such as *justice* or *democracy* and opens a space for their symbolization that departs from what they mean within a police order. Thus we need not introduce what Chambers has criticized as the "three-term model" of Rancière's politics; both Jean-Philippe Deranty and Oliver Marchart have argued that Rancière's opposition between politics and policing, to be coherent, requires the concept of a space that mediates between the two, which they call "the political" (*le politique* as opposed to Rancière's *la politique*).[6] While there are texts where Rancière does discuss the difference between *la politique* and *le politique*, Chambers notes that "Rancière's central works on politics from the 1990s were all produced *after* the 1991 lecture that had suggested three terms (in English), yet Rancière did not bother to fold that terminology into *La Mésentente*" (Chambers 2013, 56). And when the term *le politique* appears in *Disagreement*, Rancière generally uses it to signal how critics and ideologues deny the possibility of politics (as dissensus) by positing the political as an already defined, or even originary, object or place of politics.[7]

To claim though, as Rancière does, that politics has "no objects or issues of its own;" that "its sole principle, equality, is not peculiar to it and is in no way in itself political" seems to point to another three-term model: politics, policing, and equality (Rancière [1995] 1999, 31). To complicate matters, he not only claims—as we have seen—that politics is the enactment of the supposition of equality, that equality is not particular to politics, but he also states that "inequality is only possible through equality" (Rancière [1995] 1999, 17). The latter two claims seem to suggest that equality is a fundamental or original social relation, an ontological substrate that delimits human being-in-common (Deranty 2016, 66). However, this would commit Rancière to reinstating the logic of an *arkhê*. Instead, he refuses to ontologize equality; his use is functional, meaning that he focuses on how relations of equality are *enacted*.[8] On the one hand, relations of equality are not exclusive to politics. As the broader work of Rancière has shown, there can be relations of equality in pedagogy, literature, and aesthetics. Furthermore,

May (2012a) has argued that friendship can embody relations of equality. These relations, when enacted, open temporary spaces where the inequalities of policing are resisted or undermined. On the other hand, there are some actions in which no relation of equality, in Rancière's sense, is operative, such as killing. Thus far I have not discussed violence beyond the scope of command or coercion because I do not think we can outline a Rancièrean concept of violence without first examining the latent violence present in apparatuses of policing, and it is this latent violence of command and coercion that means that we are not dealing merely with a discursive or symbolic politics.

We will focus on two points in *Disagreement* where Rancière analyzes the performative contradictions of relations of command. Not only do these passages demonstrate that command and coercion are, for Rancière, part of the police order but they also echo arguments found in the rich tradition of francophone anticolonialism. The first passage appears at the end of chapter 1, when Rancière contends that all forms of inequality are historically contingent. Though the Western tradition of political philosophy has sought to naturalize these inequalities, all social stratification is premised on a contradiction:

> There is order in society because some people command and others obey, but in order to obey an order at least two things are required: you must comprehend the order and you must comprehend that you must obey it. And to do that, you must already be the equal of the person who is ordering you. It is this equality that gnaws away at any natural order. (Rancière [1995] 1999, 16)

A command institutes the difference between those who command and those whose task it is to obey. And commands are coercive because they carry the implication of retribution if they aren't carried out: unemployment is one palpable result for a worker who does not obey orders at work. And yet all commands imply a performative contradiction. On the one hand, an order indicates a power differential between those who give orders and those who are supposed to follow them. On the other hand, despite this asymmetry, those who command performatively concede that those who obey understand them. Therefore relations of command and inequality are paradoxical: to command requires dividing humanity into (at least) two categories—those who command and those who obey—but to make this division legible, those who command must assume the intellectual equality of those who command and those who obey. In the second passage, Rancière analyzes the performative contradiction of the "false interrogative" "Do you comprehend?" (Rancière [1995] 1999, 44). This analysis plays an important role in chapter 3, "The Rationality of Disagreement," situated as it is within a broader polemic against Habermas. While this polemic has drawn the attention of numerous scholars, I consider Matheson Russell and Andrew Montin's analysis to be the most concise and attentive account of their differences.[9] For Habermas, they write, the theory of communicative action is to provide the normative foundation for a discourse that aims for the mutual recognition of interlocutors "as equals with respect to their capacity for rational speech and rational evaluation of speech" (Russell and Montin 2015, 543). Though mutual recognition and the ideals of communicative action are attenuated by concrete circumstances, Habermas believes that partners to a communicative understanding cannot ultimately refuse these ideals while availing themselves of the legitimacy and warrant provided by them. Rancière, then, undermines Habermas's framework by demonstrating that, for "common understanding" to be reached by interlocutors in an intersubjective setting, "it is not necessary for the speaker to presuppose the equal standing of the hearer as a partner in dialogue. An understanding may just as well be reached on the presupposition of the hearer's incapacity as on the presupposition of their capacity to participate in rational discourse as an equal" (Russell and Montin 2015, 545–46).

To illustrate this problem, Rancière points toward the speech situation in which the question "Do you comprehend?" functions as a technique for distinguishing between those who command and those who obey. As Russell and Montin point out, the question presumes that the addressee is incapable of rationally contributing

to a dialogue about the implicit command framed as an interrogative—it is presumed that the addressee could only disagree on the
basis of a misunderstanding or failure to comprehend, but not for
good reasons (Russell and Montin 2015, 546). While I agree with
their summary of the problem, I think their interpretive choices are
not incisive enough in this case. A command need not assume prior
inequality between interlocutors; it *produces* this inequality. "Do
you comprehend?" as a command, as Rancière writes, "draws a line
of division [*partage*]" between two senses of the word *comprehend*
and two categories of speaking beings; it makes it understood to its
addressee(s) that there are those who comprehend and those from
whom the speaker expects a response and those whose task it is to
follow orders (Rancière [1995] 1999, 45).

We are, however, not only interested in how command produces
inequality but also how the implicit supposition of the equality of
intelligences that is also communicated by a command can be politicized. Rancière notes, while analyzing the meaning of "Do you
comprehend," that the term *comprendre*—like many other expressions concerning comprehension or understanding (*entendre*)—
needs to be interpreted nonliterally; instead, it should be understood
ironically (Rancière [1995] 1999, 44). More specifically, he contends that disagreement can emerge when "Do you comprehend?" is
understood (*entendre*) both literally and ironically. He argues that
addressees must understand their relation to the enunciator in order
to know whether the question "Do you comprehend?" requires a
response to the problem at hand or whether the content of the question is, "It's not up to you to comprehend; all you have to do is
obey'" (Rancière [1995] 1999, 45). But it is precisely this understanding that comes into question when politics enacts the rationality of disagreement (Rancière [1995] 1999, xii). Therefore, in what
follows, I will examine Rancière's usage of the terms *disagreement*
(*la mésentente*) and *entendre* before returning to the problem of
command, for it is through disagreement that politics symbolizes its
dissensus with a given police order.

In work subsequent to *Disagreement*, Rancière has noted that the
translation of *la mésentente* as *disagreement* loses some connota-

tions of the French.[10] An Anglophone reader could hear disagreement as a juridical dispute, given that Rancière not only characterizes, throughout *Disagreement*, politics as the litigious demonstration of a wrong but also illustrates his account of political subjectivation through a scene drawn from the 1832 trial of Auguste Blanqui (Rancière [1995] 1999, 37–38). However, a juridical interpretation carries the connotation that disagreement takes place between "specific parties that can be adjusted through appropriate legal procedures" (Rancière [1995] 1999, 39). The rationality—the measure—of politics, then, would be circumscribed within an already existing legal framework, which, on Rancière's terms, is an apparatus of policing. *La mésentente*, by contrast, is a "polemical knot" that ties together the "different senses of the word 'to understand' [*entendre*] (see, comprehend, agree) that sums up the sensible and conflictual dimension of the political community" (Rancière 2012, 83). Therefore, the politics of disagreement does not concern already constituted persons, classes, categories, or objects; for Rancière, it enacts practices through which unanticipated subjects, situations, or objects, are made manifest—political subjects are those "whose very existence is the mode of manifestation of the wrong" (Rancière [1995] 1999, 39). By Rancière's definition, disagreement disrupts or reinscribes the received meanings of a given *entendre* (understanding, agreement, and perception) of the social and sensible world; it makes these meanings political and conflictual.

It is unsurprising, then, that in a polemical text such as *Disagreement*, Rancière's use of the term *entendre* and its cognates is performative and self-reflexive, illustrating how common and contentious ideals such as *justice* and *democracy* become focal points of disagreement. Rancière uses *entendre* to signal disagreement between terms when they are politicized in contrast to their received meanings; this doubling and opposition of understandings of a given term appears in the definition of *la mésentente* itself: disagreement is "a determined kind of speech situation in which one of the interlocutors at once understands and does not understand what the other is saying [*où l'un des interlocuteurs à la fois entend et n'entend pas ce que dit l'autre]*" (Rancière [1995] 1999, x). Furthermore, the frequent use of *entendre* in chapter 3, "The Rationality of Disagreement," serves to emphasize how the politics of disagreement practices the interruption and subversion of relations of command. Before returning to "The Rationality of Disagreement," where *entendre* is frequently used, we will examine two other usages of *entendre*. When Rancière defines concepts such as equality, subjectivation, or democracy, he uses *entendre* or its cognates to signal that his definition displaces received meanings of the terms or the genealogies of these terms (Rancière [1995] 1999, 30, 35, 99). As I have argued elsewhere, when Rancière evokes Descartes in his definition of *subjectivation*, for example, this signals a subtle critique of Heideggerian and Marxist understandings of the history of modern philosophy:

> By *subjectivation* I mean [*on entendra*] the production through a series of actions of a body and a capacity for enunciation not previously identifiable within a given field of experience, whose identification is thus part of the reconfiguration of the field of experience. Descartes's *ego sum, ego existo* is the prototype of such indissoluble subjects of a series of operations implying the production of a new field of experience. Any political subjectivation holds to this formula. It is a *nos sumus, nos existimus*. (Rancière [1995] 1999, 35–36tm)

By linking political subjectivation to Descartes, Rancière shifts our attention from received interpretations—of Descartes as the modern epitome of technicity (Heidegger 1967) or of seventeenth-century bourgeois ideology (Negri 2007)—to a current of Cartesian egalitarianism that takes the supposition of "good sense" (*bon sens*) at the beginning of the *Discourse on Method* as its point of departure (see Shaw 2016a, 25–49).

In contrast to the first three chapters of *Disagreement*, the use of *entendre* is infrequent in chapters 4 through 6; it most often signals the way that political philosophy suppresses the possibility of politics. In chapter 4, for example, Rancière contends that "parapolitics" is a form of political philosophy that reduces political conflict to a conflict of interests among different parts of the community. He contends that Hobbes's modern parapolitics reinterprets politics, as the conflict between the part with no part and the police, as the threshold between the state of nature and the state of sovereignty. While human beings are by nature intellectually equal, this equality gives rise to the equality of competing interests: this "equality of hope in attaining of our Ends" provokes the enmity of those who desire the same things, leading to the war of all against all.[11] Therefore, in the state of nature, according to Hobbes, no persons are able to meet and secure their respective needs; in order to do so, individuals alienate their natural freedom to a sovereign and thus enter into a commonwealth. To suppress the possibility of politics within the commonwealth, Hobbes subsequently reinterprets disagreement as the conflict between public and private life. Rancière writes, "The truly calamitous evil, says Hobbes, is that 'private persons' take it upon themselves to decide what is just and unjust. But what Hobbes understands [*entend*] by 'private persons' is nothing other than those who . . . 'have no part' in the government of the common sphere" (Rancière [1995] 1999, 76–77). Hobbes, on Rancière's account, suppresses the possibility of disagreement by excluding equality—including that capacity to disagree over what counts as justice and injustice—from public life.

To return to "The Rationality of a Wrong," to return to the problem of how to politicize and undermine the force of command, Rancière argues that disagreement is possible insofar as those who (are supposed to) obey can simultaneously understand and not understand the command. By instituting the division between those who command and those who obey, an order also falls into a performative paradox that cannot eliminate the possibility of disagreement. That is, it is possible for those who obey to accept both the received meaning of what command entails (the distribution of command and obedience) and how command subverts itself by both presupposing and disavowing equality. In other words, an order cannot eliminate the gap between "the capacity to speak and the account of the words spoken" (Rancière [1995] 1999, 46). Rancière argues that there is a supposition of capacity—the supposition of equality—that must be assumed for an order to work. However, the supposition of equality can be *politicized* and *symbolized* by contesting the paradox between the performative and symbolic functions of an order. Rancière illustrates how disagreement can arise when those who obey receive an order:

> We comprehend that you wish to signify to us that there are two languages and that we cannot comprehend you. *We perceive that you are doing this in order to divide the world into those who command and those who obey.* We say on the contrary that there is a single language common to us and that consequently we comprehend you even if you don't want us to. In a word, we comprehend that you are lying by denying there is a common language. (Rancière [1995] 1999, 46 my emphasis)

We see in this passage evidence of the claims I made at the outset. First, while a command can reproduce the inequalities already instituted within a given police order, this passage also demonstrates that, for Rancière, in a situation where no prior relation of inequality is instituted, a command *produces* relations of inequality. Then, we also see the ambiguity of inequality: for an order to be obeyed, the addressee must comprehend the order and that it must be obeyed. However, to understand this order, the addressee must already be the equal of the enunciator. This is, he states, how equality "gnaws away at any natural order" (Rancière [1995] 1999, 17).

Through this analysis of the problem of command, it is now possible to interpret what Rancière means when he states that equality is not particular to politics—and that equality is also supposed once an order has been given. In conceptualizing the problem in this way, we adhere to a practical interpretation of equality without having to substantiate it as the ontological foundation of social order. When Rancière states that politics and policing are heterogeneous, he means that politics and policing involve different practices of relating to equality. While policing suppresses equality by imposing the division of those who command and those who obey, politics works to disrupt, undermine, and eliminate relations of command. Though politics and policing are heterogeneous, this heterogeneity must still be staged between them. By differentiating between political symbolization and practice, Rancière can paradoxically hold that politics and policing are heterogeneous while maintaining that "politics runs up against the police everywhere" (Rancière [1995] 1999, 32). It is through symbolization that a place emerges for these two heterogeneous dynamics to meet, and it is because symbolization is historically situated that Rancière need not search out political claims that explicitly take equality as their object. Instead, he argues that politics "has much more to do with literary heterology, with its utterances stolen and tossed back at their authors . . . than [contra Habermas] with the allegedly ideal situation of dialogue" (Rancière [1995] 1999, 59).

Rancière illustrates this point about heterology through Pierre-Simon Ballanche's retelling of the plebeian secession on Aventine Hill—which advances our discussion of the problem of command because the secession opened a space where previous relations of inequality were temporarily eliminated. The Roman Republic at that time was structured through a division between patricians, the elite who commanded political and economic power and possessed religious status, and plebeians, who did not. The "plebs," as Martin Breaugh points out, lacked civil and religious status; the term initially "referred to individuals who had neither names nor the right to speak in public" (Breaugh 2013, xix). Furthermore, they were "heterogeneous" in composition and in relation to the patricians: their plebeian status initially referred to their exclusion from political life rather than to any positive, shared characteristics (Breaugh 2013, 5). In 494 BCE, facing destitution and debt that could cost them their status as free men, the plebs withdrew to Aventine Hill. When Menenius Agrippa went to Aventine Hill, he saw that the plebs were acting *as if* they enjoyed the same status as patricians. The plebs, Rancière writes, were executing

> a series of speech acts that mimic those of the patricians: they
> pronounce imprecations and apotheoses; they delegate one of

their number to go and consult *their* oracles; they give themselves representatives by rebaptizing them. In a word, they conduct themselves as beings with names. Through transgression,
they find that they too, as speaking beings, are endowed with
speech that does not simply express want, suffering, or rage, but
intelligence. (Rancière [1995] 1999, 24–25tm)

On the one hand, these practices symbolized the politics of disagreement, in which plebeians acted as if they were equals to the patricians.[12] As Clare Woodford phrases it, the plebs disrupted the "existing police order because rather than relating to the dominant order
in the expected subservient manner the subjects take the rights before they are given them, asserting the equal status they should have
been accorded straightaway" (Woodford 2015, 817–18). On the other hand, Rancière also argues that the Aventine secession undermined previous relations of command. By appropriating the practices of the patricians, the plebs symbolized their equality. However,
Rancière—via Ballanche—argues that their secession makes it possible for them to stage the intersection of two distributions of
speech, not only of *what* is spoken but also *who* has a claim to
speech. The plebs stage a new distribution of the sensible, in which
plebs and patricians become equal as speaking beings, upsetting the
already constituted social order in which the plebs are merely at the
command of the patricians. Menenius concedes, performatively
speaking, when he gives an inegalitarian argument that the patricians are the belly of the republic and the plebs the extremities, that
the plebs must be reasoned with, that they must come to understand,
that they, too, are equals as speaking beings. For Rancière, "from
the moment the plebs could comprehend Menenius's apologia—the
apologia of the necessary inequality between the vital patrician principle and the plebeian members carrying it out—they were already,
just as necessarily, equals" (Rancière [1995] 1999, 25).

We must pause here to establish the political meaning of this
moment on Aventine Hill. To claim that the patricians and plebs are
equals remains ambiguous. Deranty has recently discussed
Rancière's different readings of this scene in order to claim that the

secession results in a moment of recognition. While recounting Ballanche's narrative of the secession in an earlier essay, "Heretical Knowledge and the Emancipation of the Poor," Rancière writes, "This rebellion was characterized by the fact that it recognized itself as a speaking subject and gave itself a name" (Rancière [1985] 2011, 37; Deranty 2016, 38). But the use of the term *recognition* does not constitute a theory of recognition. Rancière continues: "Roman patrician power refused to accept that the sounds uttered from the mouths of the plebeians were speech, and that the offspring of their unions should be given the name of a lineage" (Rancière [1985] 2011, 37). The passage in full indicates, instead, that these plebeian practices were a form of self-empowerment rather than a dialectic of mutual recognition between patricians and plebs. It is also telling that Rancière's narrative never indicates the subsequent changes to Roman governance that followed from the plebs returning to Rome.[13] The *political* moment of the Aventine secession is neither that of a possible mutual recognition nor of institutional transformation. There is, in the politics of disagreement, both an *aisthesis* in which the plebs emerge as speaking, intelligent beings and the enactment of a scene in which the two groups are situated as equals rather than divided as rulers and the ruled. But we must be more specific. The two groups are situated as equals not in Rome but in the division of a common world enacted by the secession. Thus the plebs *become* equals of the patricians at the moment of dissensus, when they symbolize themselves as speaking beings and when they refuse, through seceding from Rome, the latent coercion that treats them as those who merely work and not as those who act, speak, and have names.

To summarize: politics enacts both the symbolization of equality and the disruption of relations of command through the introduction of practices of equality. When, to return to one of the claims discussed above, Rancière argues that "political activity is whatever shifts a body from the place assigned to it or changes a place's destination; it makes visible what had no business being seen, and makes heard [*entendre*] a discourse where once there was only place for noise; it makes understood [*entendre*] as discourse what was once only heard [*entendu*] as noise," we should interpret these claims as entailing both a process of symbolizing an unprecedented *aisthesis* (distribution of the sensible) of socially lived experience and as the reconfiguration of social space that disrupts, reduces, or eliminates relations of command (Rancière [1995] 1999, 30tm). By outlining how politics is doubled, operating against the policing of discourses and spaces, I have shown how, for Rancière, the same command that produces inequality also presupposes the supposition of equality which undermines the very stratified order in which these commands function. I have also argued that while symbolizing equality provides the discursive space in which politics and policing meet and conflict, the respective ways that politics and policing relate to equality (as a logic, praxis, and *aisthesis*) remain heterogeneous. Thus I have shown how that politics and the police intersect while remaining heterogeneous without introducing a concept of "the political" (le *politique*) as a neutral meeting ground for politics (la *politique*) and the police. In addition, by emphasizing how politics involves both discursive and practical opposition to command and coercion, I have reinterpreted the central point of contention between Todd May and Samuel Chambers; May focuses on the enactment—in his words, the "activation"—of equality against command, while Chambers interprets May as giving an account of political *symbolization*. Finally, by emphasizing how Rancière's work challenges the latent violence and coercion of command within the stratified order of policing, we are able to distinguish his work from the various theories of recognition current in critical theory. The primary flaw of these theories is that each one presumes some historically situated social institution—the market or the state—as the neutral background or adjudicator of political agonism and recognition, whereas Rancière's attention to command shows how the state and the so-called free market (that is, capital accumulation) are, when it comes to asymmetries of power, wealth, and governance, never neutral.

## 3.4. WHY FASCISM ISN'T POLITICS

Now that I have made the case that Rancière's politics involves both the symbolization of equality and the struggle against coercion, I would like to address Jodi Dean's Leninist-Lacanian interpretation of his work.[14] Clare Woodford has already responded to Dean's critique in detail. As she points out, Dean takes what Chambers intends to be a virtue of Rancière's work—that politics can never be pure because politics takes place within spaces that are also policed—as its main failing: "'Politics' is weak and ineffective because it is always *infected* by the ordering it wishes to challenge and can never therefore overturn that ordering in a *meaningful* way" (Woodford 2015, 823). Woodford rebuts two problematic aspects of Dean's interpretation that rest upon terminological equivocations. First, Dean equivocates between two meanings of *politics*, assuming that any meaningful politics must be a politics of seizing state power, while for Rancière politics takes place through the enactment of the supposition of equality. Woodford rephrases their differences to show that Rancière's politics focuses on how the supposition of equality can be employed to undermine the stratified ordering of the police while Dean defines effective politics, in Rancière's terms, as building "better police orders" (Woodford 2015, 829).

Second, Dean equivocates between two distinct definitions of *democracy*. For Rancière, democracy is a synonym for politics: not a "set of institutions" but the "forms of expression that confront the logic of equality with the logic of the police order" (Rancière [1995] 1999, 101). By contrast, Dean argues that democracy an institution:

> If the dominant order presents itself as democratic, if the order of the police is the order of democracy, then only non-democratic stagings of disagreement can be political since only they set up a contrast with the conditions of their utterance. Far from exclusively democratic, politics can be fascist, anarchist, imperial, communist. (Dean 2011, 92)

As Woodford notes, politics in Rancière's sense cannot be fascist, anarchist, communistic, or democratic in the way we refer to these terms as forms of instituting political practices; instead, "politics is exclusively democratic (in Rancière's new usage of the term) because it is based on the universal claim to equality in a way that none of these ideologies are" (Woodford 2015, 821).

Given the very public reemergence of the Far Right in the United States, Canada, and elsewhere, I would like to dedicate my own analysis to Dean's claim that politics, in Rancière's sense, could be fascist. I think she can only arrive at this possibility through substituting a psychoanalytic concept of policing for Rancière's own. As we have seen, for Rancière, policing is both the institutionalization and symbolization of inequality. By contrast, as I suggested above, the Lacanian model conceptualizes policing *first* as a repressive force and *then* as a force that subsequently distorts all attempts to symbolize the social order. Or, in Lacanian terms, Dean argues that democratic politics—by attempting to outflank the limited form of democracy implemented by the dominant order—plays out at the level of the imaginary or the symbolic order and thus cannot challenge the real: the inequalities produced by the socioeconomic system of capitalism and imperialism. Thus, *for Dean*, while Rancière's appeals to democratic politics are already captured within the symbolic coordinates of the dominant order, fascists break the symbolic deadlock by articulating demands that undermine the conditions of their utterance. Following Rancière's terms, we would draw a different conclusion. He argues that politics is a dynamic of political subjectivation whereby the part of those who have no part asserts that what was once heard as noise is speech or what was once invisible is visible. Though the Far Right has become more visible (in terms of its public relations and media profile), it does not follow that its social mobilization is politics. No matter how many posters are put up saying "It's okay to be white," as if whiteness has been suppressed, whiteness designates *having a part* in the settler-colonial societies such as the United States and Canada.[15]

Arguing that fascism is not already part of the dominant order, especially given that the ongoing history of nation building in the

United States readily involves the ideology and institutions of white supremacy and settlerism, is a really bad take. Rancière would not draw this conclusion; nor does Žižek in a discussion of fascism that is embedded in his own critique of Rancière (Žižek 1999, 200). So how does Dean get there? In my view, at this particular point in her argument, in attempting to show how Rancière's politics is merely symbolic, she attempts to refute his work by discursive, symbolic means.

Therefore, on her terms, given that the symbolic coordinates of American political discourse are always couched in democratic terms, only political movements that symbolize their politics in antidemocratic terms do so in terms not already included in the system—hence Rancière should be led to the conclusion that fascism is, on his account, *politics.* Yet when Dean claims that fascism, especially since she seems to imply its American variants, articulates its demands in terms that cannot be accommodated by the system, I ask, Which part of the system? She cannot be referring to the parts of policing in the United States that are imbricated in structures of heteropatriarchy, settler-colonialism, and antiblack racism. (As J. Sakai observes, while discussing the failure of fascism to take root as a popular social movement in the decades before World War II, "white settler-colonialism and fascism occupy the same ecological niche. Having one, capitalist society didn't yet need the other" [Sakai (2002) 2017, 130]). The only way Dean can draw this conclusion is by reducing politics, at this point in the argument, to its symbolic and discursive elements. In other words, when Dean treats Rancière's work as abstract and symbolic, it is *her* account of politics that becomes abstract and symbolic. Given that we are diametrically opposed to everything that the Far Right, fascists, the alt-right, and their alt-light cronies stand for, the stakes are too high to concede the point on the status of their attempts at protest and social mobilization. Any kind of social mobilization that implements, or aims to implement, coercive and inegalitarian social relations cannot be politics, *nor should it be respected as such.* Thus, on Rancière's terms, the Far Right is not political; it is a form of policing that takes parapolitical and insurrectionary forms. In fact, we can phrase this more stringently—the Far Right movement cannot be political; it can only be a parapolitical or insurrectionary social mobilization aimed at policing others.

But the problems raised by the reemergence of a very public fascistic, white supremacist social movement in North America extend beyond conceptualizing the Far Right. They also bear on radical leftist politics. Hence I cannot accept Dean's assumption that any politics that does not aim at taking power is not politics. In Dean's defense, I would note that the terrain of both what the Left counts as politics and what the Left counts as policing has shifted since "Politics without Politics" was published. And I would note that I recognize the so-called crisis of the Left as Dean articulates it; it stems from a frustration with how the antiglobalization movement that shut down the World Trade Organization meeting in Seattle in 1999 was unable to relay that victory into a broader political movement, and with how the antiwar movement following 9/11 was largely phrased as registering dissent against the Bush administration's version of American imperialism.

Today, however, I would hardly say that the Left (as broadly speaking as possible, as either organizers or accomplices) is in a crisis of praxis—as numerous movements such as #blacklivesmatter, #idlenomore, #NoDAPL, the prison abolitionist movement, and antifascism, among others, take aim at the forms of latent state and capitalist violence that I have discussed above—while also situating the injustices of the state or the police as they are operative within a broader system of imperialist, antiblack, heteropatriarchal, settlerist norms. My point isn't that any of these movements or the motives of their organizers are "Rancièrean," but rather that they are guided by a similar discontent with the status quo *and* with prominent reformist frameworks such as the politics of recognition. And that it would inimical to the way these movements are organized and to their goals (combatting forms of state and capitalist coercion and violence) to suggest that taking power is immediately more *political* than combatting the kinds of violence and injustice enacted by both the state, capital accumulation, and the parapolitical mobilization of the alt-right. And given that many of the movements that I've mentioned have roots in decades of political practices in North America, it seems that any discussion of the "crisis of the left" must always self-reflexively implicate the way that our perceptions of politics—what, precisely, has *value* and what doesn't; what makes the antiglobalization movement a synecdoche of the Left rather than some other movement; or what leads authors, as even I claimed above, to claim that the terrain of politics has shifted without stipulating *for whom*, when often the *for whom* is in question—are often shaped by our own positions in academia and society in general. When Dean contends that the Left has played into its own victimization and when she suggests the metonymic chain "We protest. We talk. We complain. We undercut our every assertion, criticizing its exclusivity, partiality and fallibility in advance as if some kind of purity were possible" (Dean 2011, 82) epitomizes leftist criticism, she's not sensitive to the way that this characterization can be used, has been used, and could continue to be used *by leftists* to forestall direct action from marginalized groups and their accomplices and silence leftist criticism from marginalized voices within our often tenuous communities of solidarity.

## NOTES

1. Note that I have silently modified the translation of *Disagreement* (1995) so that instances of *comprendre* and its cognates are translated as *to comprehend* while instances of *entendre* and its cognates are translated as *to understand*.
2. Given that he does not use *symbolization* as a technical term in *Disagreement*, I have adopted this usage following his remarks in Rancière (2012) 2016, 119–21.
3. The primary difference between Aristotle and social contract theory, Rancière contends, rests on whether the agonism of competing interests is framed as competition between different parts of society (the rich and the poor, according to Aristotle) or between self-interested individuals (modern social contract theory).
4. On Rancière's refusal to ontologize politics and aesthetics, see Rancière 2009, 476–77; Rancière 2011b, 11–16; Chambers 2013 18–21; and "1.2. Toward a Philosophy of Antifascism," in this volume.

5. "Equality turns into its opposite the moment it aspires to a place in the social or state organization" (Rancière [1995] 1999, 34).

6. See Marchart 2011; Deranty 2003a, 144–45; and Deranty 2003b. Similarly, drawing on Deranty's earlier work, Katia Genel reifies the police as "the social" and politics as "the political," terminological substitutions that are not found in Rancière's work (Genel 2016, 19–20, 25–27, 32).

7. Since translator Julie Rose renders both "la politique" and "le politique" as "politics" in the passages in question, the following references to *Disagreement* list the pagination of the English translation followed by that of the French original. Rancière differentiates between his account of "la politique" and the use of "le politique" by others to signal his differences with Aristotle's and Hobbes's parapolitics (72–73, 79 / 108, 115), Marxist metapolitics (81–83, 85–86 / 119–20, 123–24), and the general contours of what he calls "consensual democracy" (chapter 5, especially 99 / 139).

8. I have framed this by analogy to Rancière's discussion of the "functional" definition of dissensus in *The Method of Equality*. See note 10 below.

9. See Russell and Montin 2015, 543–54; Deranty 2003a; Dean 2011, 89; Patton 2012, 132–33.

10. While he states that *la mésentente* is "untranslatable," he notes that introducing the term *dissensus* in its place opens the "possibility of a functional definition," of political rationality that, aside from the activation of the supposition of equality, cannot be defined in advance (Rancière [2012] 2016, 83).

11. Hobbes 1996, 87. Hobbes then inadvertently concedes that "there is no natural principle of domination by one person over another" (Rancière [1995] 1999, 79).

12. Breaugh notes one feature from Livy's account of the secession that is not explicitly thematized by Rancière: Aventine Hill was organized as a military camp "without any officer to direct them" (Breaugh 2013, 11).

13. Cf. Breaugh 2013, 10: "The patricians agreed to create specifically plebeian magistracies. The raison d'être of the plebs' 'tribunes' was to defend against the consuls. The new tribunals were 'inviolable,' and patricians could not . . . hold office there. The two tribunes of the plebs were granted the Sacred Law and thereby became 'inviolable' in religious terms. The plebs thus emerged from 'nonbeing' and acceded to a double status in Rome: political and religious."

14. Judging from her comments in *The Communist Horizon*, the formulation "politics without politics" echoes Žižek's claim that "the key 'Leninist' lesson today is: politics without the organizational form of the Party is politics without politics" (Dean 2012, 9; Žižek 2002, 297).

15. The posters said, "It's Okay To Be White" in black on white 8 1/2" x 11" paper. Some were printed in comic sans. They appeared beginning in late October 2017 on campuses across North America, including in Canada at the University of Toronto, the University of Alberta's Faculty of Native Studies at University of Alberta, and the University of Regina's Office of Indigenization in the Research and Innovation Centre (Balgord 2017, CBC News 2017, Fung 2017). A poster campaign was also mounted after the shooting at the Tree of Life Synagogue in Pittsburgh, Pennsylvania, on October 27, 2018 (Brake 2018).

# 4

# PUNCHING NAZIS

## 4.1. THE REASON FOR MILITANT ANTIFASCISM

**M**ilitant antifascism is separated from liberal antifascism by its willingness to use a diversity of tactics in opposing fascism—and the most controversial of these numerous tactics is the use of physical confrontation, up to and including "punching nazis." This contemporary usage of "nazis" is not intended to designate exclusively Nazis and neo-Nazis. Instead, its use is patterned on the German joke which goes,

> Q: What do you call ten people sitting at a dinner table with a Nazi?
> A: Eleven Nazis.

The joke, of course, makes fascist sympathizers uncomfortable because it implicates them in extending civility to fascists and normalizing fascism. But this usage is not as slippery as critics allege. The "nazis" at issue in punching nazis could include individuals wearing National Socialist symbols, prominent white nationalist or white supremacist activists or organizers, or participants marching with or participating in Far Right street mobilization, whether they are attacking members of local community or participating in producing propaganda based on events, *but in general, the reference is specific to willing collaborators with Far Right and fascist groups in the midst of social mobilizations.* Perhaps the most famous incident involved an anonymous antifascist punching Richard Spencer in the middle of a television interview on January 20, 2017. The moment had a galvanizing effect on radical opposition to the rise of the alt-right (among other factions of the Far Right) and the way that mainstream media collaborated toward normalizing the alt-right during the election cycle of 2016. The spectacle offered a stark contrast between militant antifascist direct action and the mainstream, ostensibly liberal, normalization of the alt-right as dapper bigots with edgy haircuts.[1] Moments like this have been rare, so more commonly "punching nazis" refers to physical confrontations occurring between Far Right street mobilizations and antifascist countermobilizations. By the time this chapter concludes, I will have argued that generally we can include punching nazis under an antifascist concept (though not exclusive to antifascism) of physical confrontation as part of community self-defense.

Yet the militant commitment to a diversity of tactics has given rise to a number of misconceptions of the movement. The most obvious misconception, which I think is made entirely in bad faith, is the accusation that "antifascism is the real fascism." This claim is commonly made when street fighting breaks out between Far Right groups and antifascist counterprotesters. As I have already noted in "1.1.2. Demarcating Antifascism and Fascism," both antifascism and fascism are insurrectionary insofar as they challenge or reject the legitimacy of the state's monopoly on violence. Many other movements besides are insurrectionary. Therefore identifying fascism with merely insurrectionary violence empties it of its specific ideological content as an insurrectionary form of right-wing populism, "inspired by a totalitarian vision of collective rebirth, that challenges capitalist political and cultural power while promoting economic and social hierarchy" (Lyons 2018, 253). When critics allege that "antifascism is the real fascism," they are positioning their respective ideology against militant antifascism as part of a broader political strategy. Fascists accuse antifascists of being the real fascists to position themselves as a legitimate faction of law and order, and liberals make the accusation to present institutional engagement as the only legitimate route to stopping fascism. Both sides reframe "fascism" as merely the use of violence in order to delegitimize militant antifascist tactics in political conflict. Not only does this claim conflate insurrectionism with fascism but it also removes the specific ideological content that differentiates fascism from both liberal antifascism and militant antifascism, while occluding both the history of the long collaboration between capital and settler-colonialism in North America and the ways that settler-colonialism enables white supremacy. Finally, this claim equates antifascism with violence when physical confrontation, and especially punching nazis, is relatively uncommon compared to other tactics that advance antifascist goals—for example, letter-writing and social media campaigns, no-platforming Far Right speakers, doxing, or the more recent phenomenon of "milkshaking nazis."

Another frequent mischaracterization of militant antifascism concerns its goals. For example, in "Violence Will Only Hurt the Trump Resistance," Erica Chenoweth evaluates militant antifascism (which she characterizes as "black bloc") as a "violent flank" in proximity to a broader coalition of liberal civil disobedience campaigns (Chenoweth 2017). We should briefly consider her analysis, because her book *Why Civil Resistance Works* (coauthored with Maria J. Stephan) has been influential on Todd May's quasi-Rancièrian concept of nonviolent resistance. There Chenoweth and Stephan make two central claims. First, based on an analysis of 323 nonviolent and violent movements from 1900 to 2006, they conclude that nonviolent campaigns are relatively more successful than violent campaigns (Chenoweth and Stephan 2011, 5–15). Then they argue that high levels of participation correlate to a higher likelihood of success in nonviolent campaigns (Chenoweth and Stephan 2011, 39–41). When Chenoweth considers militant antifascism in light of this evidence, she contends that violent tactics hurt participation and thus undermine the legitimacy of the broader resistance. But it is incorrect to conclude that violence will *only* hurt the campaign; as Mark Bray observes, she should have concluded that "violence will *likely* hurt the Trump Resistance" (Bray 2017, 179)—as the main contention of *Why Civil Resistance Works* remains that nonviolent campaigns are *relatively* more successful than violent campaigns.

More importantly, though, Chenoweth does not evaluate whether militant antifascism has the same strategic goals as the Trump resistance.[2] It doesn't. One would presume that the broader goal of a liberal coalition would be to elect a Democratic candidate in the presidential election of 2020 while gaining a majority in Congress. Civil disobedience campaigns might also work to pressure the government or elected officials to prevent or reduce the implementation of Trump administration policies. At each point this coalition must "ensure that their methods of resistance communicate that vision in a way that attracts rather than repels adherents, while building capacity to continually maintain resilience, project legitimacy to those in the center, and build power from below" (Chenoweth 2017). In Chenoweth's vision, despite the fact that civil disobedience movements are "noninstitutional and generally confrontational" (Chenoweth and Stephan 2011, 12), in the context of the Trump Resistance their energies are funneled back toward institutional forms of hegemony.

These are not the goals of militant antifascism. In addition, Chenoweth is wrong to reduce militant antifascist actions to black bloc tactics: while both types of affinity groups use black bloc tactics to evade surveillance and police, and sometimes involve the same participants, we can understand them as prioritizing different tactics within the diversity of tactics. According to Francis Dupuis-Déri, a black bloc action produces a "spectacle" of antisystemic social mobilization. If we consider an event such as the J20 (2017) action in Washington, DC, black bloc actions sought to produce a counterspectacle to the spectacle of the presidential inauguration. Dupuis-Déri summarizes the general logic of the tactic: "In the face of the official spectacle designed to legitimize and glorify power, the . . . counter-spectacle strives to demonstrate the power of protest and to chip away at the aura of legitimacy of official power" (Dupuis-Déri 2013, 78). This counterspectacle is realized through breakaway marches (when they are part of larger and/or permitted marches) and targeted destruction of the property of large corporations. I should also note that it is typically assumed that participants in black bloc actions will stand their ground to shield other protesters from police violence.

The priorities of militant antifascism are somewhat different than what is typically assumed of black bloc actions (though, again, these distinctions are not as clear in practice). Broadly speaking, the goal of antifascism is to build fully nonfascist and emancipatory communities. To this end antifascists are often involved with political movements that are emancipatory but not necessarily, in technical terms, militant antifascist affinity groups. When militant antifascists mobilize against the Far Right or fascism, their goal is emancipatory community self-defense, building spaces of solidarity through organizing to stop Far Right recruitment while supporting targets of right-wing scapegoating and policing. While building communities through organizing and solidarity work remains the ultimate goal of militant antifascism, and there are many different tactics available to frustrate recruitment efforts of the Far Right (from rehabilitation to doxing), here I will focus on one of the more controversial: physical confrontation to combat Far Right street mobilization. I will argue that physical confrontation, including punching nazis, must be understood as a method of emancipatory community self-defense.

In this chapter I aim to bring the philosophy of antifascism, as developed through the work of Beauvoir and Rancière, into dialogue with discussions of militant antifascists. In order to do so, however, we must first critique nonviolent interpretations of their respective approaches: in existentialism, Ronald Santoni advocates nonviolence in his *Sartre on Violence: Curiously Ambivalent* (2003) and "The Bad Faith of Violence: And Is Sartre in Bad Faith Regarding It?" (2005), and in Rancière studies, Todd May does so in *Nonviolent Resistance: A Philosophical Introduction* (2015). Santoni and May level, in effect, two questions at our analysis that we must address before concluding: Is militant antifascism in bad faith? And is militant antifascism anti-egalitarian?

## 4.2. PUNCHING NAZIS IS NOT IN BAD FAITH

Punching nazis is not in bad faith on Beauvoir's terms—nor on Fanon's, nor, in my view, on Sartre's. This claim, especially concerning Sartre, is not without controversy. Ronald Santoni argues, on the basis of a broad survey of Sartre's works, that Sartre is both "curiously ambivalent" and in bad faith in his discussions of violence. In *Sartre on Violence*, he contends that Sartre's works are often marked by a "justificational ambivalence" toward revolutionary violence. That is, Sartre uses weasel words or justificatory euphemisms in his discussions of violence—such as referring to violence as "necessary," "acceptable," or "legitimate" (Santoni 2005, 70)—that elide whether his claims are descriptions of revolutionary violence or justifications thereof (Santoni 2003, 154–62). In "The Bad Faith of Violence," he claims that violence is an action in bad faith and that Sartre is, on his own terms, in bad faith in his discussions of violence. In short, violent action is in bad faith because it reduces a human freedom to a thing (whether I objectify the other in my actions or seek to destroy my own freedom through violence), and Sartre is in bad faith because his justifications of violence rely on "selective evidence" concerning its meaning, downplaying the dehumanization carried out by revolutionary violence—in other words, to paraphrase his epistemological characterization of bad faith, Sartre is lying to himself. If Santoni is correct, then to be consistent Sartre would have to hold that punching nazis is in bad faith. I disagree.

Here I will briefly address Santoni's critique of Sartre's account of violence in order to compare his conclusions to those that we have drawn from Beauvoir. Santoni himself notes that the first problem, of justificational ambivalence, does not apply to Beauvoir (Santoni 2003, 154n46). In "An Eye for an Eye," it is not difficult to discern her approbation toward the execution of Mussolini or the vengeance carried out by concentration camp survivors against their former jailers. In *The Ethics of Ambiguity*, she explicitly provides justification for the use of *emancipatory* violence. But Beauvoir recognizes that violence is ambiguous, and thus the meaning of emancipatory violence must constantly be "won": first, the oppressed must measure the means of violent praxis against their emancipatory ends; and second, they must defend the meaning of emancipatory violence against the discourses and the outright violence of the oppressors. While Beauvoir justifies emancipatory violence, it is against the context of the many kinds of oppressive violence that operate in our societies despite being both undesirable and unjustifiable. And thus part of the meaning of violence is shaped by the agonistic character of discursive justification itself. As discussed in "2.3.1. Discourse and Disagreement," Beauvoir shows that the discourse of justifications is itself shaped by social relations of power, access, and oppression—and the terms of the debate are loaded in the oppressor's favor. From this vantage point, we could conclude, contra Santoni, that Sartre's so-called ambivalence is the result not of moral uncertainty but of his attempt to navigate the power dynamics of discursive justification. We face similar obstacles when defending militant antifascism.

Santoni's second contention is that violence is an action in bad faith and that Sartre is in bad faith regarding it. He could not make a similar claim in Beauvoir's case, though one might expect that Beauvoir's justification of emancipatory violence would, on the terms established in Santoni's account, fall into bad faith. Santoni is explicit that his inquiry is focused on whether or not Sartre is in bad faith "given Sartre's own grounds, terms, and analysis of bad faith" (Santoni 2015, 76). In other words, Santoni reconstructs a Sartrean critique of violence and then considers whether Sartre's various criticisms, descriptions, or justifications of violence are consistent with one another. Comparing Sartre (via Santoni) and Beauvoir requires a different approach: we must examine two competing views and then evaluate how they deal with violence. Matthew Eshleman sketches four positions one might take toward Santoni's theses: (1) one can agree; (2) one can argue that violence necessarily involves bad faith but certain mitigating conditions warrant violence; (3) one can argue that there are relevant kinds of violence that are not necessarily in bad faith; or (4) one can argue that the category "bad faith" is unhelpful in analyzing violence. Eshleman defends positions 2 and 3 (by reference, in part, to *The Ethics of Ambiguity*); here I will follow up on his suggestion that "there is something to be said for the fourth" (Eshleman 2015, 62–63).

Santoni argues that there is a continuity in Sartre's *oeuvre* concerning violence. His claim, however, has two components. On the one hand, he claims that Sartre's descriptions and justifications of violence generally demonstrate the ambivalence of his attitude toward the use of revolutionary violence throughout his work. On the other hand, Santoni maintains that Sartre adheres to the *value* of violence as it is defined in *Notebooks for an Ethics* (1992; written in 1947–1948 but published posthumously) throughout his later writings. While there are important continuities in Sartre's thought—elsewhere I have argued that there is a continuity in Sartre's critique of "identity" as a function of oppressive or exploitative social relations, though he frames this critique in terms of bad faith in *Being and Nothingness* and seriality in the *Critique of Dialectical Reason* (Shaw 2016a, 52–81)—I think that Sartre deliberately drops the value-laden language of bad faith due to its individualistic moralism. In other words, what the later Sartre says of Albert Memmi's account of colonialism applies to the relationship between the later Sartre and the early Sartre's definitions of violence: "The only difference between us is perhaps that he sees a situation where I see a system" (Sartre [1957] 2006, 62n1).

I provisionally accept, based on Santoni's evidence, that there is a strong continuity between *Being and Nothingness* and the *Notebooks*, and thus I will focus on problems that follow from reconstructing Sartre's attitude toward violence on the basis of those works. First, Santoni avers that Sartre's descriptions of being-for-others and concrete relations with others in *Being and Nothingness* anticipate his more specific comments on violence in the *Notebooks*. While he notes that Sartre does not characterize the conflictual relationships between being-for-itself and others as *violence*, Santoni states,

> The Other's original refusal of me, the Other's "looking" at me
> as object, the Other's "objectification" of me, and, conversely,

my counterrefusal and counter-"objectification" of the other *violate* me, as well as the Other, as *being-for-itself,* as free conscious being, as subject, as human reality, or—to repeat Sartre's idiomatic usage of the word—as *a freedom.* . . . [It] seems clear that these mutual violations have a claim to that word [violence], for, etymologically, to violate (*violare*)—in this case, to violate free, conscious subjects—is at the root of the word "violence." . . . In fact, it is not, in my judgment, too extreme to suggest . . . that "violence" is at the core of my "original fall" and my original "being-for-others." (Santoni 2003, 19)

He observes, like Thomas Flynn (see "2.2. Ambiguity and Solidarity," in this volume), that when Sartre inscribes conflict as original ontological meaning of intersubjective relations, his account precludes the possibility of solidarity. To counterbalance this pessimistic view of intersubjectivity, Santoni suggests that this description applies only to social relationships of those "who are in natural bad faith and have not yet converted to an authentic way of being" (Santoni 2003, 20). For Santoni, the importance of these passages lays in how they anticipate Sartre's explicit discussion of violence in the *Notebooks*; thus he does not evaluate the merit of this presumed position. From our standpoint, following Beauvoir, violence must be evaluated vis-à-vis social relations of solidarity, conflict, *and* systemic oppression as they are historically situated. Therefore, the brief outline of violence in *Being and Nothingness,* along with its implied ethical consequences, is incomplete and should not subsequently be applied to evaluate Sartre's later philosophy—or Beauvoir's.

Santoni's interest in *Being and Nothingness,* in the case of violence, is limited to the degree that it anticipates the claims of the *Notebooks.* A critique of Sartre's concept of violence in the *Notebooks* poses a number of different, more interesting interpretive problems. While we might dispense with the problems of *Being and Nothingness* by showing how they are subsequently criticized and revised in the later work of Sartre or Beauvoir, with the *Notebooks,* we are faced with the fact that Sartre abandoned what Sartre scholarship has called his "first ethics."[3] Santoni's argument rests on the assumption that if there is a continuity in Sartre's justificational ambivalence, then that must be based to some degree on his recognition that violence is in bad faith; hence it is irrelevant that Sartre did not complete and publish the *Notebooks*. But from our perspective, we are presented with *two*, presumably incompatible, existentialist interpretations of violence dating from the late 1940s: Sartre's *Notebooks* or Beauvoir's *Ethics of Ambiguity*. Only the latter, if we take Santoni's reconstruction of Sartre's account at its word,[4] provides an account of violence that situates it within social relations of solidarity, conflict, and oppression. Indeed I would suggest that Sartre abandoned the ethical system of the *Notebooks* because it did not satisfactorily develop these social relations systematically. (I would also suggest that if it had, Sartre would have arrived at the conclusions of *The Ethics of Ambiguity*.) If Sartre abandoned the *Notebooks* for these reasons, then it is problematic to judge his subsequent work on the basis of an abandoned set of concepts and value judgments.

Yet the *Notebooks* serves as the linchpin of Santoni's argument; there, "Sartre most frequently and even explicitly refers to violence as instantiating bad faith" (Santoni 2005, 63). Furthermore, the framework he reconstructs on the basis of the *Notebooks* grounds Santoni's overall judgment that Sartre lapses into bad faith in his account of violence. Santoni bases this framework on the ethical and epistemological conclusions he derives from Sartre's claim that "in violence, one treats a freedom like a thing, all the while recognizing its nature as freedom" (Sartre 1992, 193; Santoni 2005, 63). In other words, violence acts to dehumanize the other, treating them as a thing, though the violent person recognizes, in the mode of bad faith, the freedom of the other. Santoni first reconstructs the content of a violent action. Violence is both a relation to the world and a relation to others. On the one hand, the "violent man" affirms a "divine right of the human person" to destroy the world—that is, the violent man considers the world as merely an obstacle to realizing his will (Sartre 1992, 174; Santoni 2003, 24). Sartre adds that violence, as destructive, "cannot *produce* an object" (Sartre 1992, 174).

In my view, Sartre's claim that violence cannot produce an object precludes conceptualizing systemic violence, where, for example, the violence of economic exploitation is productive—at least to the degree, for example, that it can maintain and re-*produce* the material conditions necessary to continue the expropriation of surplus-value. We might better understand such passages to indicate a typology of a certain kind of attitude toward violence, not dissimilar to the typologies found in chapter 2 of *The Ethics of Ambiguity*. That Santoni adopts this particular description of violence as the ground of violence in general indicates how he fails to place individual violence in a systemic context.

Then Santoni notes that for Sartre, violence is also a particular kind of intersubjective relation to the other. One who commits violence against another human treats that human as an "inessential" means to accomplish one's will. There is an ambiguity to violence, because it must treat the other as an inessential means while demanding the other's assent (or free choice) of recognition of the violent agent's will. Santoni writes, "I want the freedom of the Other to 'give way' to mine; I want to possess and be 'master' of the freedom from whom I wish to be recognized as free" (Santoni 2005, 63). Thus the violent agent is, epistemologically speaking, in bad faith: the agent's actions vacillate between treating the other as an inessential means while demanding the recognition of the other to justify the violence. In other words, when the perpetrator of violence demands the recognition of the other through violence, this action both treats the other as inessential (a mere means or instrument of violent action) and as essential (an impossible equal, capable of recognition). Sartre elucidates this contradiction by distinguishing between force and violence. Force is lawful, while violence is not (though Santoni notes the ambiguities in Sartre's use of the term *lawfulness*, in 2003, 24). Violence produces the "abjectness" of the other, and the perpetrator of violence then adduces this abjectness as the reason for treating other humans as beasts or things. This vacillation is in "bad faith," and while violence, Sartre continues, "wants to be force, deep down it is violence for it is addressed to the freedom of the Other, both to destroy it and to obligate it to freely acknowledge this force" (Sartre 1992, 178). Santoni concludes, in his analysis of these passages, that "we have a case, here, not only of bad faith as (duplicitously) objectifying and using the Other's freedom as means, but also of bad faith as 'lying to oneself' by a consciousness that 'half-persuades' itself on the basis of 'selective' evidence" (Santoni 2005, 64). For Santoni, these passages provide the ground for his subsequent judgments concerning the bad faith of the later Sartre's descriptions and judgments of violence (Santoni 2005, 72ff). In sum, for Santoni, because Sartre in the *Notebooks* recognizes the bad faith of violence, and because there are similarities in his ambivalent attitude toward violence throughout his work, his subsequent work is colored by this prior judgment.

Though it is beyond the scope of this study to reconstruct Sartre's first ethics, our examination of Santoni's argument casts some light on the philosophical problems of the *Notebooks*. To some degree, Sartre struggles to situate individual acts of violence in relation to systemic violence, and indeed Santoni's reconstruction of his argument amplifies those problems. As I have already noted, it is problematic to accept, as Santoni does, that violence is purely *destructive*, for then we cannot explain how the violence of economic exploitation could be system-sustaining. In addition, he fails to note that Sartre's claim that the perpetrator demands the victim to recognize violence as force could function as a description of the ideological *naturalization* of systemic violence, much like Beauvoir's claim that "one of the ruses of oppression is to camouflage itself behind a natural situation since, after all, one cannot revolt against nature" (Beauvoir [1947] 1976, 83). These failures are indicative of Santoni's appropriation of the individualism of the earlier Sartre—that is, generally centering meaning in being-for-itself outside of its social relations—to such a degree that this individualism affects even his interpretation of Sartre's later work on collective group agency.[5] In both *Sartre on Violence* and "The Bad Faith of Violence," in his discussion of the *Notebooks*, Santoni treats social oppression as a secondary consideration in Sartre's account of violence: in the former it is one of two "transitional considerations" between the *Note-*

*books* and Sartre's later work (Santoni 2003, 28ff), and in the latter he refers to oppression as "one other important but predictable illustration" (Santoni 2005, 64). In contrast to Sartre, Beauvoir does not categorize violence as a form of bad faith. While indeed one might take an attitude in bad faith *toward* violence, she does not categorize violence itself as bad faith.[6] She avoids this conclusion by categorizing, in political terms, violence as either oppressive violence or emancipatory violence. Unlike Santoni, who relegates the problem of systemic violence to a secondary philosophical concern, Beauvoir prefaces her remarks on emancipatory violence with a theory of systemic oppression. We cannot, in fidelity to Beauvoir, abstract the political and moral evaluations of violence from their respective systemic contexts: "We challenge every condemnation as well as every *a priori* justification of the violences [*sic*] practiced with a view to a valid end. They [these violences] must be legitimized concretely" (Beauvoir [1947] 1976, 148tm). It is unsurprising, then, when Beauvoir's programmatic statements about emancipatory violence (in *The Ethics of Ambiguity*) or revenge (in "An Eye for an Eye") foreground how oppression shapes the meaning of the praxis of the oppressed, that she draws fundamentally different conclusions than Santoni does. To demonstrate this contrast, I have chosen two passages that play an important role in Santoni's account. Compare the first to the following passage from *The Ethics of Ambiguity*:

• Sartre: "Violence is an ambiguous notion. We might define it something like: to make use of the facticity of the other person and the objective from the outside to determine the subjective to turn itself into an inessential means of reaching the objective. In other words, bring about the objective at any price, particularly by treating man as a means, all the while preserving the *value* of its having been chosen by some subjectivity. The impossible ideal of violence is to constrain the other's freedom to choose freely what I want" (Sartre 1992, 204).
• Beauvoir: "By virtue of the fact that the oppressors refuse to co-operate in the affirmation of freedom, they embody, in the

eyes of all men of good will, the absurdity of facticity; by calling for the triumph of freedom over facticity, ethics also demands that they be suppressed; and since their subjectivity, by definition, escapes our control, it will be possible to act only on their objective presence; others will here have to be treated like things, with violence. . . . Since we can conquer our enemies only by acting upon their facticity, by reducing them to things, we have to make ourselves things; in this struggle in which wills are forced to confront each other through their bodies, the bodies of our allies, like those of our opponents are exposed to the same brutal hazard" (Beauvoir [1947] 1976, 97, 99).

Compare the second to "An Eye for an Eye":

- Sartre: "Destructive of the human world, it [violence] needs the human world to acknowledge its destruction. At the same time that it means to establish its absolute right over men by the spectacle it presents to itself of their abjectness. In this way, violence demonstrates to itself that it can treat them as things or beasts. . . . But here again is its *bad faith*" (Sartre 1992, 178, my emphasis).
- Beauvoir: "An abomination arises only at the moment that a man treats fellow men like objects, when by torture, humiliation, servitude, assassination, one denies them their existence as men. Hatred grasps at another's freedom insofar as it is used to realize the *absolute evil* that is the degradation of a man into a thing. And it calls immediately for a revenge that strives to destroy that evil at its source by reaching the freedom of the evildoer" (Beauvoir 1946, 248, my emphasis).

We have already examined Beauvoir's argument in chapter 2 (especially "2.3. The Antinomies of Action" and "2.4. Vengeance, Violence, and the State"), but a few additional comments are in order. First, it is evident that, while both Sartre (in parts of the *Notebooks*) and Beauvoir maintain that violence involves the degradation of a human being as a thing or object, from this claim they draw fundamentally different political and ethical conclusions. In "An Eye for an Eye," Beauvoir pronounces a much stronger moral judgment on what I have called "existential violence," calling it an "absolute evil"—and yet revenge is not (see "2.4.1. An Eye for an Eye"). And for both Sartre and Beauvoir, violence is marked, even though she distinguishes between oppressive violence and emancipatory violence, by ambiguity. But for Sartre, violence is an "ambiguous notion" because it treats others as by turns inessential and essential to one's will. For Beauvoir, violence is ambiguous in the same way that all human actions are ambiguous, meaning that there is no objective, impartial standpoint to evaluate it. In other words, when we evaluate the value of human actions, we take a side about them.

This point returns us to considering how, for Beauvoir, political subjectivity arises as part of a social totality. On her account, oppression divides humanity into two groups: oppressor and oppressed; oppression is a system that reduces the oppressed to mere instruments for the material benefit of the oppressor at the same time it suppresses the possibility of an open future for the oppressed; the oppressor then "feeds" on both the material means and the open future of the oppressed. In such a situation, Beauvoir affirms the right of the oppressed to revolt and the right for them to use violence to overthrow a situation of oppression. But she acknowledges that the meaning of this violence must be subject to scrutiny: when one deploys emancipatory violence, one risks instrumentalizing the actions of one's comrades (and for Beauvoir this instrumentalization itself, as *The Blood of Others* shows, is not necessarily unjustified); or the oppressed could lapse into oppressive violence. Therefore, she contends, emancipatory violence must be guided by a frank assessment of means and ends within the broader social totality constituted by systemic oppression; it must either broaden the horizon of an open future *in the present* or defend already "won" spaces of egalitarian freedom. As I have repeatedly stated, the Far Right is social mobilization for the cause of re-entrenching various kinds of oppression already present in our societies, and thus antifascists have the "right," as it were, to the diver-

sity of tactics for community self-defense. Beauvoir's argument is
not that emancipatory violence is *necessary* in this situation—where
one might have physically confronted fascists with physical violence to break their line as they march, one might also, if it serves
the same purpose, throw a milkshake—she merely defends the view
that it cannot be excluded from political praxis on a priori grounds.
And thus punching nazis, from Beauvoir's standpoint, is not in bad
faith.

## 4.3. PUNCHING NAZIS IS NOT ANTI-EGALITARIAN

From the outset, I have held that the antifascist commitment to
egalitarianism distinguishes it fundamentally from fascism. This
commitment places militant antifascism in a seemingly paradoxical
position: if punching nazis is anti-egalitarian, then doing so contradicts the spirit of antifascism. In this section I will dispel this seeming paradox.

One might draw the conclusion that physical violence is anti-
egalitarian on the basis of the discussion in chapter 3, where I contend that Rancière's politics enacts both the discursive symbolization of equality and a praxis that combats or undermines policing as
it institutes and implements social relations of command and coercion. The reasoning might run as follows: if Rancière's politics
fights coercion, then it must be that the use of physical violence in
the antifascist diversity of tactics is entirely off the table. This objection, in my view, abstracts coercion from the dialectic of command and coercion that is, on Rancière's account, part of policing. I
pair the two terms for several reasons. By differentiating between
them, it emphasizes their dialectical relation: command *produces* or
*institutes* social relations of inequality, and coercion gives command
its *force* (see "2.1. Existentialism Is an Antifascism"). But command
is reinforced when the person or group does not have the discursive
means to formulate command or coercion as a *wrong*. The dialectic
of command and coercion is a dialectic of the implementation and
reinforcement of social oppression. We can observe, furthermore,

that advocates of nonviolence, such as Todd May, argue that nonviolent actions or campaigns are permitted to use some degree of coercion to accomplish their political aims. When one is coerced, he writes, "One is blocked from acting as one would otherwise want to act. One's preferred course of action is made impossible, or at least very difficult. . . . Is nonviolence coercive? It often is, and in fact often is meant to be" (May 2015, 49). Demonstrations and boycotts, for example, both apply a degree of coercive pressure to impinge on the actions of bystanders or adversaries, but unlike relations of command-coercion, they intend to make visible the choices and motivations that guide one's actions and offer alternatives for social and political change. This use of coercion contrasts starkly with the way that the dialectic of command-coercion functions to prevent the discursive formulation of alternatives or of a wrong. To return to May's account, then, this nonviolent use of coercion does not violate the egalitarianism that guides *nonviolence*. Thus, if Rancière maintains that political praxis fights coercion, this must be understood within the context of systemic oppression—in other words, politics combats the ways that policing implements a dialectic of command and coercion, a dialectic of the implementation (command) and reinforcement (coercion) of social oppression.

Despite our shared interest in Rancière, May and I differ about the use of violent tactics. In *Nonviolent Resistance*, May argues that Rancière's "politics seems to necessitate a nonviolent approach as the first and default option" (May 2015, 147). In other words, for May, Rancière's egalitarianism functions normatively as a "nonviolent orientation" toward politics (May 2015, 147). I understand May's argument to mean that egalitarianism commits us, politically speaking, to nonviolent resistance. I will dispute May's claims in two steps. First, I will argue that Rancière's own concept of politics does not preclude the use of violence, up to and including insurrectionary violence. Then, given their differences about the status of violence, I will identify where May diverges from Rancière: in sum, May's claims rest on a Kantian reconstruction of Rancière's concept of equality.

To my knowledge, there are only two occasions in which Rancière suggests that egalitarian politics involves violence; his other references remain oblique.[7] The two exceptions both focus on the meaning of workers' publications and insurrections in France from 1830 to 1834, a period bookended by the July Revolution and the violent suppression of the Lyon insurrection of 1834: his "Introduction" to *La parole ouvrière* (1976) and chapter 2.2 of *On the Shores of Politics*, "The Uses of Democracy" (2007a; originally published in the first French edition of *Aux bords du politique* in 1992). While some essays collected in the various editions of *On the Shores of Politics* develop conceptual distinctions that Rancière later dispenses with (noted in "3.3. Disagreement and Command"), "The Uses of Democracy" is largely congruent with Rancière's politics in *Disagreement* and the "Ten Theses on Politics." Therefore an analysis of this second section of chapter 2, "The Use of Words and the Syllogism of Emancipation," will further develop our earlier discussion of Rancière's politics. Indeed, this essay is unique in that Rancière explicitly holds that political mobilizations such as strikes and insurrections *supply* the persuasive force of the political symbolization of dissensus and equality.

Workers played a prominent role in the insurrections of July 1830, which led to the abdication of Charles X and the installation of a constitutional monarchy under Louis-Philippe. Enabled by liberal reforms guaranteeing freedom of the press and encouraged by "public recognition of their pivotal role in the revolution, Parisian workers now felt they could legitimately and publicly put forward the demands they had hitherto pursued quietly within their trades" for the government to "outlaw machines, to raise wages, to establish uniform tariffs, to shorten the workday, and so on" (Sewell 1980, 195). These demands were ignored by authorities and further workers' demonstrations were met with government suppression; militant workers became convinced that "events since the July Revolution had demonstrated the need for an independent working-class voice" (Sewell 1980, 197). It was a particularly important task because, as William H. Sewell Jr. contends, the "corporate idiom" derived from conventions of the old regime was by 1830 "without moral or even cognitive force in the public sphere" (Sewell 1980, 194–95).

Rancière contends that the discussion of equality, as worked out in a proliferating number of working-class publications, pamphlets, and newspapers in the aftermath of these events, takes the "approximate form of a syllogism" that formulates the *wrong* committed by social inequality. The major premise of the syllogism "is simple: the Charter promulgated in 1830 says in its preamble that all French people are equal before the law" (Rancière 2007a, 45). The minor premise is adduced from the direct experience of social inequality. Though he does not cite his point of reference, Rancière provides three examples from two texts by the militant tailor Grignon (reproduced in Faure and Rancière 2007, 55–63): first, workers have made demands to the masters, but the head of the master tailors association refuses the workers a hearing; second, the law prohibits associations, and while workers are prosecuted for forming associations, the masters are not; finally, the indictment of prosecutor Persil against the town crier denies that workers are "*men just like those others* [the others being "a more elevated class of men"], and that they have the right to enjoy the same things" (quoted in Rancière 2007a, 46). In each case, the minor premise contradicts the major premise by demonstrating that workers are not the equals of other citizens. In each case, the syllogism articulates how social inequality perpetrates a wrong against the working class—in this particular case, workers were demanding the right to association. For Rancière, we must take this syllogism at its word. On the one hand, it establishes a language of the political subjectivation of the working class; workers coalesce as a class around a shared language that, according to Sewell, enables the "emergence of class consciousness." On the other hand, this dynamic of political subjectivation is grounded in a sense of solidarity and social equality that is irreducible to its legal inscription in the Charter. Rancière writes, "*Social equality* is neither a simple legal/political equality nor an economic levelling. It is an equality enshrined as potentiality in legal/political texts, then translated, displaced and maximized in everyday life" (Rancière 2007a, 48). When he conceptualizes political subjectivation as self-recognition through solidarity, Rancière here truly writes in the wake of Beauvoir and Fanon. The "demonstration" of the syllogism of emancipation is not, for Rancière, purely logical. The workers' discourse often goes "hand-in-hand with strike movements or other kinds of movements" (Rancière 2007a, 45), or, as the French has it, "political conflicts" (Rancière 2004, 85). While Rancière claims that the Parisian tailors' strike of 1833 takes the form of a "logical proof," he maintains that it gets its *force* from political mobilization: one verifies words "through one's actions" (Rancière 2007a, 47). The most telling passage, in my view, though, is Rancière's contention that the syllogism of emancipation "opposes word to word *and* deed to deed" (Rancière 2007a, 47, my emphasis). I understand the parallel of words and deeds to anticipate what I have developed as the double conflict of *Disagreement*: egalitarian politics involves both the symbolization of equality (words opposed to words) and political mobilization against social inequality (deeds opposed to deeds). Here, though, Rancière verges on providing a direct causal formulation of their relationship; the syllogism of equality draws its force from political mobilization, if not violent insurrection. He writes,

> Proving one is correct has never compelled others to recognize they are wrong. In order to uphold one's correctness other kinds of arguments have always been needed. The affirmation of the right to be correct is dependent on the violence of its inscription. Thus, the reasonable arguments of the strikers of 1833 were audible, their demonstration visible, only because the revolutionary events [*événement révolutionnaire*] of 1830, recalling those of 1789, had torn them from the nether world of inarticulate sounds and ensconced them by a contingent forced entry in the world of meaning and visibility. The repetition of egalitarian words is a repetition of that forced-entry, which is why the space of common meaning [*sens commun*] it opens up is not a space of consensus. Democracy is the community of sharing [*du part-age*], in both senses of the term [that is, the French *partager* and its cognates connote both sharing and dividing]: a membership in a single world which can only be expressed in adversarial

terms, and a coming together which can only occur in conflict. To postulate a world of common meaning [*sens commun*] is always transgressive. It assumes a symbolic violence both in respect of the other and in respect of oneself. (Rancière 2007a, 49tm / 2004, 92)

He later glosses, in similar terms, modern forms of political subjectivation:

Against hierarchies of consensus and the passions of exclusion, the occupation of the street by the anonymous multitude reaffirms the community of sharing [*du partage*]. And this it can do only by tracing that violent inscription which made the contingent site of the negotiation of knowledge into a place for the exercise of egalitarian transgression. (Rancière 2007a, 58 / 2004, 106)

Aside from the rhetoric of transgression, and despite the fact that Rancière does not explicitly characterize social inequality here as "policing," the similarities between these passages and *Disagreement* are clearly evident.[8] Politics takes place in a "contingent site" as a form of dissensus over how speech and praxis are distributed— shared or divided, as the French verb *partager* and its cognates suggest. Furthermore, Rancière characterizes politics as the seizure of a common language to demonstrate a wrong through conflict, and then he likens politics to the intersection of two worlds (one organized *as if* the supposition of equality were fully enacted and one governed by social inequality) in one common space.

Where, indeed, "The Uses of Democracy" differs with *Disagreement* or "Ten Theses on Politics" is the explicit acknowledgement of the role of violence in political subjectivation. Let us look first at his reference to "symbolic violence." Any given regime of policing or social inequality implements distinctions between those words and activities that are meaningful and those that are merely noise (that are, at best, articulations of nonpolitical interests). Politics attacks this stratification of meaning/noise through an "egalitarian transgression." Though Rancière rarely conceptualizes politics as "transgression," it here signals how the language of dissensus forces its way into discourse, thus it "assumes a symbolic violence both in respect of the other and in respect of oneself" (Rancière 2007a, 49). To use the terminology of *Disagreement*, political subjectivation transforms the part of those who have no part into a subject; in other words, a political subject does not precede its subjectivation through political mobilization. At the same time, politics imposes or forces the transformation of the given contours of a discourse. Rancière writes that equality and freedom "are *forces* engendered and augmented by their own actualization" (Rancière 2007a, 50, my emphasis).

Certainly, Rancière's reference to symbolic violence of political subjectivation serves to reinforce how politics and dissensus involve conflict. Our rejoinder to May, however, hinges on whether this violence is merely *symbolic*. At two points Rancière evokes the violent "inscription" of political mobilization. We might treat "violence" as a metaphor, similar to Jean-Philippe Deranty's use of "battle" in his description of the discourse of justifications: "Politics in *Disagreement* is a battle of justifications, mainly a battle about what counts as justification and who is entitled to proffer and expect justifications" (Deranty 2016, 54). Drawing this conclusion would return us to Deranty's version of the politics of recognition (alluded to in "3.1. Demarcating Egalitarianism" in this volume). By contrast, I have argued that Rancière's politics opposes word to word and deed to deed. Therefore, we can accept that the revolutionary rhetoric of the July Revolution offered a language for egalitarian political mobilization for the strike of 1833, but Rancière also asserts that "the *revolutionary events* of 1830, recalling those of 1789, had torn them from the nether world of inarticulate sounds and ensconced them by a contingent forced entry in the world of meaning and visibility" (Rancière 2007a, 49tm). Rancière must mean the *events* of 1789, for his reference to discursive possibilities opened by the French Revolution is equivocal: in 1791 the National Assembly passed laws prohibiting workers' "coalitions," which runs counter to later appeals to workers' right to association, although *fraternité*, which was "always the unaccented term of the revolutionary trinity in the liberal version of the revolutionary idiom, became dominant in the workers' version" of the early 1830s (Sewell 1980, 88, 205).

Rancière could have evoked events closer to 1833, and indeed he does in his introduction to *La parole ouvrière*. There were insurrections in Lyon in 1831 and 1834, and Rancière took an interest in this period of workers' history because the young Marx draws on them in formulating his account of revolutionary struggle (Rancière 2007b, 338): Marx calls these insurrections "the first outbreaks of the French proletariat" (Marx [1844a] 1967, 355; see also Bezucha 1974). In November 1831, after the government attempted to suppress a strike by Lyonnais silk workers, the silk workers led an armed insurrection and seized control of Lyon for six days. Their motto became a rallying cry for other workers. As Grignon wrote in 1833, "If our right to associate in our common interest is called into question . . . we would have, like our brothers in Lyon, to cry out in distress: *Live working or die fighting*" (quoted in Faure and Rancière 2007, 59). Summarizing this period of workers' writings, he states that these workers

> speak to be understood. If, in the aftermath of 1830, they can forcefully name their identity and assert their demands, it is undoubtedly because the July Revolution proved that it is they who, in the last instance, made and defeated kings. It is also because the insurrection of Lyon in 1831 proved the impact of their words and their deeds. . . . The desire to be recognized is bound up with the refusal to be misunderstood. The will to convince others of a right can entail a resolution to defend it by taking up arms." (Rancière [1976] 2007, 9, 12)

Rancière notes a complex relationship between speech and violence in working-class organizing of the early 1830s, which has been subsequently obscured. These worker-critics did not view their appeals to right or equality as precluding insurrectionary violence. They presented social equality in general, and specific rights such as the right to association, as just and reasonable terms for a society

that claimed to enshrine legal equality. As we have seen, the syllogism of emancipation seeks to demonstrate that society wrongs
workers by permitting social inequality. Insurrectionary violence
protects the rights that workers already have and that the rich deny:
"Let us not forget," Grignon writes, "that the rich alone make the
law, and that we will free ourselves definitively from the yoke of
misery only by exercising, like them, our rights as citizens" (quoted
in Faure and Rancière 2007, 60–61). It is only after the failures of
the insurrections of the 1830s and a turn toward workers' education
by utopians and bourgeois republicans that speech and violence
became dissociated; Rancière evokes Marx when he then states that
the bourgeoisie subsequently sought to deepen the "breach . . . between the weapon of criticism and the criticism of weapons"
(Rancière [1976] 2007, 10).

If these two discussions of working-class struggle, from *La parole ouvrière* to *On the Shores of Politics*, are congruent, we can use
his earlier analyses to interpret the latter.[9] When he states that "other kinds of arguments have always been needed" to make the syllogism of emancipation heard, he does not merely mean that the militant tailors built off the rhetorical and conceptual language of 1789
and 1830 (or even 1831); he means, echoing the young Marx, that
"the weapon of criticism obviously cannot replace the criticism of
weapons" (Marx [1844b] 1994, 34). In other words, for Rancière,
political mobilization does not win its adversaries over by consensus or purely logical appeals. Words must be accompanied by direct
action: "Those who act *as if* the other can always understand their
arguments increase their own strength—and not merely at the level
of argument" (Rancière 2007a, 50tm, my emphasis). In "The Uses
of Democracy," Rancière examines both working-class insurrectionism and student demonstrations in 1986. He theorizes them in
similar terms, even though we would not consider the latter to be
violent in the manner of the former. In my view, the parallel shows
that Rancière is agnostic about violence when examining egalitarian
politics. I only needed to show, as a rejoinder to May, that
Rancière's politics of equality does not default to nonviolence as its
norm.

We must now ascertain how May arrives at the normative priority of nonviolent resistance (what he abbreviates as "nonviolence").

The argument of his *Nonviolent Resistance* operates at two levels: first, he seeks to outline the moral grounds of nonviolence, and then he defends the thesis that nonviolence is "morally superior to violence in respecting two related values: dignity and equality" (May 2015, 161). We will not challenge his account of the moral grounds of nonviolence; however, we must dispute his claim that nonviolence is morally superior to violent resistance. While May's argument is built in part on Rancièrean grounds (developed further in May 2016), we have seen that Rancière's account of emancipatory politics does not preclude the use of violence. Thus we must examine how May arrives at the conclusion that nonviolence is "the moral default in cases of resistance" (May 2015, 161).

We must first examine May's account of the "space of reasons" animating nonviolence.[10] He defines nonviolence as "political, economic, or social activity that challenges or resists a current political, economic, or social arrangement while respecting the dignity . . . of its participants, adversaries, and others" (May 2015, 59). In other words, nonviolence applies social and political pressure—without violating the dignity of participants, adversaries, or bystanders—to shift public support toward social or political change; it affects political change through sit-ins, demonstrations, boycotts, or other means by remaining morally steadfast in the face of suppression by force or by disrupting business as usual; in general, it places a moral and/or political cost on maintaining the status quo. May argues that in nonviolent actions one acts as a "moral exemplar," willing to undergo suffering when the adversary uses violent suppression while refusing to violate the dignity of the other. The violence of the adversary has (or ought to have) a double effect: On the one hand, "its members are seen not as interested in justice but only in their own self-interest" (May 2015, 78). On the other, the willingness of nonviolent participants inspires (or ought to inspire) admiration in bystanders, fostering sympathy for or lending credibility to the movement's goals. When they choose to use coercive tactics, such as boycotts, nonviolent movements can also place an economic cost on the status quo. In any case, nonviolence seeks to provoke a crisis of moral or political legitimation for the status quo in order to shift consensus toward social justice.

This brief account tells us how nonviolent resistance works but not how May conceptualizes its moral basis. He defends nonviolence on quasi-Kantian and quasi-Rancièrean grounds, which marks a significant departure from Rancière's own work. May argues that nonviolence respects the dignity and equality of participants, adversaries, and bystanders. We will focus on May's definition of dignity, which he defines as having

> a human life to lead, more specifically the ability to engage in projects and relationships that unfold over time; to be aware of one's death in a way that affects how one sees the arc of one's life; to have biological needs like food, shelter, and sleep; to have basic psychological needs like care and a sense of attachment to one's surroundings. (May 2015, 117)

May argues that part of the moral force of nonviolent action rests on the fact that it respects the dignity of the adversary. This respect extends even to adversaries who seek to provoke violence in order to discredit a nonviolent campaign—meaning that participants could not engage in violent self-defense, which would disrespect the adversary (May 2015, 53). One might defend May's conclusion that violent self-defense would discredit participants in a nonviolent campaign on purely tactical grounds. For example, I have been a non-Indigenous participant in demonstrations for Indigenous rights where organizers required nonviolence on the part of all participants to avoid feeding stereotypes of violent "natives" (in other words, they adopted this approach because violence on the part of *any* participant would redound against the Indigenous participants). Though this particular reasoning was tactical, it fits within the general moral universe enacted in nonviolent actions. May notes, within this space of reasons, that disrespect for a particular adversary cuts against the moral exemplarity of the nonviolent action, for "inasmuch as it countenances physical violence toward adversaries, it winds up disrespecting those other adversaries who have not sought to provoke violence" (May 2015, 54).

May's reasoning here also fits within the quasi-Kantian justifications for nonviolence he provides throughout the book. He writes, for example, that "nonviolence does not concern the dignity of *this* or *that* group. . . . It concerns the dignity of all people" (May 2015, 58). Later, in more explicitly Kantian terms, May writes that respect for the adversary involves treating the adversary as having "intrinsic value" as a human deserving of dignity, and this respect treats the Other as an end and not merely as a means. Finally, in nonviolent action, he argues, "one acts, as one is to act in Kant's view, *as though* one lived in a kingdom of ends, not *because* one lives in such a kingdom"; one does so "simply in order to be a moral exemplar" (May 2015, 115). While May provides Kantian formulations of nonviolent principles, he argues that these principles "function performatively" (May 2015, 139). In other words, nonviolent actions or campaigns enact a particular kind of moral space of reasons in order to build support for their causes or goals. And again, I do not dispute this outline of the politics and ethics of nonviolence. Instead, I believe that while this space of reasons builds the moral force of nonviolence, it cannot be applied to evaluate movements that opt for the diversity of tactics—so I will conclude by examining the space of reasons constructed by militant antifascist organizing.

May's application of the space of reasons operative within a nonviolent campaign to his concept of politics in general is mistaken. In other words, politics, even in Rancière's narrow sense, can employ a variety of tactics and strategies. I have argued thus far that nonviolence enacts a particular space of reasons—one engages with other participants, adversaries, and bystanders *as if* one lived in a kingdom of ends, while recognizing that one does not—that are not necessarily applicable in all political and social situations. May also recognizes the difference between the space of reasons of nonviolence and the lived experience of social oppression but tends to apply the space of reasons operative in nonviolence to broader political analysis, and thus he concludes that nonviolence is "morally superior" to violence because it respects the dignity and equality of all participants, adversaries, and bystanders.

The existentialist standpoint that I have defended throughout rejects the possibility that one is able to respect the dignity of all human beings in a situation of oppression. As Beauvoir argues, no action can be taken, no choice can be made, without potentially acting against some others within the situation. When one acts in solidarity with the oppressed, for example, one contests the interests of the oppressor. This standpoint does not preclude nonviolent campaigns; it merely situates the nonviolent space of reasons within a broader social context. We accept that nonviolence could be more successful in campaigns where one seeks to shift public opinion or legitimacy toward social justice or reform, but the moral values of a nonviolent space of reasons do not necessarily translate in movements, such as militant antifascism, which are not oriented toward public consensus. On this point, May's interview with the *Los Angeles Review of Books* (2018) is telling. There he reiterates his normative commitment to nonviolence—prescribing adherence to respect for the dignity and equality of adversaries—and advocates nonviolent resistance to the rise of the Far Right but fails to either outline concrete practices that could stem the rise of the Far Right or address what alternatives nonviolence might offer to militant antifascist diversity of tactics. In other words, May stops short at the crux of the problem:

> When a movement of equality is forced into a position where it must be violent, does that undermines its character as a movement of equality? It is, admittedly, a vexed question, one that I have struggled to answer in a way that I am finally comfortable with. (May 2018)

I hold that militant antifascism, though it uses a diversity of tactics, remains egalitarian. We have two avenues to resolve May's "vexed question." The first attempts to resolve the problem on his terms by accepting, for the sake of argument, that we can define Rancière's concept of equality through the paradigm of "meaningful lives":

May glosses this equality of intelligences as the presupposition that each person, "unless we are somehow damaged emotionally or intellectually, can envision meaningful lives for ourselves and sort out to one extent or another with others how to carry out or conduct those lives" (May 2015, 141). This definition is similar to how he defines dignity. To resolve the problem on May's terms, I would suggest that while we might owe respect to all other persons as capable of living meaningful lives, not all *projects* that might guide a meaningful life are worthy of respect. May anticipates this difference, arguing that while a commitment to equality requires that we extend respect to the adversary, this does not entail deference: "To respect that specific others have a life to lead does not require that we defer to every desire they possess. If it were then . . . nonviolent coercion would be impossible" (May 2015, 51). He then contends that in a nonviolent campaign, we may only frustrate or interfere with the actions of the adversary as long as our actions maintain respect for their dignity. But I do not see how this point places a similar obligation on political actions that do not constitute the nonviolent space of reasons. I think we can demarcate between respect for the capacity to lead a meaningful life and whether or not a particular *project* that guides a meaningful life is worthy of respect. I doubt that May would agree, to paraphrase his own definition of dignity, that "the *fascist* deserves the ability to engage in projects and relationships that unfold over time" if these projects are fascistic. I do not believe that we owe fascists respect insofar as they lead a life as *fascists*. We don't, because we understand that the project that guides a meaningful life for a fascist *as fascist* involves, when given the means, the oppression and genocide of others—more than likely it is a project in which white supremacy is intensified in North America either through state repression and/or ethnic cleansing, the re-entrenchment of heteropatriarchal gender roles, and a reliance on state violence to accomplish these goals. This project is not only unworthy of respect but harmful to others. On this view, our obligation to respect the other's dignity extends to an acknowledgment of the capacity of adversaries to revise their morally reprehensible views and opt for better, nonfascist projects. There must be, as part of an antifascist political program, opportunities for rehabilitation for those who seek to leave Far Right movements. That said, we do not owe them further respect when they refuse this possibility and seek to realize their project through recruitment, intimidation, or mobilization in our communities. Indeed, I believe that if we truly take their autonomy seriously, then we cannot paternalistically dismiss their projects as atavism or pathology; we must meet their actions with community self-defense.

Alternatively, we could jettison the "meaningful lives" paradigm for understanding equality, which would bring our discussion of Rancière closer to the militant antifascist line. I prefer this approach. May's interpretation of the equality of intelligences as the capacity to live a meaningful life constitutes an important exception to his generally anarchist reading of Rancière. As Rachel Magnusson contends, May opts for a figurative interpretation of the equality of intelligences rather than a literal meaning. She notes that before May defines equality according to the meaningful life criteria, he concedes that there might be fields of expertise that fall outside the ambit of intellectual equality. May writes that equality of intelligences "has nothing to do with standardized tests or with the ability to do advanced math or physics. Instead, it has to with the ability of people to shape their lives" (May 2007, 111; see also May 2008, 57–60). Magnusson then observes that May's caveat that equality "has nothing to do . . . with the ability to do advanced math or physics" undermines the subversive and disruptive force of Rancière's declaration of intellectual equality—and according to Joseph Jacotot, the protagonist of Rancière's *The Ignorant Schoolmaster,* there are no fields of expertise that fall outside the reach of his egalitarian methods. By contrast, by prioritizing the equality of *autonomy* rather than *intelligence*, May's reinterpretation of what Rancière means by the equality of intelligences reads as, in Magnusson's terms, "simply another declaration of the fundamental liberal tenet that we are all the best governors of our own lives" (Magnusson 2015, 204). The differences between the figurative and literal interpretations of equality become more pronounced when we consider Rancière's research on nineteenth-century French workers' movements. Magnusson considers the worker-poets and autodidact critics who populate the discussions of Rancière's *Proletarian Nights*, who asserted that they were both workers and intellectuals—artists, poets, and philosophers. If we treat this assertion figuratively, we might conclude that their endeavors gave an intellectual meaning and sense of autonomy to their lives. However, this figurative reading blunts the subversive sting of Rancière's reading: these workers became artists or intellectuals; they both subverted the social categories that distinguished between those whose task it is to think and those whose task it is to work, and they undermined the distinctions between "poetic art" and the "mechanical art" of labor. As William H. Sewell observes, independently of Rancière,

> the very existence of worker-poets, the coupling of the terms *poête* and *ouvrier*, was itself a novel and potent statement about labor. That manual labourers were capable of poetry, the most esteemed of the arts in this age of high romanticism, that mechanical art and poetic art could be mastered by the same person, signified that the long-presumed opposition between vile labor and lofty creativity was false, that labor and poetry were not opposite but basically the same. The worker-poets, whatever the subjects of their poetry, revealed the exalted mission of labor by their very existence. They were living representations of a great new truth: the labor was synonymous with creativity and an emanation of the sublime. (Sewell 1980, 236–37).

From this discussion we draw the following conclusion: the worker-poets forced a different, more egalitarian distribution of the sensible—a different, more egalitarian *aesthetics*—within the broader parameters of a policed distribution of the sensible premised on the opposition between intelligence and labor. The simultaneous existence of this egalitarian aesthetics and the police suggests an ongoing conflict between two kinds of social forces (or sets of social relations), and that, to take the worker-poets at their word, to acknowledge them as worker-poets, means rejecting the normative conventions of the opposition intelligence-labor.

In other words, I believe that we cannot reduce what Rancière means by equality to May's quasi-Kantian principles. While the meaningful life paradigm might animate the space of reasons for nonviolent resistance, we must situate the enactment of this paradigm as involving a *choice* about how to apply egalitarianism. In my view, we cannot respect all humanity in our choices and our actions—thus to apply the norms of the nonviolent space of reasons to all forms of political struggle and conflict is mistaken. As Beauvoir contends, in a situation or system of social oppression, we cannot even choose solidarity with others striving for an open future without choosing against the interests of the oppressors. In a parallel manner, I believe that we cannot fight, even on Rancière's terms, for emancipation without fighting against the oppressive institutions of policing and the supererogatory bigotry of the Far Right.

I have sought to show how Rancière's egalitarian politics can involve some degree of force or violence—as he writes, that equality and freedom are *forces* that are engendered and augmented by their enactment against forces of policing and oppression—in order to build an egalitarian case for community self-defense. This case departs from Rancière on one key point—not because community self-defense involves the willingness to use force, but because Rancière maintains "equality turns into its opposite the moment it aspires to a place in the social or state organization" (Rancière [1995] 1999, 34). Thus in Rancière's terms, practices of community self-defense could paradoxically involve protecting sedimented practices that are instituted and maintained in stratified social structures of policing rather than a politics opposed to policing. Here I think we must modify Rancière's work, shifting from the binary model of oppressor-oppressed (in his terms, those who "have a part" and "the part-with-no-part") toward the three-way fight. This involves situating dissensual political organizing against the Far Right and state institutions. These spaces of community self-defense, then, must be more egalitarian than state institutions while willing to defend these spaces from the violence of the Far Right through direct action. As J. Clark writes in "Three-Way Fight: Revolutionary Anti-Fascism and Armed Self-Defense," militant antifascist organizing must, on the one hand, "oppose, disrupt, and undermine the fascist/insurgent right and their organizing, as well as help build support for the targets of right-wing violence and scapegoating. On the other, we must organize to fight the conditions from which fascism grows" (Clark 2018, 56).

I argued in chapter 3 that the politics of dissensus involves both the symbolization of equality and practices that subvert or combat practices of command-coercion. There are two passages in Rancière's *Disagreement* that could constitute a starting point for discussing, on his terms, how dissensus might be sustained through community self-defense. First, he suggests that politics—while it is on principle heterogenous to policing—nonetheless leaves a "trace" on a given distribution of the sensible (Rancière [1995] 1999, 34). Second, he contends that "politics is aesthetic in principle" (Rancière [1995] 1999, 58). In my view, we can then hold that, in the wake of any given political mobilization, there remain practices of an egalitarian politics, in discursive, aesthetic, and practical terms, that serve as the "traces" that constitute "a kind of community of sense experience that works on the world of the assumption [of the equality of intelligences], of the *as if* that includes those who are not included by revealing a mode of existence of sense experience that has eluded" a given order of policing (Rancière [1995] 1999, 58tm). This egalitarian *as if* impinges on the policing of a given distribution of the sensible and constitutes a point of resistance and critique. And if this egalitarian aesthetic is a "community of sense experience" and a "mode of existence," there must be some temporal stability to these modes of existence imbricated in egalitarian practices that are defined by the refusal or forestalling of domination, exploitation, command, and coercion. And if they are, to some degree, constitutively temporally or spatially stable, then attacks on these egalitarian practices warrant self-defense—because otherwise these egalitarian practices would cease to exist.

Whence the differences between May and myself? Let us recall that May accepts in his pragmatic defense of nonviolence (which I have not discussed here) a reliance on Chenoweth and Stephan's metrics for success (May 2015, 71–72, 100–104). In Chenoweth's critique of the black bloc, which we discussed above, she reprimands militants for harming consensus building from the "center," or within established institutions of power; she concludes that the diverse coalition of the Trump Resistance must communicate their "vision in a way that attracts rather than repels adherents, while building capacity to continually maintain resilience, *project legitimacy to those in the center*, and build power from below" (Chenoweth 2017). From a militant antifascist standpoint, the strategy of the Trump Resistance concedes the terms of struggle to the norms of settler-colonial hegemony. May, who has been influential in studies of poststructuralist anarchism, ought to be skeptical of the way that appeals to the "center" not only normalize state power and the policing operative in appeals to discursive "civility" but also enable the normalization of the Far Right. The differences between our positions will continue to rest on the different goals of nonviolent resistance in liberal antifascism and militant antifascism: whereas nonviolent resistance is ultimately a model of building consensus, militant antifascism is driven by dissensus.

## 4.4. MILITANT ANTIFASCISM IS COMMUNITY SELF-DEFENSE

I have argued that punching nazis, should the need arise, is neither in bad faith nor anti-egalitarian. I have sought to show that militant antifascism is not only compatible with existentialism and egalitarianism but that it ought to follow for those who find existentialism or Rancière's egalitarianism compelling. The case for militant antifascism has been built philosophically but also implicitly according to the space of reasons of academic philosophical discourse. Here I will shift the perspective and examine militant antifascism and the use of the diversity of tactics through a reconstruction, to some degree, of the space of reasons operative in antifascist organizing.

The guiding premise of antifascist organizing is that militant action is a practice of emancipatory community self-defense. In other words, when antifascists organize to oppose fascist street mobilization, their practices and choices are guided and criticized according to two questions: What tactics will stop, or are most successful in stopping, fascists from recruiting or organizing? What tactics will build support for targets of right-wing intimidation, scapegoating, and violence? Before situating punching nazis within this space of reasons, we must first define the concept and practice of emancipatory community self-defense—how it departs from, and emerges in opposition to, commonsense notions of the right to self-defense.

Commonsense notions of the right to armed self-defense define it as individuals' natural or state-sanctioned right to protect themselves, their family, or their property, in the absence of state protection. Defining the right to armed self-defense in terms of natural or self-evident right dehistoricizes and depoliticizes how the concept has been shaped by the settler-colonial project in North America, especially by a "dangerous gun culture [which] has emerged in the United States, one that has entitled white nationalism, racialized dominance, and social control through violence," not to mention a masculinist, misogynistic, homophobic, and transphobic culture of violence (Dunbar-Ortiz 2018, 25). The right to armed self-defense is only "self-evident" for those who were first extended the right to bear arms: white settlers who were prepared to use violence to steal Indigenous land to the west of the United States or patrol slaves (and free blacks) within. These are the typically unacknowledged sociohistorical roots of what Chad Kautzer calls the "sovereign subject" of self-defense, "which is the centerpiece of authoritarian political ideologies and motivates so many reactionary movements," such as white militias and the sovereign citizen movement (Kautzer 2018, 46).

The practice of community self-defense emerges against the background of this system of oppression. For example, in his landmark *Negroes with Guns* (1962), Robert F. Williams situates the use of self-defense against systemic and state-sanctioned racist violence, noting that black community self-defense challenges "the exclusive monopoly of violence practiced by white racists" (Williams [1962] 1998, 76).[11] Williams here also disputes the identification of state power and the monopoly on violence by locating the state's own legitimacy in a broader project of white supremacy and, in our terms, settler-colonialism. In general, much of the discourse and practice of emancipatory community self-defense has been developed on the basis of the armed defense of the black civil rights movement and national liberation struggles, though I do not want to diminish the broader importance and influence of Indigenous struggles for self-determination, militant feminism, or the organizing of groups such as Anti-Racist Action or the 43 Group on contemporary antifascism. Kautzer notes that community self-defense involves defending a marginalized or beleaguered community against both bodily harm and the dominant culture that "others" them, meaning "their self-defense also undermines existing social hierarchies, ideologies, and identities" (Kautzer 2018, 36). To place Kautzer's observation in Beauvoir's terms, community self-defense has a dual character: it asserts the agency of communities treated as "others," while protecting spaces of solidarity.

Three comments are in order before we address antifascist community self-defense. First, I do not want to suggest that community self-defense is restricted to geographically bounded neighborhoods such as black communities in the era of American segregation. Accepting this restriction entails accepting a difference between public spaces of protest and private spaces of self-defense. The latter is, of course, important: Williams credits armed self-defense with ending armed Ku Klux Klan incursions into Monroe, North Carolina's black community and leading to a city ordinance banning the Klan from Monroe unless they had a special permit from the police chief. But Williams foregrounds his entire argument, in chapter 1 of *Negroes with Guns*, by showing how self-defense was necessary to protect the black community's public picket of Monroe's segregated swimming facilities. In addition, Charles E. Cobb Jr., in his *This Nonviolent Stuff'll Get You Killed*, has documented the tacit acceptance of armed civil rights activists at public, avowedly principled nonviolent actions (Cobb 2016, especially 187–226). Thus community self-defense rejects the idea of a public/private distinction grounding its use.

Second, we cannot delimit a community merely according to homogenous, sociologically identifiable groups. This comment rests on arguments I have made elsewhere but which are consistent with the present discussion, that political subjectivation involves a dynamic of disidentification with roles and identities assigned to individuals and groups within police orders (Shaw 2016a, chapter 2). In other words, political subjectivation is not merely the assertion of an identity but transforms subjects and their presumed identities through the assertion of political agency. For our purposes here, I will adopt scott crow's working definition of liberatory community armed self-defense: "The collective group practice of temporarily taking up arms for defensive purposes, as part of larger engagements of self-determination in keeping with a liberatory ethics" (crow 2018, 8). The framework developed by crow is built on four principles, which are consistent with the concept of egalitarianism that I have developed here: "Mutual aid (cooperation), direct action (taking action without waiting on the approval of authorities), solidarity (recognizing that the well-being of disparate groups is tied together) and collective autonomy (community self-determination)" (crow 2018, 11). In sum, an antifascist organizing seeks to build community as a form of collective autonomy (through instituting forms of participation that are more open and egalitarian than liberal mechanisms of participation), mutual aid, and solidarity across lines of racial, gender, class, and ability in order to combat fascist organizing through direct action. Optimally, this practice of community building demands a greater level of self-critical vigilance than is observed in movements directed toward mainstream forms of institutional representation. As Kautzer notes, "Since the social structures and identities of race, gender, class, and ability intersect in our lives, practices of self-defense can and often must challenge structures of oppression on multiple fronts simultaneously," including the principled self-criticism of antifascist organizing itself (Kautzer 2018, 36; on intersectionality, see "2.2.2. Beauvoir's Critique of Marxism").

Third, we must note that antifascist community self-defense departs from these other practices in that it is typically unarmed. There have been occasions in open-carry jurisdictions in the United States where groups such as the John Brown Gun Club have counterdemonstrated against armed Far Right open-carry groups, but these demonstrations are the exception. The norm is to opt for nonviolent tactics first, such as public-awareness campaigns, before shifting to physical confrontation, and even then, physical confrontation has been largely restricted to blocking march routes or street skirmishes. The observance of this norm does not necessitate that we evaluate antifascist organizing according to the nonviolent space of reasons, as the commitment to diversity of tactics signals a willingness to use force to disrupt Far Right organizing.[12]

Instead, we must interpret punching nazis within the parameters of community self-defense. We observe, first, that, typically, punching nazis is one tactic in a broader strategy of physically confronting Far Right street mobilization. The goal of this strategy is to stop or undermine Far Right recruitment and the mobilization of public violence, harassment, or intimidation of marginalized communities. Therefore, militants measure the success of physical confrontation against two factors: First, does physical confrontation hurt the recruitment or stymie organizing among the Far Right? And, second, are there other tactics that would do equivalent work that do not carry the risks (such as arrest, prosecution, or retaliation) associated with physical confrontation?

We might provisionally answer the second question first. Generally speaking, militant antifascists deploy tactics that raise the cost of participation for those involved, or interested in getting involved, in Far Right or fascist organizing. Campaigns against Far Right events raise public awareness of the presence of Far Right activities in our communities, and counterprotesting places pressure on organizers and complicit organizations, and organizations such as colleges, universities, and libraries are then (potentially) held accountable for platforming groups in direct opposition to mission statements of inclusion, diversity, and open public participation and in possible violation of, as some union activists have noted, workplace protections. Shane Burley notes that doxing (releasing personal information of) specific members of the Far Right "has been an incredibly potent tool for antifascist organizing, as it plays heavily on the fact that most [white] nationalist activists cannot afford to be outed to their professional or social networks" (Burley 2017, 203). There was a brief time during the spring and summer of 2019 where antifascists were out "milkshaking" nazis as a disruptive tactic. When deciding about which tactics to deploy, antifascists must consider the specific circumstances of militant actions. Effective as public awareness campaigns or doxing may be, they do not deter the most militant of the Far Right from continuing to organize street demonstrations to further recruitment while intimidating or harassing the public in general and marginalized communities in particular. Militant antifascist counterdemonstrations seek to place a cost on street-level mobilization, and Far Right organizers know that antifascist organizing interferes with and undermines fascist social mobilization. Militant antifascists have—or *should have*—studied discussions of community self-defense rooted in traditions such as the armed factions of the black civil rights movement. Thus I think Robert Williams describes the conflict between racist vigilantism and community self-defense well: vigilantism is carried out by "people who would like to do violence to others but want to have immunity from violence themselves" (Williams [1962] 1998, 62). The contemporary Far Right, especially in its rhetoric, embraces aspects of white vigilantism that were once public, widespread, but operative only as long as there was a white monopoly on violence. Community self-defense breaks this presumed monopoly—and, importantly, it prevents fascists from projecting an image of uncontested power in public spaces, which itself discourages potential recruits. Contemporary antifascists are quite close to Williams in their assessments of militant physical confrontation. A Washington, DC, antifascist, Chepe, calls it the "it's not worth it principle": since new fascists come looking "to identify with the most powerful kid on the block," Chepe explained that in his experience, "when they are defeated in conflict or find their brethren run off, they feel like 'it's not worth it' and a lot of them leave" (Bray 2017, 175).

Militant antifascists are aware that the reasons for physical confrontation must be tested against results. On the one hand, organizers and journalists track patterns of Far Right street-level participation across time. This involves tracking how many people show up at particular rallies and variation of attendance over time (and in relation to antifascist participation); the demographics of participation (for example, whether participation is regional or not); what their rallies accomplish (whether or not they meet their strategic goals); and whether there are mitigating factors outside of the control of organizers (interventions by governments or police or events that happen elsewhere). Organizers and outside observers need to account for each factor. The last major Far Right rally to be held, as I write, was the cynically or disingenuously titled "End Domestic Terrorism" rally, organized by the Proud Boys and Patriot Prayer, and which included the participation of the American Guard (two other groups, the Oath Keepers and the Washington III% militias pulled out).[13] Though the rally was, according to journalist Shane Burley, one of the largest in Portland, Oregon, in recent memory, numbers alone do not indicate success—as the Far Right participation was greatly outnumbered by a coalition of militant and nonmilitant groups.[14] The fact that the rally ended after thirty minutes signals a recruitment and organizational failure for the Right. Several factors probably had an effect on participation: increased press and public scrutiny toward right-wing violence in general after several mass shootings, a number of arrests related to a Far Right attack on the local establishment Cider Riot on May 1, 2019, and pressure exerted by local politicians and civic groups. Burley had previously reported on the recent decline of Patriot Prayer and indicates that the size of the rally points to a reversal of this trend (Burley 2019a; direct messages to author, August 2019). I would suggest that if initial reports are correct and the rally's attendance was boosted by participation of individuals from outside the region, then this model of recruitment involves financial and logistical costs that might not be sustainable in the face of mounting opposition. In any case, the counterdemonstration against the Far Right brought out more than one thousand people, including militant community self-defense groups and a number of nonmilitant organizations such as the local chapters of the NAACP and the IWW, the Portland DSA, the labor coalition Portland Jobs with Justice, the Buddhist Peace Fellowship, and other groups—despite calls by mayor Ted Wheeler for Portlanders to stay home. I doubt the rally would have been so brief if the Far Right had not been clearly outnumbered. The increasing willingness of nonmilitant groups to participate in counterdemonstrations signals an important shift toward a broader vocal and local political base for antifascist organizing, and brings increased scrutiny toward local police, who have been accused of closely collaborating with Far Right groups and effectively acted as a Far Right propaganda outlet when spreading allegations that antifascists had been milkshaking nazis with vegan milkshakes blended with quick-drying cement in a counterdemonstration on June 29, 2019 (see Shepherd 2019a, 2019b).

On the other hand, antifascists also consider their assessments against internal discussions among the Far Right, who have repeatedly admitted that militant organizing has undermined their efforts. According to Richard Spencer, rallies aren't "fun" anymore (quoted in Lennard 2018). Spencer is not alone. Matt Parrott (a white nationalist and cofounder of the Traditionalist Workers Party) wrote on Gab, a social media platform popular among the Far Right: "The antifa [*sic*] has pretty much succeeded in achieving what the progressive left cannot, which is fully and finally de-platforming the hard right"; "they demoralized and disabled the majority of the 'alt-right,' driving most of them off the streets and public square" (quoted in Burley 2018b). Though we ought to evaluate these admissions with some skepticism, insofar as they double as propaganda tools signaling social persecution and victimhood to their social base, we should note that they also vindicate the analyses of antifascists such as George Ciccariello-Maher, who argues that

> the effects that punching Nazis creates include, first, as Richard Spencer through his own absurd inability to think strategically has admitted, it has made his life a living hell already. He admitted that it's making it very difficult for them to organize. He's admitted, in other words, everything that many of us have said about how Nazis need to be treated and about this famous apoc-

ryphal quote from Hitler that says, "If someone had recognized early on and crushed our movement with the utmost brutality of violence, then we would never have been able to grow." (Ciccariello-Maher 2017b)

And yet despite the evidence supporting militant antifascism thus far, there remains a seemingly intractable liberal argument against physical confrontation and punching nazis: violence, critics allege, only serves to instigate or feed a spiral of escalating recriminatory violence. However, if this were true, how does the critic explain the lack of such escalation over more than two years of fascist and antifascist street-level mobilization? As I conclude in August 2019, even when the Far Right *has already escalated* (resulting in the death of Heather Heyer and injuries to more than a dozen others during the Unite the Right events in Charlottesville, Virginia, in August 2017, not to mention mass shootings committed by individuals espousing Far Right and incel ideologies), antifascists still organize around building popular support for street mobilizations and unarmed physical confrontation. The argumentative burden ought to be on liberal critics, who must answer for what particular, concrete action(s) they *can do* to fight fascism beyond abstract appeals to the benevolent mechanisms of civil society or demands for more state and police power—the latter of which will more likely redound on marginalized and beleaguered communities before it ever does something about fascism.

I believe that the liberal critic remains mistakenly committed to the idea that physical confrontation reflects individual frustrations rather than a principled commitment to stopping Far Right popular mobilization. Among Continental philosophers, it's a dogma inherited from Hannah Arendt, who defines violence as "incapable of speech" (Arendt [1963] 2006, 9). By contrast, Ciccariello-Maher argues that emancipatory violence "speaks volumes" (Ciccariello-Maher 2017a, 48)—and within militant space of reasons, there is a fundamental opposition between the ends of emancipatory community self-defense and fascistic violence, and this difference has been a point of critical discussion among antifascists for decades. Don Hamerquist, for example, writes,

> Fascism is fundamentally a doctrine of justified force to advance selected special interests. Fascists do not worry too much about who and what is injured by their use of force. The left must, if it is to be true to a universal vision of liberation. When we abandon this vision and rationalize non-combatant casualties and collateral damage as the fascists might, the heart goes out of both our confrontation with fascism and our radical critique of capitalism. The prime beneficiaries of this will be the various liberal ideologists who are promoting the notion of the essential unity of the radical extremes. (Hamerquist [2002] 2017, 72)

Fascists praise violence as an instrument of social domination (though often in plausibly deniable terms when such statements are made for public consumption and recruitment) and, as Walter Benjamin showed many decades ago, venerate it as an aesthetic object. By contrast, antifascists must engage in open self-criticism to prevent martial values from superseding political objectives, in other words, to prevent violence from superseding the diversity of tactics. Furthermore, antifascism must continue to offer spaces for and meaningful participation from and support for the marginalized and beleaguered communities who are the targets of Far Right harassment and scapegoating. But we must always remember that antifascism is part of a three-way fight against fascism and liberalism, two social forces that coalesce—at points converging and at others diverging—around the broader projects of capital accumulation and settler-colonialism. Fascism cannot be defeated until the conditions that enable it are overthrown. Until then, we assert a political claim to emancipatory community self-defense.

## NOTES

1. I cannot emphasize enough that the liberal fascination with figures like Spencer is a product of their own paternalistic views of fascists and

racists as backward hicks rather than a product of a coherent theory of the Far Right or fascism.

2. This point, along with several other important objections that I will not consider here, are detailed in Bray 2017, 178–87.

3. The "second ethics," as it were, is then elaborated in Sartre's 1964 Rome lectures (Sartre 2015) and/or his undelivered 1965 Cornell lectures (Sartre 2005).

4. Eshleman (2015, 65) addresses a number of implicit interpretive decisions that guide Santoni's reconstruction of the *Notebooks*.

5. For example, Santoni writes, "In the *Critique* [*of Dialectical Reason*], given material scarcity and the related inhumanity of exploitation, oppression, objectification, and necessity, the only human option is *individual* violence" (Santoni 2005, 70, my emphasis).

6. For example, "one must retreat from neither the outrage of violence nor deny it, or, which amounts to the same thing, assume it lightly" (Beauvoir [1947] 1976, 133).

7. A third possibility is his essay "The Cause of the Other" (1998a), which focuses on how French citizens mobilized against the French state during the Algerian war. However, Rancière introduces a number of interpretive caveats that preclude him from drawing conclusions about the Algerian struggle itself or a general theory of the relationship between politics and war. See also Shaw 2016a, 72–76.

8. See Chambers 2013, 54–57, concerning the differences between the various editions of *Aux bords du politique* and the English translation (which is based on the first edition, but with revisions by Rancière). He also notes how "police/policing" is not explicitly conceptualized in *On the Shores of Politics* (183n7).

9. Reflecting on the differences between *La parole ouvrière* and his more recent work, Rancière argues that the former presumed that workers' speech affirms the collective experiences of workers, whereas he later began from the idea that workers' speech is a dynamic of disidentification that breaks with the given identity of "the worker" through a "transgression that takes place on the terrain of the thought and speech of others" (presumably, a transgression of the system of social inequality that had established the given identity of the worker) (Rancière 2007b, 341).

10. May 2015, 134. He borrows the phrase from Wilfrid Sellars. May writes, "Humans occupy the space of reasons in the sense that we can give reasons to one another for what we believe as well as understand reasons

given by others. . . . We might think of it as an inferential space . . . where, from being committed to certain beliefs, other commitments follow" (May 2015, 134).

11. It has subsequently been acknowledged that the book is the product of collaboration between Robert and Mabel Williams.

12. May argues that nonviolence must disavow the threat (a loaded term that undermines the legitimacy of a "willingness to use") of violence (May 2015, 62–63).

13. In this account, I rely on three sources: journalists Shane Burley (2019b), Christopher Mathias and Andy Campbell (2019), and the antifascist website It's Going Down (This Week in Fascism 2019).

14. Burley estimates that the rally drew from 250 to 300 supporters, while reporting from It's Going Down pegs the number around 200.

# 5

# FIGHTING WHITE SUPREMACY

From Antifascism to Decolonization

## 5.1. FROM ANTIFASCISM . . .

Throughout the present study I have argued that the Far Right is a social movement that coalesces around two strategies: parapolitical social mobilization and insurrectionism. Thus far I have focused on its parapolitical strategies because they contribute to our understanding of how the Far Right attempts to normalize its extremist views or alibi the forms of social oppression that it seeks to reentrench in our societies. These parapolitical strategies open a parliamentary or institutional path for rooting in the political system. At the same time, when the Far Right presents its project in terms of so-called grievances, this co-optation of the language of oppression deliberately occludes how white supremacy and white privilege—in the form of sovereign possession and a "public and psychological wage"—operate within the settler-colonial societies of the United States and Canada.

Here I would like to situate militant antifascist theory and practice within a broader struggle against white supremacy while outlining, in more detail than in chapter 1, how settler-colonial hegemony coalesces around compromises between liberalism and white settlerism or white supremacy. In what follows, I outline a theory of settler-colonialism while reconceptualizing the antifascist intellectual tradition. Given that fascist movements emerged in numerous European countries and succeeded in seizing power in Germany and Italy, and that these countries were, broadly speaking, part of the European metropole of colonialism and imperialism, one is entirely warranted in attempting to make sense of the social conditions within these countries that gave rise to fascism. There's more to the story, however. From a time nearly contemporary with the emergence of fascism, and indeed, already alert to protofascist movements such as the Ku Klux Klan, political theorists situated outside the European tradition had ascertained a transformation of the meaning of whiteness that originated in black emancipation in the United States and the expansion of European and American colonialism and imperialism across the globe.

Antifascist movements must integrate within the "larger legacy of resistance to white supremacy in all its forms" (Bray 2017, xvii). It is not uncommon to see antifascists in North America cite Aimé Césaire's *Discourse on Colonialism*, where the great Martinician poet and critic contends that fascism, "Hitlerism," took the practices of colonialism, oppression, and genocide, and turned them against Europe itself. He writes that the "very distinguished, very humanistic, very Christian bourgeois of the twentieth century" had tolerated Nazism "before it was inflicted on them, that they absolved it, shut their eyes to it, legitimized it, because, until then, it had been applied only to non-European peoples" (Césaire [1950] 2000, 36). Published in 1950, the *Discourse*, when extracted from the transatlantic black, creole, and Indigenous intellectual traditions from which it arose, appears a retrospective summary of the relation between colonialism and fascism, when in fact it is better understood as a *culmination* of at least four decades of a critique of the interlocking structures of whiteness, imperialism, and colonialism. We find similar remarks in the work of W. E. B. Du Bois, who, in *Dusk of Dawn*, contends, "Hitler is the late crude but logical exponent of white world race philosophy since the Conference of Berlin in 1884" (Du Bois [1940] 2007, 86). But Du Bois had analyzed this "white world race philosophy" in detail even earlier, in chapter 2 of *Darkwater: Voices from Within the Veil* (1920), and the first publication of that chapter as a short essay, "The Souls of White Folk," in 1910.

Just as neglecting the role of colonialism and imperialism limits our understanding of conditions that made fascism possible in the decades between the end of World War I and the end of World War II, we cannot understand the contemporary rise of the Far Right and fascism in North America without considering settler-colonialism. The philosophers we have studied thus far do not provide much assistance in this direction. Though Sartre wrote about the United States, to my knowledge, he did not thematize settler-colonialism, and his equivocations about Palestinian political struggle represent a serious theoretical and political failure (see Arthur 2010, 147–49). Nor has Rancière discussed settler-colonialism in a North American context, though a critical theory of settler-colonialism and race is pertinent to his own discussions of the aesthetics of Emerson, Whitman, and James Agee and Walker Evans (see Rancière [2011a] 2013, 55–74; 245–62). Beauvoir has discussed settler-colonialism in *America Day-by-Day*, but she fails to bring anti-Indigenous racism into theoretical focus. While she notes how the American reservation system is predicated on the expropriation of Indigenous land, her descriptions of visiting Taos evoke a number of colonial stereotypes of the "Vanishing Indian." At one point, she wonders "if they [the Taos] will come to terms with the fate reserved for them in this pueblo, which is artificially cut off from the world, yet beleaguered by modern civilization" (Beauvoir [1948] 1999, 192). Then, evoking the image of the stolid but silent "Indian," she observes of the children of the pueblo that "it's difficult to make out what's going on behind those young brown foreheads" (Beauvoir [1948] 1999, 192). Finally, when she literally trespasses on Indigenous land—"We have violated the boundaries assigned to whites"—she evinces colonial attitudes similar to her American acquaintances. As Sonia Kruks notes, "Perhaps oddly and certainly troublingly, Beauvoir does not appear to recognize the behavior of the Taos residents as a form of very justifiable resistance, and she aligns her perspec-

tive with that of her Anglo acquaintances and informants . . . and
she seems unconscious of her position as a member of the privileged
racial 'caste'" (Kruks 2012, 77).

Thus our account of settler-colonialism requires reorienting our
theoretical signposts. There is, however, a line of analysis in which
black political thought, existentialism, critiques of settler-colonialism, and Indigenous political thought intersect. Du Bois, in "The
Souls of White Folk," sets—though does not fully theorize—that
agenda.[1] In both versions of "The Souls of White Folk," Du Bois
contends that *personal* whiteness emerges in the late nineteenth
century as the claim to two types of possession: a claim of Euro-
peans (and those of European descent), as *white*, of being the right-
ful titleholder of title, sovereignty, and ownership the world over
(implemented through imperialism) and whiteness as a form of entitlement, as a "public and psychological wage" or, as Cheryl Harris
phrases it, "status property." Du Bois's account of possessive whiteness precedes Sartre's discussion of the anti-Semite's ideology of
possession by several decades and has had a lasting influence in
whiteness studies. Harris, in "Whiteness as Property," develops this
theoretical program to demonstrate how whiteness and property
were codified in social and legal terms in opposition to Indigenous
sovereignty and "Blackness."[2] In *The White Possessive*, Quanda-
mooka scholar Aileen Moreton-Robinson observes that much of
whiteness research has neglected to situate the development of
white supremacy within settler-colonialism, despite the fact that the
"existence of white supremacy as hegemony, ideology, epistemolo-
gy, and ontology requires possession of Indigenous lands as its pro-
prietary anchor within" settler-colonial capitalist economies such as
the United States, Canada, and Australia (Moreton-Robinson 2015,
xix). Harris, Moreton-Robinson notes, is one exception in this literature, and for this reason her work has been an important point of
reference for those who have dealt with the relationship of whiteness to possession, title, status, and Indigeneity in the settler-colonial societies of Australia, Canada, Israel/Palestine (Moreton-Robinson 2015; Bhandar 2018) and concerning the Far Right in the United States (Inwood and Bonds 2017).

Militant antifascism is part of a broader array of radical political movements that seek to build nonfascist, emancipatory communities. In the previous chapter, I argued that militant antifascist organizing contributes to movement building by frustrating and undermining Far Right efforts at recruitment. Therefore, militant antifascism must be understood within the parameters of emancipatory community self-defense. To conclude, I will argue that the communities that we build through alliances and solidarity work must aim to be antifascist, emancipatory, and decolonized. Decolonization is not a metaphor, as Unangax scholar Eve Tuck and K. Wayne Yang (2013) argue. There is no meaningful way that white supremacy can be defeated in settler-colonial societies without decolonization. Decolonization requires, among other things, dismantling the ideologies and institutions of possessive whiteness—in theory, this involves the critique of the ideology of possessive whiteness; in antifascist practice, it involves organizing and action, building solidarity movements, or directly aiding Indigenous resurgence and self-determination.

## 5.2. WHITENESS AS POSSESSION AND ENTITLEMENT

In *Anti-Semite and Jew*, Sartre argues that the ideology of possession plays an important role in the anti-Semitic worldview. Though I have been critical of some of Sartre's main claims in that book, it is worth remembering that even for Frantz Fanon, "certain pages of *Anti-Semite and Jew* are some of the finest we have ever read" (Fanon [1952] 2008, 158). By examining both the psychological motives and the socioeconomic conditions that make anti-Semitism and racism possible, Sartre's *Anti-Semite and Jew* foreshadows elements of Fanon's sociogenic analysis of antiblack racism. Sartre contends that "it is the antisemite who *makes* the Jew" (Sartre [1946a] 1995, 69); Fanon contends that "it is the racist who creates his inferior" (Fanon [1952] 2008, 73tm). However, as noted in "The Three-Way Fight and No-Platforming the Far Right," section 2.5 of this volume, Sartre separates antiracist practice into two phases: he severs the dialectical unity of ideological combat (posed as a program of "concrete liberalism") from anticapitalist politics (fighting the conditions that make racism possible), which on his own terms is self-defeating. Fanon's sociogeny corrects Sartre's mistake by placing this ideological combat in dialectical relation to anticolonialism and anticapitalism. Nonetheless, Fanon uses Sartre's analyses to compare and contrast anti-Semitism and antiblackness, to differentiate concrete, particular forms of racism within the totality of white supremacist ideology. It is possible that Fanon had in mind the passages on Frenchness and the ideology of possession when he contends that, for the anti-Semite, it is "because the Jews commandeer a country that they are dangerous" (Fanon [1952] 2008, 138). Anti-Semitism is a direct ancestor of the contemporary white supremacist conspiracies about white genocide and the so-called replacement "theory."

Sartre contends that the French anti-Semitism views Frenchness as a kind of property or possession. In his view, anti-Semitism functions as a "safety valve" that redirects social struggle away from fighting class domination and toward racial scapegoating (Sartre [1946a] 1995, 44). While at points he specifically identifies anti-Semitism as a product of bourgeois ideology, he argues that it meets an ideological and psychological need of the lower middle class or petty bourgeoisie. As we know from *The Communist Manifesto*, the petty bourgeoisie typically sink into the proletariat "partly because their diminutive capital does not suffice for the scale on which Modern Industry is carried on" (Marx and Engels [1848] 1994, 172). Anti-Semitism offers an ideological refusal of the status subordination that follows from economic immiserization; it evokes a claim to a primitive or magical form of possessing the property of Frenchness. Sartre writes, "It is in opposing themselves to the Jew that they [functionaries, office workers, small-businessmen, in short, the petty bourgeoisie] suddenly become conscious of being proprietors . . . they have chosen antisemitism as a means of establishing their status as possessors" (Sartre [1946a] 1995, 25). Anti-Semitism, then, is a claim to possession of the property of Frenchness. The anti-Semite, Sartre argues, lays claim to a "magical rapport" to their culture or history: "His virtue depends on the assimilation of the qualities which the work of a hundred generations has lent to the objects which surround him"; on an anti-Semitic view, the Jew never possesses a title to French heritage in the way that a Frenchman of many generations does (Sartre [1946a] 1995, 23). This magical rapport to Frenchness cannot be dispossessed like real property or wealth, for "by treating the Jew as an inferior and pernicious being," the anti-Semite affirms his self-perceived elite status; "this elite, in contrast to those of modern times which are based on merit or labor, closely resembles an aristocracy of birth" (Sartre [1946a] 1995, 27). In sum, Frenchness is not determined by the adaptation of customs or the mastery of French grammar and literature; it signifies the possession of an intangible but exclusive membership in a nation or history.

Sartre, then, provides a case study of how a particular manifestation of whiteness, as *Frenchness*, works. Yet his analysis remains hampered by a number of problems. Most importantly, from a materialist standpoint, he struggles to explain what anti-Semites receive from their purported superiority over the Jew. That is to say, in Du Bois's terms, in what way might anti-Semitism function as "a sort of public and psychological wage" for the white, French petty bourgeoisie or working class? Because Sartre fails to identify the materialist bases of anti-Semitism beyond a very schematic Marxist analysis, Sartre appears to overemphasize the psychological, and *pathological*, characteristics of this claim to Frenchness-as-possession. He treats French anti-Semitism as a self-justification for one's mediocrity, "a poor man's snobbery," or a variation on bad faith (that is, the refusal of one's freedom and responsibility), but one is left wondering why individuals in bad faith *choose* this particular kind of bad faith (Sartre [1946a] 1995, 26). In other words, on Sartre's account, all anti-Semites are in bad faith, but not all individuals who act in bad faith are anti-Semites—so why *choose* that particular kind? What if racism isn't merely a psychological pathology but becomes *personal* as an individual's investment in institutional forms of racism and white supremacy?

Here I will examine three works where Du Bois seeks to answer these questions: "The Souls of White Folk" (1910), a revised and expanded version of this essay published as chapter 2 of *Darkwater* (1920), and (albeit too briefly) *Black Reconstruction* (1935). Du Bois is best known in philosophical circles for *The Souls of Black Folk* (1903). While a growing number of scholars recognize that his description of double consciousness found therein anticipates Sartre's concept of the gaze, and his and Fanon's later analyses of how the gaze of the racist constitutes the racialized Other as inferior, it is less often recognized that in the "The Souls of White Folk" Du Bois reverses this gaze to analyze whiteness.[3] He positions his black gaze, focused on whiteness, between a disinterested sociological standpoint (represented by his claim to observing from the position "high in the tower") and that of a socially subjugated black "other" in a segregated white supremacist society.[4]

In "The Souls of White Folk," Du Bois outlines a theory of what he calls personal whiteness, which evokes both Protestantism's idea of a personal relationship with God and the ideology of manifest destiny. I will also refer to personal whiteness as possessive whiteness, to evoke the regime of private property from which it has arisen, that is, capital. Possessive whiteness has two characteristics. First, it asserts whiteness as dominion, sovereignty, and ownership—as Du Bois writes, "I am quite straight-faced as I ask soberly: 'But what on earth is whiteness that one should so desire it?' Then always, somehow, some way, silently but clearly, I am given to understand that whiteness is the ownership of the earth forever and ever, Amen!" Later, he adds, whiteness is "title to the universe" (Du Bois [1910] 1982, 26; [1920] 2007, 16). And then possessive whiteness refers to whiteness as entitlement. Whiteness is both socially and legally codified, but it is also *personal*—it interpellates some individuals as white and accords them both title and entitlement. This latter characteristic presents us with an important interpretive problem. Du Bois avers that "the discovery of personal whiteness among the world's peoples is a very modern thing,—a nineteenth and twentieth century matter, indeed" (Du Bois [1910] 1982, 25; [1920] 2007, 15). To date personal whiteness as a nineteenth- and early twentieth-century phenomenon presents us with a historicointerpretive problem that Du Bois does not resolve until *Black Reconstruction*: What is *personal* whiteness? Answering this question will contribute to our understanding of the emergence of fascism and the Far Right in American and Canadian settler-colonialism.

The social and legal institution of whiteness preceded the "discovery" of personal whiteness by several centuries. Laws codifying the "stratified social and legal status" between "white" racial identity and "black" racial identity in the American colonies date to the latter half of the seventeenth century.[5] Thus, while personal whiteness rests on these social and political codifications of white supremacy, it emerges as a social phenomenon at a much later date. Indeed, Du Bois suggests that personal whiteness marks a stark departure from the Enlightenment project, which sought to forge the figure of "Universal Man" which "ignored color and race even more than birth"; now "the world in a sudden, emotional conversion has discovered that it is white and by that token, wonderful!"[6] There are clues in the 1910 version of "The Souls of White Folk" that indicate that part of personal whiteness involves a level of status anxiety rooted in the negative perceptions of whites toward social equality. At the outset, Du Bois suggests that his interest is not with the "souls of them that are white, but souls of them that have become *painfully conscious* of their whiteness; those in whose minds the paleness of their bodily skins is *fraught* with tremendous and eternal significance" (Du Bois [1910] 1982, 25; my emphases). *Those*, he notes, "when black Jack Johnson beat a white man at a white man's game before an audience of a hundred millions, with what mingled motive did *those* millions, from the United Society of Christian Endeavor to the hoodlums of the nation, join hands to shout 'Shame!'" (Du Bois [1910] 1982, 28). To historicize the "discovery" of this personal whiteness by its very method undermines this so-ascribed eternal significance. He adds, "white folk today are suffering from this attempt to transmute a physical accident into a moral deed" (Du Bois [1910] 1982, 28).

In sum, Du Bois contends that among white supremacist societies, the claim that "I am white" is "the one fundamental tenet of our practical morality" (Du Bois [1910] 1982, 28; [1920] 2007, 17). In the 1910 version, he focuses on how this tenet functions to reinforce whiteness in the segregation-era United States. In the 1920 version, he expands the scope of the essay to situate the emergence of personal whiteness within class struggle and European and American imperialism. Though Du Bois contrasts the high ideals of the American republic and the European polity with the barbarism of segregation and colonialism, he refuses to reduce this discordance to mere hypocrisy. Instead, he argues that the political and moral calculus of white supremacy frames practical morality according to a series of emphases and omissions that always situate whiteness on the side of civilization, history, and virtue. White supremacy, in cultural terms, functions by identifying European history as history writ large—omitting or ignoring the cultural and historical achievements of nonwhite peoples. For example, this categorization serves to identify whiteness with civilization and virtue while minimizing the cruelty or barbarism of white Americans as accidental; by contrast, if violence is perpetrated by a black American, it is identified as blackness itself (Du Bois [1910] 1982, 28; [1920] 2007, 17). It is not incidental that even now, violence committed by a racialized person is held to be indicative of the race, whereas white supremacist violence (fomented by and through online communities) is repeatedly characterized as accidental, lone-wolf violence as opposed to the substance of historical progress.

Though this discussion continues to examine the conditions or systemic features of white supremacy that make personal whiteness possible, it does not explain personal whiteness itself. Based on the numerous examples provided by Du Bois, I believe that personal whiteness involves individuals as they uphold the entitlements or status which are the property of whiteness (whether this property is maintained through social convention or legal codification). As we will see, civilian settlers effectively acted as paramilitary agents in Indigenous dispossession and genocide. Du Bois's own examples are of white Americans intervening in social situations to enforce the norms and codes of segregation (Du Bois [1910] 1982, 26–27; [1920] 2007, 16–17). These interventions occur especially when black Americans "dispute the white man's title to certain alleged bequests of the Fathers in wage and position, authority and training" (Du Bois [1910] 1982, 26; [1920] 2007, 16). Whiteness, to refer back to our initial distinction, is not merely the capacity to hold title over the earth but also a form of entitlement or status. In Cheryl Harris's terms, whiteness has become status property. She argues that the law has, in legitimating a racialized regime of slavery and the seizure of Indigenous lands, "established and protected an actual property interest in whiteness itself" (Harris 1993, 1724). For example, whiteness "defined the legal status of a person as slave or free" (Harris 1993, 1726). And the patterns of white settlement constitute the norm around which the law demarcates property rights and adjudicates claims of Indigenous title (Harris 1993, 1721–24; see also Bhandar 2018). The property of whiteness, however, extends beyond the rights a group or individual has over a thing; it also confers status property to whiteness, as the norm for concepts of identity, privilege, and expectation. As Harris notes, one such privilege involves the right to self-definition. Whiteness is defined against an "other." But those who are not white have been subject to regimes of racial classification that are inimical to their own definitions of group inclusion or exclusion. In Canada and the United States, the ideology of blood quantum has been used to define blackness and/or the legal recognition of Indian status. But, as has been often noted, blood quantum was counted differently in the case of blackness and Indianness in ways that advanced the goals of the settler-colonial project: a minimum of black "blood" (eventually referred to as the "one drop rule") excluded one from political agency and numerous entitlements offered to whites (and during slavery increased the property of white slaveowners), while setting higher thresholds of Indigenous "blood" to maintain legally recognized Indian status functioned as forms of forced assimilation, depopulating Indigenous nations to reduce their claim to title over the lands invaded by settlers (Wolfe 2016).

In *Darkwater*, Du Bois argues that the status or entitlement of whiteness is bought at the cost of the "darker peoples" across the globe. In the late nineteenth century, whiteness worked to align the white bourgeoisie and working classes against nonwhite workers. In the United States, this racial alignment either interrupted or prevented alliances between black and white workers in the South (studied in depth in his *Black Reconstruction in America*) while integrating Irish, German, Jewish, Slavic, and Italian immigrants as "'new' white people" (Du Bois [1920] 2007, 25; see also Roediger 1999). Du Bois writes,

> It is plain to modern white civilization that the subjection of the white working classes cannot much longer be maintained. Education, political power, and increased knowledge of the technique and meaning of the industrial process are destined to make a more and more equitable distribution of wealth in the near future. The day of the very rich is drawing to a close, so far as individual white nations are concerned. But there is a loophole. There is a chance for exploitation on an immense scale for inordinate profit, not simply to the very rich, but to the middle class and to the laborers. This chance lies in the exploitation of darker peoples. It is here that the golden hand beckons. Here are no labor unions or votes or questioning onlookers or inconvenient consciences. These men may be used down to the very bone, and shot and maimed in "punitive" expeditions when they revolt. In these dark lands "industrial development" may repeat in exaggerated form every horror of the industrial history of Europe, from slavery and rape to disease and maiming, with only one test of success,—dividends! (Du Bois [1920] 2007, 21)

Capitalism is plagued by crises endemic to its modes of exploitation and accumulation. And capital's own modes of production and managing labor abet the conscientization and organization of the proletariat. Due to the growing strength and number of the proletariat, capitalism cannot be perpetuated indefinitely. But, Du Bois writes, "There is a loophole": the realignment of sociopolitical hegemony along the racial lines of whiteness rather than interracial working-class solidarity. Far from asserting proletarian internationalism against capital, the European working classes aligned themselves with the European bourgeoisie around the "theory" of colonialism that "it is the duty of white Europe to divide up the darker world and administer it for Europe's good" (Du Bois [1920] 2007, 20). European imperialism and World War I are products of this racial realignment of class struggle. Imperialism is enabled by national working classes forsaking internationalism for national colonial competition—and World War I is the arrival of this barbarism in Europe itself. World War I, Du Bois writes, is "not Europe gone mad; this is not aberration nor insanity; this *is* Europe; this seeming Terrible is the real soul of white culture" (Du Bois [1920] 2007, 19). Three decades later, Césaire returns a similar verdict on Hitlerism and World War II.

While Karl Marx observes that European colonial expansion is premised in part on "conquest, enslavement, robbery, murder, in short, force," Du Bois emphasizes that whiteness is given, when force is supposed to accede to so-called right, as the *right* to possession as title, sovereignty, and ownership (Marx [1867] 1990, 874). We will return to this claim—that whiteness signifies the right to title, sovereignty, ownership—in examining settler-colonialism, below. It must be acknowledged first that Du Bois's suggestion that whiteness is a form of entitlement or status is developed in more detail in *Black Reconstruction*, where he argues that whiteness functions as "a sort of public and psychological wage":

> It must be remembered that the white group of labourers, while they received a low wage, were compensated in part by a sort of public and psychological wage. They were given public deference and titles of courtesy because they were white. They were admitted freely with all classes of white people to public functions, public parks, and the best schools. The police were drawn from their ranks, and the courts, dependent upon their votes, treated them with such leniency as to encourage lawlessness. Their vote selected public officials, and while this had small effect upon the economic situation, it had great effect upon their personal treatment and the deference shown them. White schoolhouses were the best in the community, and conspicuously placed, and they cost anywhere from twice to ten times as much

per capita as the coloured schools. (Du Bois [1935] 2007, 573–74)

*Black Reconstruction* is a nuanced and complicated work, so I can only briefly summarize Du Bois's account of the formation of white hegemony through the public and psychological wage. Du Bois argues that the re-entrenchment of white supremacy in the United States, through a political alliance between the white bourgeoisie and the white working class (especially the white working class in the South), foreclosed on the possibility of a broader working-class movement that could have challenged the dictatorship of capital, a coalition that he calls "abolition democracy."[7] A new form of white hegemony was forged by aligning property interests of the bourgeoisie (though these interests were also divided between Northern industry and Southern planters) with the perceived fears of Southern whites, who envisioned social equality as economic and/or status subordination to former slaves. Du Bois accurately perceives that this racial alignment of poor whites against their ostensible class interests nonetheless produces some degree of economic benefit: the public and psychological wage. Harris argues that these wages of whiteness have been maintained despite the end of the system of segregation: "After legalized segregation was overturned, whiteness as property evolved into a more modern form through the law's ratification of the settled expectations of relative white privilege as a legitimate and natural baseline" (Harris 1993, 1714). It is also crucial to note that white hegemony coalesces around the implementation of new forms of racist social control. I think it is no accident that this point is made most forcefully by black prison abolitionists. As Angela Davis observes, Du Bois "pointed out that in order to fully abolish the oppressive conditions produced by slavery, new democratic institutions would have to be created. Because this did not occur, black people encountered new forms of slavery—from debt peonage and the convict lease system to segregated and second-class education. The prison system continues to carry out this terrible legacy" (Davis 2005, 69–70). Michelle Alexander then notes that the implementation of mass incarceration in the United States is the New Jim Crow. We have examined Du Bois to show how the critique of possessive whiteness precedes Sartre's account of anti-Semitism and possession by several decades. More importantly, Du Bois provides a touchstone to evaluate Sartre's claims. Though Sartre sketches the class character of the anti-Semite in broad outline, he overemphasizes the pathological aspect of anti-Semitism by psychologizing the anti-Semite's claim to possession. In other words, Sartre equivocates between mystification and ignorance: "The antisemite can conceive only of a type of primitive ownership of land based on a veritable *magical* rapport, in which the thing possessed and its possessor are united by a bond of mystical participation" (Sartre [1946a] 1995, 23–24 my emphasis). Du Bois, by contrast, demands that we explain this attitude on the basis of some prior entitlement or public or psychological wage. As Steve Martinot writes, Sartre's antiracist program "reveals little sense of the profound cultural transformation necessary [to eliminate racism]. It is not only the denigration of an other that counts for the racist, but a larger complex of social structures by which the racist (or antisemite) constructs his/her own social identity" (Martinot 2008, 64).[8]

But Du Bois's own account of whiteness as possession also remains incomplete. In "The Souls of White Folk," he outlines *two* forms of possession: whiteness as "ownership of the earth," as sovereignty, dominion, and the right to property, and whiteness as entitlement. While *Black Reconstruction* adds considerable historical and conceptual depth to his initial formulations of whiteness as entitlement, the problem of whiteness, dominion, and the right to property remains largely undeveloped. In other words, Du Bois does not provide a thematic examination of the failures of black Reconstruction in relation to the expansion of settler-colonialism in the formation of white hegemony. David Gilbert notes that

> as materialists we have to wonder why such a formidable consensus of a class and its organizations would hold a position over a long period of time that was opposed to their interests. . . .

> Certainly the issue in relationship to the Native Americans is clear: genocide provided the land which allowed many white workers to "rise" out of their class (which also strengthened the bargaining power of the remaining laborers). This reality firmly implanted one of the main pillars of white supremacy. (Gilbert 2017, 26)

While the violent dispossession of Indigenous land provides the material bases for class "mobility" in the settler-colonial societies of Canada and the United States, we must also recognize how it set in motion an ideology of entitlement and white settler identity that underlies white supremacist insurrectionism in these societies. As Kevin Bruyneel observes, "Du Bois saw land as central to the story of the Civil War, Reconstruction, and post-Reconstruction eras. However, in terms of defining the *political identity* of the white worker, the white settler desire for land does not come into play for him in trying to make sense of the white worker's racial alliance with white elites across class lines rather than one based on class solidarity across racial lines" (Bruyneel, forthcoming; my emphasis). Bruyneel argues that white settlerism (the desire for land) is an important factor for understanding the racial alliance between the white bourgeoisie and white workers. White settlers were not merely the recipients of land under the Homestead Act of 1862 or the Southern Homestead Act of 1866 but also acted as active paramilitary agents, "citizen-deputies," of Indigenous dispossession and genocide. Volunteer militias raised in the West, ostensibly to fight the Confederacy in the western territories, turned their weapons against Indigenous peoples (see Dunbar-Ortiz 2014, 136–40). After the Civil War, the United States pursued the ethnic cleansing of Indigenous lands through continued homesteading by civilian-deputies of colonialism in order to disrupt Indigenous ways of life and their access to resources, as well as outright war, waged by the US Army, to break armed Indigenous resistance (not to mention the destruction of buffalo populations to starve Indigenous peoples).

Du Bois's description of the public and psychological wage that accrues to whiteness focuses on points where white workers are offered points of institutional and cultural access, to goods such as education, denied to others. Bruyneel's critique of Du Bois seeks to show how the political identity of the white worker *also* entailed an entitlement to land—an opportunity for class "mobility" opened by settler-colonial expansion during and after the Civil War: homesteading and allotment "provided significant material and sociopsychological enticement to white workers to think and act as settlers as a critical feature of their whiteness" (Bruyneel, forthcoming). Indeed, we can understand, then, Du Bois's concept of "personal whiteness" as the indication of *agency* as citizen-deputy of colonialism and segregation. But we cannot view the emergence of personal whiteness and the wages of whiteness as merely an adaptation of a prior American or white identity: if we leave aside the black regiments known as "buffalo soldiers," the Indian Wars were fought by Irish and German immigrants who would (presumably) come to understand their American identity in terms of *whiteness* and as *settlers* (Dunbar-Ortiz 2014, 148).

## 5.3. WHITENESS AS SETTLER-COLONIAL SOVEREIGNTY

The impact of this paramilitary role played by civilian settlers during the colonization of what is currently the western United States extends far beyond the nineteenth century, which is why it must be considered as part of the public and psychological wages of whiteness. As Inwood and Bonds show, the ideology of the Patriot movement—perhaps, due to the January 2016 occupation of the Malheur National Wildlife Reserve, the best-known Far Right movement before the rise of the alt-right—borrows freely from the providential myths of American manifest destiny (Inwood and Bonds 2017, 262–64). Thus when the Patriot movement is categorized as a Far Right movement, we must be specific in our reasoning: the movement is not Far Right because it evokes settler mythologies of manifest destiny but because of its insurrectionary character when it perceives the settler-colonial state to have failed to provide the wages of whiteness.

From the standpoint of the three-way fight, then, we must show how settler expectations to property are codified within the liberal-institutional side of settler-state hegemony. Here, I will shift the analysis to the Canadian context, because Canadians typically position themselves and their system of governance as more progressive and inclusive than the American system of settler-colonialism. I will focus on the codification of possessive whiteness as (white) settler futurity against Indigenous futurity and sovereignty, even in the so-called era of Reconciliation. This requires, as part of the concluding remarks, a high degree of simplification—thus it must be noted at the outset that this account is necessarily incomplete, having not addressed, for example, the imposition of Western structures of heteropatriarchy on Indigenous peoples in order to destroy Indigenous forms of governance (Simpson 2017, 95–144) or systemic antiblack racism in Canada (Maynard 2017). The foregoing simplifications are made so that I can focus on outlining the relation of antifascism to decolonization; further and more detailed arguments can be found in my sources. Finally, I take it as an axiom that "neither legal relations nor political forms could be comprehended whether by themselves or on the basis of a so-called general development of the human mind, but that on the contrary they originate in the material conditions of life" (Marx [1859] 1994, 210).

Canada is a settler-colonial project premised on the dispossession of Indigenous land and the replacement of First Nations, Métis, and Inuit through genocide or coerced assimilation. In the Constitution Act (1982), the Canadian settler-colonial state (which I will also refer to as the Crown) explicitly claims to recognize aboriginal rights.[9] More recently, the Crown has also attempted a process of reconciliation between the Crown and First Nations, Métis, and Inuit. Many Indigenous critics have pointed out that despite these reconciliatory gestures, the ultimate policy of the Crown continues to be the extinguishment of aboriginal rights or title claims other than those explicitly negotiated in modern treaties or comprehensive land claims.[10] In lieu of negotiations conditional on extinguishment, some Indigenous nations have opted to litigate title claims through the Canadian legal system. I will briefly examine the Canadian Supreme Court's decision in *Tsilhqot'in Nation v. British Columbia* (2014), which is typically considered a victory for Indigenous rights: by recognizing "aboriginal title over a two thousand square kilometre section of Tsilhqot'in territory, the court has shown that extinguishment is far from the only option in Canada" (Manuel 2017, 109). Nonetheless, Brenna Bhandar (whose work in part applies Harris's analyses of whiteness and property within the context of British Columbia) argues, "The court fails to fundamentally alter legal precedent that has continually reinscribed the primacy of Crown control over Indigenous land in conjunction with the racialization of First Nations and their ways of life as inferior to settler society" (Bhandar 2018, 63). When the court describes the "aboriginal perspective" of the Tsilhqot'in toward title claims as that of a seminomadic people, it tacitly accepts the Eurocentric concepts of land use, cultivation, and improvement that have been normalized and codified through the settler-colonial project. First, Bhandar suggests, this choice fails to render how Tsilhqot'in people see themselves.[11] And then, she contends, describing the Tsilhqot'in people as seminomadic situates them incorrectly as a primitive or atavistic society that could be "improved" or "modernized"—in other words, assimilated to settler society.

Furthermore, the *Tsilhqot'in Nation* decision also asserts Crown primacy despite acknowledging the aboriginal rights that *preexisted* colonialism: "At the time of assertion of European sovereignty, the Crown acquired radical or underlying title to all the land in the province. This Crown title, however, was burdened by the pre-existing legal rights of Aboriginal people who occupied and used the land prior to European arrival" (quoted in Manuel 2017, 110). In sum, aboriginal title precedes Crown sovereignty, though from the point of its assertion forward, Crown sovereignty takes precedence over and is "burdened" by aboriginal title. This assertion of radical Crown title functions as a legal fiction: radical title underlies all other forms of title, including aboriginal title. In *The Reconciliation Manifesto*, Sécwepemc activist Arthur Manuel observes that "the decision is still a decision of a colonial court": because the court is part of the settler-colonial government, it will not undercut the legal basis of its own jurisdiction. But the decision extends beyond issues of jurisdiction; it speaks to the meaning and ends of the settler-colonial project itself. Manuel continues:

> Here the court is saying, without any explanation or reasoned argument, that settler property rights are higher than Indigenous property rights. In fact, there is no "reason" at all. . . . What is at its heart is racism—the idea that white people have the inherent right to claim title to Indigenous lands, or the lands of black or brown peoples, and rule them as colonial masters. (Manuel 2017, 110–11)

Manuel echoes, nearly a century later, Du Bois's observation that whiteness is possession, sovereignty, and "ownership of the earth." Indeed, Manuel contends that whiteness has been codified as legal fiction when settler-colonial states dispense with appeals to the doctrine of discovery or terra nullius. The decision frames the Crown as burdened with resolving aboriginal land claims within the settled expectations of settler-colonial sovereignty, governance, and land use. Harris, as I have noted, examines a number of aspects of whiteness as property—as noted above, whiteness is the possession of the capacity for self-definition and the capacity to determine group inclusion and exclusion. Whiteness as property also confers certain expectations. Harris writes,

> Because the law recognized and protected expectations grounded in white privilege (albeit not explicitly in all instances), these expectations became tantamount to property that could not permissibly be intruded upon without consent. As the law explicitly ratified those expectations in continued privilege or extended ongoing protection to those illegitimate expectations by failing to expose or to radically disturb them, the dominant and subordinate positions within the racial hierarchy were reified in law. When the law recognizes, either implicitly or explicitly, the settled expectations of whites built on the privileges and

benefits produced by white supremacy, it acknowledges and reinforces a property interest in whiteness. (Harris 1993, 1731)

By analogy, in a settler-colonial society, where the law has codified
and protected settler expectations throughout the process of settler-
colonialism, the court reinforces a property interest in being a settler. The court, then, is "burdened" with settling, to some degree,
aboriginal rights within the already established expectations of settler-colonial property rights expressed in the court's assertion of
Crown-settler radical title. In other words, to decide aboriginal
rights in such a way as to upset the settled norms or expectations of
property law risks conflict with the legal precedent that has established the property interest in white-settler possession. While *Tsilhqot'in Nation* is often hailed as an ideal against which to judge
subsequent (typically police) actions of the Crown, Manuel contends that it affirms the same social and legal norms as the Crown
when it negotiates land claims or modern treaties—ultimately leaving Indigenous peoples under the control of settler-state sovereignty. By contrast, he contends, "Our leadership must continually assert
that Aboriginal title is the underlying title in our territory and that all
other property rights are layers of property rights that rest on underlying Aboriginal title" (Manuel 2017, 111).

As a settler writing about Indigenous struggles and decolonization, I want to be clear that I am not criticizing efforts of Indigenous
peoples who pursue redress through the legal system. That is not my
goal. As Manuel notes, these legal avenues may advance Indigenous
struggles insofar as they return land to Indigenous nations or provide leverage for further struggles. But, he cautions, they cannot
replace or preempt the work of self-determining Indigenous political organizing, what others have called *Indigenous resurgence* (e.g.,
Simpson 2008). I have argued that these legal remedies are limited
because they rest on legal fictions that serve to maintain Crown
sovereignty and settler expectations or futurity. If the Crown continues to maintain extinguishment—or the "modification" of aboriginal title (see Mackey 2016, 60–67)—as a condition of so-called
nation-to-nation negotiations, and if Canada's courts continue to

uphold and protect settler expectations, then we can expect that the Crown will not recognize aboriginal title to a degree that overturns that prior settler property interest grounded in Crown title. Thus settlers are mistaken to believe that the *only* legitimate or justifiable channels of Indigenous politics are those that are funneled through the institutions of the settler state. Without countervailing political organizing, without Indigenous resurgence, we can expect that Crown recognition of Indigenous rights will always be shaped by the priorities of the settler-colonial project. It is the right of Indigenous peoples to formulate and assert their demands for resurgence and liberation through any means that they deem necessary. As for settlers, Fanon's guidance remains indispensable: "One of the first duties of intellectuals and democratic elements in colonialist countries is unreservedly to support the national aspirations of colonized peoples" (Fanon [1957] 1988, 76).

We are now prepared to offer an antifascist account of the settler-colonial state and its relation to the Far Right. I have argued, against a broadly liberal interpretation of state power, that the state is not a neutral or objective arbiter of the rule of law. Here we can render this critique in concrete detail. The critical legal theory developed from Du Bois to Manuel shows how white supremacy is codified into law in settler-colonial societies. Their work shows how the oppression of black and Indigenous peoples was, historically speaking, "implemented by force and ratified by law" (Harris 1993, 1715). The dialectic of codifying property interests has codified a property interest in whiteness itself. This dialectic is not merely a historical artifact of settler-colonial societies. As their work demonstrates, these forms of protecting possessive whiteness are ongoing, though they are typically codified in officially "color-blind" terms. Michelle Alexander's *The New Jim Crow* (2012) demonstrates how the caste system of segregation in the United States has been reentrenched—and subsequently intensified—in the American legal system in the so-called color-blind or neutral language of fighting crime or law and order. Settler-colonialism is treated as if it were an issue of disputes over land title.

Earlier, I noted that state power constitutes a line of adjacency between liberalism and white supremacy. At this point, I would like to formulate a thesis concerning the contemporary settler-state in North America. *Settler states are institutionalized systems of white supremacy; settler-state hegemony is constituted by the interests of capital and whiteness.* I do not want to overstate the common interests of the bourgeoisie and the Far Right, but I do not want to deny that these social forces also converge. They have a common interest in the political economy of the settler-state, which constitutes their line of adjacency. However, because hegemony is constituted in ideological and discursive forms, in opposing settler-state hegemony, we must take their self-ascribed ideological distinctions seriously. Liberalism views state power as the realization of objective right or the rule of law. By contrast, for the Far Right, state power ought to advance the interests of the white settler-colonial project. But the difference between liberalism and fascism is far neater in ideology than in practice. The authors we have examined demonstrate that contemporary liberalism is willing to formalize or codify white supremacy insofar as the norms of the latter can be codified in color-blind terms.

In his analysis of why fascism failed to emerge as a mass social movement in the United States in the 1930s and 1940s, J. Sakai observes that "white settler-colonialism and fascism occupy the same ecological niche. Having one, capitalist society didn't yet need the other" (Sakai [2002] 2017, 130). During that period, the settler-colonial societies of the United States and Canada had already implemented the reservation system and codified the dispossession of Indigenous land and had introduced the "public and psychological wage" of whiteness that had cemented an alliance between the white bourgeoisie and working classes. Again, though, we must observe that hegemony is not immune to crisis. Sakai's historical observations must be situated within his broader analysis of the relation of settler-colonialism to fascism. Though fascism did not emerge as a political force in the United States at that particular moment does not mean that subsequently it will not at a different conjuncture. Settler-state hegemony is not immune to economic crisis. If the Far

Right is drawn primarily from the petty bourgeoisie, then its members' social and economic status is, according to Marx and Engels, always tenuous. In addition, economic crisis imperils the public and psychological wage upon which white hegemony is built. If, historically speaking, fascism has not taken root in the settler-colonial societies of North America, this must be because there have continued to be new paths for intensified accumulation by dispossession of Indigenous lands and resource extraction to stave off crisis. This does not preclude a crisis—or perceived crisis—that breaks this cycle.

This study began by drawing on theorists of the three-way fight to observe that contemporary Far Right and fascist movements deviate from their historical antecedents in their insurrectionary character. Here we can formulate a thesis about the relationship between Far Right and fascist insurrectionary movements and settler-colonial hegemony: *Far Right movements are system-loyal when they perceive that the entitlements of white supremacy can be advanced within settler-colonial institutions, and they become insurrectionary when they perceive that these entitlements cannot be thus advanced.* The emphasis on *perception* is fundamental to our thesis, for as we have seen, whiteness as property and entitlement remains normatively and legally codified within settler-colonial societies. Fascism has been described as revolutionary or insurrectionary, but it is neither emancipatory or antistatist; it is premised on the re-entrenchment of the settler-colonial project itself.

## 5.4. ... TO DECOLONIZATION

There is no meaningful sense in which fascism can be defeated in North America without overthrowing the conditions that make it possible: namely, capital accumulation and settler-colonialism. Thus, in a settler-colonial society, militant antifascism necessitates (at least) two lines of mobilization. On the one hand, we must break the hegemony of whiteness, which has assuaged parts of the working class and the petty bourgeoisie with the privileges of a public and psychological wage. On the other hand, we must fight against the settler-colonial state's program of resource extraction and the ongoing dispossession of Indigenous peoples.

In the past, the relationships between anarchist and communist militants and Indigenous militants has been marked by tension and failure. As Glen Sean Coulthard notes, the debates between Marxists and Indigenous theorists have been marked by a hostility which "has led to the premature rejection of Marx and Marxism by some Indigenous studies scholars on the one side, to the belligerent, often ignorant, sometimes racist dismissal of Indigenous peoples' contributions to radical thought and politics by Marxists on the other" (Coulthard 2014, 8). And there are many warranted criticisms of socialist movements in settler-colonial North America. As Tuck and Yang note, "The Occupy movement for many economically marginalized people has been a welcome expression of resistance to the massive disparities in the distribution of wealth; for many Indigenous people, Occupy is another settler re-occupation on stolen land. The rhetoric of the movement relies upon problematic assumptions about social justice and is a prime example of the incommensurability between 're/occupy' and 'decolonize' as political agendas" (Tuck and Yang 2012, 23). Examining more recent antifascist mobilization and theory, Rowland "Enāēmaehkiw" Keshena Robinson writes, "A socialism, whether marxist or anarchist, that does not, at the deepest possible level, engage with and seek to combat the fact of settler colonialism can only result in its own reconfiguration of the arrangements of settler power into a new form, nominally in the hands of the working class" (Robinson 2019). Furthermore, Robinson notes, the white Left, even when it has sought to decolonize, has often continued to set the agenda of anticapitalist and antifascist struggle. Nonetheless it would be incorrect to draw the conclusion that ultimately antifascism and decolonization are inimical. It would deny the anticapitalist Indigenous engagement with these movements, to deny the work of Coulthard, Dunbar-Ortiz, Nick Estes, or Robinson (to name but a few authors), to deny the efforts of those sometimes anonymous Indigenous antifascists involved in organizing. It would also imprison us in the presentism of contemporary political imagination, when the work of theory and praxis should aim to redraw the possibilities of our political imagination, and who "we" ourselves are. The first step involves accounting for both the past failures and the temporary successes. But conscientization of the lines of adjacency between antifascist, antiracist, and anticolonial movements does not replace mass, militant organization—*that* must be built from a broad array of insurrectionary and revolutionary movements. These are the emancipatory communities we must build. In this book, I have only aimed to show, through a reconsideration of militant antifascist philosophy, that the diversity of tactics does not preclude a commitment to radical egalitarianism.

## NOTES

1. The purpose of tracing this critique back to at least 1910 is not to establish patrimony over the concepts but to emphasize the history of the critique of whiteness.

2. Harris discusses *Black Reconstruction*, and while there are similarities between her argument and "The Souls of White Folk," she does not discuss the latter. See Harris 1993, 1740–44.

3. Du Bois writes, "It is a peculiar sensation, this double consciousness, this sense of always looking at one's self through the eyes of others, of measuring one's soul by the tape of a world that looks on in amused contempt and pity. One ever feels his twoness,—an American, a Negro; two souls, two thoughts, two unrecognized strivings; two warring ideals in one dark body, whose dogged strength alone keeps it from being torn asunder" ([1903] 2007, 8).

4. He writes: "In my presence [as the subjugated] they [white folk] tend to lay aside all their little lies and hypocrisies and bathe in brutal frankness" (Du Bois [1910] 1982, 28).

5. As Cheryl Harris writes, "By the 1660s, the especially degraded status of Blacks as chattel slaves was recognized by law. Between 1680 and 1682, the first slave codes appeared, codifying extreme deprivations of liberty already existing in social practice. . . . Racial identity was further merged with stratified social and legal status: 'Black' racial identity

marked who was subject to enslavement; 'white' racial identity marked who was 'free' or, at minimum, not a slave" (1993, 1718).

6. Du Bois [1910] 1982, 25; [1920] 2007, 15. Du Bois overstates the Enlightenment's commitment to its own "universal" pretensions, but it is worth noting the contrast because some contemporary Western chauvinists—who have more in common with the Far Right than these Enlightenment ideals—attempt to clothe their programs and ideologies in the periwigs and breeches of the late eighteenth century.

7. Du Bois wants to show both that the political vision articulated by black politics of the time evidences a greater threat to property than what white America had recognized while showing that Northern capital had sought to reconstruct the South on advantageous terms. Thus Du Bois: "The machinery they [abolition-democracy] were compelled to set up, with the cooperation of Northern industry, was a dictatorship of far broader possibilities than the North had first contemplated, [but] . . . the temporary dictatorship set up by the Federal government represented and had to represent, in essence, the attitude of Northern capitalists" ([1935] 2007, 476, 498).

8. These failings, Martinot argues, are corrected in Sartre's play *The Respectful Prostitute*.

9. The Constitution Act (1982), Section 35(1–2) reads, "The existing aboriginal and treaty rights of the aboriginal peoples of Canada are hereby recognized and affirmed. In this Act, 'aboriginal peoples of Canada' includes the Indian, Inuit and Métis peoples of Canada."

10. As Eva Mackey summarizes it, extinguishment means that the Crown "requires that Indigenous peoples sign away (surrender) future and potential Aboriginal rights or title, other than those specified in the agreement" (2016, 61).

11. Bhandar writes, "According to one journalist who interviewed chief Roger Williams . . . '[t]hat's why the habit of government officials, of media and even of supreme court judges to call the Tsilhqot'in 'nomadic' bothers Williams so much: his people have lived on these lands for thousands of years, while it is non-natives who are constantly moving and resettling. And what could be more nomadic and transient than the extractive industry itself—grabbing what resources and profits it can before abandoning one area for another'" (2018, 73).

# REFERENCES

Abensour, Miguel. 2011. *Democracy against the State: Marx and the Machiavellian Moment*. Translated by Max Blechman and Martin Breaugh. Malden, MA: Polity Press.

Alexander, Michelle. 2012. *The New Jim Crow: Mass Incarceration in the Age of Colorblindness*. Rev. ed. New York: New Press.

Ami du Radical. 2018. "We Finally Know What 'Free Speech' Means." It's Going Down. June 18, 2018. https://itsgoingdown.org/we-finally-know-what-free-speech-means.

Anti-Fascist Forum, ed. 2003. *My Enemy's Enemy: Essays on Globalization, Fascism and the Struggle against Fascism*. 3rd ed. Montreal: Kersplebedeb.

Antifascist Front. 2015. "Alternative Internet Racism: Alt Right and the New Fascist Branding." *Antifascist News*, December 18, 2015. https://antifascistnews.net/2015/12/18/alternative-internet-racism-alt-right-and-the-new-fascist-branding.

Arendt, Hannah. (1963) 2006. *On Revolution*. New York: Penguin.

Arendt, Hannah. 1970. *On Violence*. New York: Harcourt.

Arp, Kristana. 2001. *The Bonds of Freedom: Simone de Beauvoir's Existentialist Ethics*. Chicago: Open Court.

Arthur, Paige. 2010. *Unfinished Projects: Decolonization and the Philosophy of Jean-Paul Sartre*. London: Verso.

Balgord, Evan. 2017. "Eye on Hate: The White Supremacists behind Alt-Right Posters, Revealed." *The Torontoist*, November 8, 2017. https://torontoist.com/2017/11/revealed-white-supremacists-behind-alt-right-posters-around-city.

Beauvoir, Simone de. (1945) 2004. "Moral Idealism and Political Realism." In *Philosophical Writings*, edited by Margaret A. Simons with Marybeth Timmermann and Mary Beth Mader, 175–93. Urbana: University of Illinois Press.

Beauvoir, Simone de. (1946) 2004. "An Eye for an Eye." In *Philosophical Writings*, edited by Margaret A. Simons with Marybeth Timmermann and Mary Beth Mader, 245–60. Urbana: University of Illinois Press.

Beauvoir, Simone de. (1947) 1976. *The Ethics of Ambiguity*. Translated by Bernard Frechtman. New York: Citadel.

Beauvoir, Simone de. (1949) 2011. *The Second Sex*. Translated by Constance Borde and Sheila Malovany-Chevallier. New York: Vintage.

Beauvoir, Simone de. (1948) 1999. *America Day-by-Day*. Translated by Carol Cosman. Berkeley: University of California Press.

Beauvoir, Simone de. (1960) 1965. *The Prime of Life*. Translated by Peter Green. London: Penguin.

Beauvoir, Simone de. (1963) 1968. *Force of Circumstance*. Translated by Richard Howard. New York: Penguin.

Belew, Kathleen. 2018. *Bring the War Home: The White Power Movement and Paramilitary America*. Cambridge, MA: Harvard University Press.

Benjamin, Walter. (1940) 2003. "On the Concept of History." In *Selected Writings*, edited by Howard Eiland and Michael W. Jennings, 4: 389–400. Cambridge, MA: Belknap Press.

Bezucha, Robert J. 1974. *The Lyon Uprising of 1834: Social and Political Conflict in the Early July Monarchy*. Cambridge, MA: Harvard University Press.

Bhandar, Brenna. 2018. *Colonial Lives of Property: Law, Land, and Racial Regimes of Ownership*. Durham, NC: Duke University Press.

Bowman, Paul, and Richard Stamp, eds. 2011. *Reading Rancière: Critical Dissensus*. London: Continuum.

Brake, Justin. 2018. "'It's Okay to Be White' Posters an Educational Opportunity, Say Professors," APTN. November 8, 2018. https://aptnnews.ca/2018/11/10/its-okay-to-be-white-posters-an-educational-opportunity-say-professors.

Bray, Mark. 2017. *Antifa: The Anti-Fascist Handbook*. Brooklyn, NY: Melville House.

Breaugh, Martin. 2013. *The Plebeian Experience: A Discontinuous History of Political Freedom*. Translated by Lazer Lederhendler. New York: Columbia University Press.

Bruyneel, Kevin. Forthcoming. *Settler Memory: The Disavowal of Indigeneity in the Political Life of Race in the United States*. Chapel Hill: University of North Carolina Press.

Burley, Shane. 2017. *Fascism Today: What It Is and How to End It*. Chico, CA: AK Press.

Burley, Shane. 2018a. "Against the Alt-Right: An Interview with Shane Burley." Interview by Josh Robinson. *Abolition Journal*, May 7, 2018. https://abolitionjournal.org/against-the-alt-right-an-interview-with-shane-burley.

Burley, Shane. 2018b. "The Fall of the 'Alt-Right' Came from Anti-Fascism." Truthout, April 5, 2018. http://www.truth-out.org/news/item/44079-the-fall-of-the-alt-right-came-from-anti-fascism.

Burley, Shane. 2019a. "Far-Right Group Patriot Prayer Is Declining. Thank Anti-Fascists." Truthout, June 25, 2019. https://truthout.org/articles/far-right-group-patriot-prayer-is-declining-thank-anti-fascists.

Burley, Shane. 2019b. "Portland Anti-Fascist Coalition Shows Us How We Can Defeat the Far-Right." Truthout, August 20, 2019. https://truthout.org/articles/portland-anti-fascist-coalition-shows-us-how-we-can-defeat-the-far-right.

CBC News. 2017. "'It's Okay to Be White' Posters Pop Up at U of R; Security Investigating." CBC News, November 23, 2017. http://www.cbc.ca/news/canada/saskatchewan/it-s-okay-to-be-white-poster-pops-up-at-u-of-r-security-investigating-1.4415514.

Césaire, Aimé. (1950) 2000. *Discourse on Colonialism*. Translated by Joan Pinkham. New York: Monthly Review Press.

Chambers, Samuel A. 2013. *The Lessons of Rancière*. Oxford: Oxford University Press.

Chenoweth, Erica. 2017. "Violence Will Only Hurt the Trump Resistance." *New Republic*, February 7, 2017. https://newrepublic.com/article/140474/violence-will-hurt-trump-resistance.

Chenoweth, Erica, and Maria J. Stephan. 2011. *Why Civil Resistance Works: The Strategic Logic of Nonviolent Conflict*. New York: Columbia University Press.

Ciccariello-Maher, George. 2017a. *Decolonizing Dialectics*. Durham, NC: Duke University Press.

Ciccariello-Maher, George. 2017b. "Nazi-Punching Praxis: Against the Liberal Theology of Reason and Non-Violence." Interview by Daniel Denvir. *Abolition Journal*, February 25, 2017. https://abolitionjournal.org/nazi-punching-praxis-against-the-liberal-theology-of-reason-non-violence.

Clark, J. 2018. "Three-Way Fight: Revolutionary Anti-Fascism and Armed Self-Defense." In *Setting Sights: Histories and Reflections on Community and Armed Self-Defense*, edited by scott crow, 49–67. Oakland, CA: PM Press.

Cobb, Charles E., Jr. 2016. *This Nonviolent Stuff'll Get You Killed: How Guns Made the Civil Rights Movement Possible*. Durham, NC: Duke University Press.

Cohen-Solal, Annie. 2005. *Jean-Paul Sartre: A Life*. Edited by Norman Macafee. New York: New Press.

Cooper, Anna Julia. (1892) 1998. *A Voice from the South*. In *The Voice of Anna Julia Cooper*, edited by Charles Lemert and Esme Bhan, 45–196. Lanham, MD: Rowman & Littlefield.

Coulthard, Glen Sean. 2014. *Red Skin, White Masks: Rejecting the Colonial Politics of Recognition*. Minneapolis: University of Minnesota Press.

Crenshaw, Kimberlé. 1989. "Demarginalizing the Intersection of Race and Sex: A Black Feminist Critique of Antidiscrimination Doctrine, Feminist Theory and Antiracist Politics." *University of Chicago Legal Forum*, 139–67.

crow, scott. 2018. "Liberatory Community Armed Self-Defense: Approaches toward a Theory." In *Setting Sights: Histories and Reflections on Community and Armed Self-Defense*, edited by scott crow, 7–13. Oakland, CA: PM Press.

Davis, Angela Y. 2005. *Abolition Democracy: Beyond Empire, Prisons, and Torture*. New York: Seven Stories Press.

Dean, Jodi. 2011. "Politics without Politics." In *Reading Rancière: Critical Dissensus*, edited by Paul Bowman and Richard Stamp, 73–94. London: Continuum.

Dean, Jodi. 2012. *The Communist Horizon*. London: Verso.

Deranty, Jean-Philippe. 2003a. "Jacques Rancière's Contribution to the Ethics of Recognition." *Political Theory* 31 (1): 136–56.

Deranty, Jean-Philippe. 2003b. "Rancière and Contemporary Political Ontology." *Theory and Event* 6, no. 4.

Deranty, Jean-Philippe. 2016. "Between Honneth and Rancière: Problems and Potentials of a Contemporary Critical Theory of Society." In *Recognition or Disagreement: A Critical Encounter on the Politics of Freedom, Equality, and Identity*, edited by Katia Genel and Jean-Philippe Deranty, 33–80. New York: Columbia University Press.

Descartes, René. 1985. *Discourse on the Method*. In *The Philosophical Writings of Descartes*, vol. 1, translated by John Cottingham, Robert Stoothoff, and Dugald Murdoch, 111–51. Cambridge: Cambridge University Press.

Deutscher, Penelope. 2008. *The Philosophy of Simone de Beauvoir: Ambiguity, Conversion, Resistance*. Cambridge: Cambridge University Press.

Dimitrov, Georgi. (1935) 1972. "The Fascist Offensive and the Tasks of the Communist International in the Struggle of the Working Class against Fascism." *Selected Works*, vol. 2. Sofia: Sofia Press. https://www.marxists.org/reference/archive/dimitrov/works/1935/08_02.htm.

Du Bois, W. E. B. (1903) 2007. *The Souls of Black Folk*. Edited by Brent Hayes Edwards. Oxford: Oxford University Press.

Du Bois, W. E. B. (1910) 1982. "The Souls of White Folk." In *Writings by W. E. B. Du Bois in Periodicals Edited by Others*, Vol. 2: 1910–1934, edited by Herbert Aptheker, 25–29. Millwood, NY: Kraus-Thomson.

Du Bois, W. E. B. (1920) 2007. *Darkwater: Voices from Within the Veil*, edited by Henry Louis Gates Jr. Oxford: Oxford University Press.

Du Bois, W. E. B. (1935) 2007. *Black Reconstruction in America: An Essay Toward a History of the Part Which Black Folk Played in the Attempt to Reconstruct Democracy in America, 1860–1880*. Edited by Henry Louis Gates Jr. Oxford: Oxford University Press, 2007.

Du Bois, W. E. B. (1940) 2007. *Dusk of Dawn: An Essay Toward an Autobiography of a Race Concept*. Edited by Henry Louis Gates Jr. Oxford: Oxford University Press.

Dunbar-Ortiz, Roxanne. 2014. *An Indigenous Peoples' History of the United States*. Boston: Beacon Press.

Dunbar-Ortiz, Roxanne. 2018. *Loaded: A Disarming History of the Second Amendment*. San Francisco: City Lights.

Dupuis-Déri, Francis. 2013. *Who's Afraid of the Black Blocs? Anarchy in Action around the World*. Toronto: Between the Lines.

Eshleman, Matthew C. 2015. "Is Violence Necessarily in Bad Faith?" *Sartre Studies International* 21 (2): 60–73.

Fanon, Frantz. (1952) 2008. *Black Skin, White Masks*. Translated by Richard Philcox. New York: Grove.

Fanon, Frantz. (1957) 1988. "French Intellectuals and Democrats and the Algerian Revolution." In *Toward the African Revolution*, translated by Haakon Chevalier, 76–90. New York: Grove.

Faure, Alain, and Jacques Rancière, eds. 2007. *La parole ouvrière*. Paris: La fabrique.

Flynn, Thomas R. 1984. *Sartre and Marxist Existentialism*. Chicago: University of Chicago Press.

Fraser, Nancy. 2003. "Social Justice in the Age of Identity Politics: Redistribution, Recognition, and Participation." In Fraser and Axel Honneth, *Redistribution or Recognition? A Political-Philosophical Exchange*, 7–109. London: Verso.

Fung, Nathan. 2017. "'It's OK to Be White' Posters, Offensive Pumpkin Found on Campus." *The Gateway*, November 1, 2017. https://www.thegatewayonline.ca/2017/11/posters-offensive-pumpkin.

Genel, Katia. 2016. "Jacques Rancière and Axel Honneth: Two Critical Approaches to the Political." In *Recognition or Disagreement: A Critical Encounter on the Politics of Freedom, Equality, and Identity*, edited by Katia Genel and Jean-Philippe Deranty, 3–32. New York: Columbia University Press.

Gilbert, David. 2017. *Looking at the White Working Class Historically*. 2nd ed. Montreal: Kersplebedeb.

Gordon, Lewis R. 2015. *What Fanon Said: A Philosophical Introduction to His Life and Thought*. New York: Fordham University Press.

Griffin, Roger. 1991. *The Nature of Fascism*. London: Pinter Publishers.

Hamerquist, Don. (2002) 2017. "Fascism and Anti-Fascism." In *Confronting Fascism: Discussion Documents for a Militant Movement*, edited by Don Hamerquist, J. Sakai, Anti-Racist Action Chicago, and Mark Salotte, 27–93. 2nd ed. Montreal: Kersplebedeb.

Hamerquist, Don, J. Sakai, Anti-Racist Action Chicago, and Mark Salotte. 2017. *Confronting Fascism: Discussion Documents for a Militant Movement*. 2nd ed. Montreal: Kersplebedeb.

Harris, Cheryl. 1993. "Whiteness as Property." *Harvard Law Review* 106, no. 8 (June): 1701–91.

Heidegger, Martin. 1967. *What Is a Thing?* Translated by W. B. Barton and Vera Deutsch. Chicago: Henry Regnery Company.

Hobbes, Thomas. 1996. *Leviathan*. Rev. student ed. Edited by Richard Tuck. Cambridge: Cambridge University Press.

Honneth, Axel. 2016. "Of the Poverty of Our Liberty: The Greatness and Limits of Hegel's Doctrine of Ethical Life." In Honneth and Jacques Rancière, *Recognition or Disagreement: A Critical Encounter on the Politics of Freedom, Equality, and Identity*, edited by Katia Genel and Jean-Philippe Deranty, 156–76. New York: Columbia University Press.

Honneth, Axel, and Jacques Rancière. 2016. *Recognition or Disagreement: A Critical Encounter on the Politics of Freedom, Equality, and Identity*, edited by Katia Genel and Jean-Philippe Deranty. New York: Columbia University Press.

Inwood, Joshua F. J., and Anne Bonds. 2017. "Property and Whiteness: The Oregon Standoff and the Contradictions of the U.S. Settler State." *Space and Polity* 21 (3): 253–68.

Kautzer, Chad. 2018. "Notes for a Critical Theory of Community Self-Defense." In *Setting Sights: Histories and Reflections on Community and Armed Self-Defense*, edited by scott crow, 35–48. Oakland, CA: PM Press.

Kruks, Sonia. 2012. *Simone de Beauvoir and the Politics of Ambiguity*. Oxford: Oxford University Press.

Lee, Butch. 2015. *Jailbreak Out of History: "The Re-Biography of Harriet Tubman" and "The Evil of Female Loaferism."* Montreal: Kersplebedeb.

Lennard, Natasha. 2018. "Is Antifa Counterproductive? White Nationalist Richard Spencer Would Beg to Differ." The Intercept, March 17, 2018. https://theintercept.com/2018/03/17/richard-spencer-college-tour-antifa-alt-right.

Lowndes, Joseph. 2017. "From New Class Critique to White Nationalism: *Telos*, the Alt Right, and the Origins of Trumpism." *Konturen* 9, 8–14.

Lyons, Matthew N. 2018. *Insurgent Supremacists: The U.S. Far Right's Challenge to State and Empire*. Montreal: Kersplebedeb.

Mackey, Eva. 2016. *Unsettled Expectations: Uncertainty, Land and Settler Decolonization*. Halifax and Winnipeg: Fernwood Publishing.

Magnusson, Rachel. 2015. "A Politics in Writing: Jacques Rancière and the Equality of Intelligences." In *Thinking Radical Democracy: The Return to Politics in Post-War France*, edited by Martin Breaugh, Christopher Holman, Rachel Magnusson, Paul Mazzocchi, and Devin Penner, 189–209. Toronto: University of Toronto Press.

Manuel, Arthur. 2017. "The Reconciliation Manifesto." In Arthur Manuel and Grand Chief Ronald Derrickson, *The Reconciliation Manifesto: Recovering the Land, Rebuilding the Economy*, 47–292. Toronto: James Lorimer and Co.

Marchart, Oliver. 2011. "The Second Return of the Political: Democracy and the Syllogism of Equality." In *Reading Rancière: Critical Dissensus*, edited by Paul Bowman and Richard Stamp, 129–47. London: Continuum.

Marcuse, Herbert. (1969) 2007. "Repressive Tolerance." In *The Essential Marcuse: Selected Writings of Philosopher and Social Critic Herbert Marcuse*, edited by Andrew Feenberg and William Leiss, 32–59. Boston: Beacon Press.

Marso, Lori Jo. 2017. *Politics with Beauvoir: Freedom in the Encounter*. Durham, NC: Duke University Press.

Martinot, Steve. 2008. "Skin for Sale: Race and *The Respectful Prostitute*." In *Race after Sartre: Antiracism, Africana Existentialism, Postcolonialism*, edited by Jonathan Judaken, 55–76. Albany: State University of New York Press.

Marx, Karl. (1844a) 1967. "Critical Notes on 'The King of Prussia and Social Reform.'" In *Writings of the Young Marx on Philosophy and Society*, edited by Loyd D. Easton and Kurt H. Guddat, 338–58. Garden City, NY: Doubleday and Co.

Marx, Karl. (1844b) 1994. "Toward a Critique of Hegel's *Philosophy of Right*: Introduction." In Marx, *Selected Writings*, edited by Lawrence H. Simon, 27–39. Indianapolis: Hackett.

Marx, Karl. (1859) 1994. "Preface to *A Contribution to the Critique of Political Econo-my*." In Marx, *Selected Writings*, edited by Lawrence H. Simon, 209–13. Indianapo-lis: Hackett.

Marx, Karl. (1867) 1990. *Capital*, vol. 1. Translated by Ben Fowkes. London: Penguin.

Marx, Karl. 1994. *Selected Writings*. Edited by Lawrence H. Simon. Indianapolis: Hackett.

Marx, Karl, and Friedrich Engels. (1848) 1994. "The Communist Manifesto." In Marx, *Selected Writings*, edited by Lawrence H. Simon, 158–86. Indianapolis: Hackett.

Mathias, Christopher, and Andy Campbell. 2019. "Proud Boys, Outnumbered by Anti-fascists, Get Police Escort after 30 Minute Rally." Huffington Post, August 18, 2019. https://www.huffingtonpost.ca/entry/proud-boys-portland-rally_n_5d59390ee4b0eb875f2539c4.

May, Todd. 2007. "Rancière in South Carolina." In *Jacques Rancière: History, Politics, Aesthetics*, edited by Gabriel Rockhill and Philip Watts, 105–19. Durham, NC: Duke University Press.

May, Todd. 2008. *The Political Thought of Jacques Rancière: Creating Equality*. Uni-versity Park: Pennsylvania State University Press.

May, Todd. 2012a. *Friendship in an Age of Economics: Resisting the Forces of Neolib-eralism*. Lanham, MD: Lexington Books.

May, Todd. 2012b. "Rancière and Anarchism." In *Jacques Rancière and the Contempo-rary Scene: The Philosophy of Radical Equality*, edited by Jean-Philippe Deranty and Alison Ross, 117–27. London: Continuum.

May, Todd. 2015. *Nonviolent Resistance: A Philosophical Introduction*. Malden, MA: Polity Press.

May, Todd. 2016. "Nonviolence, Disidentification, Equality." Satyagraha Foundation for Nonviolence Studies, July 28, 2016. http://www.satyagrahafoundation.org/nonviolence-disidentification-and-equality.

May, Todd. 2018. "Histories of Violence: Nonviolence and the Ghost of Fascism." Interview by Brad Evans. *Los Angeles Review of Books*, May 21, 2018. https://lareviewofbooks.org/article/histories-of-violence-nonviolence-and-the-ghost-of-fascism.

Maynard, Robyn. 2017. *Policing Black Lives: State Violence in Canada from Slavery to the Present*. Halifax and Winnipeg: Fernwood Publishing.

Mill, J. S. 2015. *On Liberty, Utilitarianism, and Other Essays*. Edited by Mark Philp and Frederick Rosen. Oxford: Oxford University Press.

Moreton-Robinson, Aileen. 2015. *The White Possessive: Property, Power, and Indige-nous Sovereignty*. Minneapolis: University of Minnesota Press.

Moufawad-Paul, J. 2019. *Demarcation and Demystification: Philosophy and Its Limits*. Winchester, UK: Zer0 Books.

Murphy, Ann V. 2006. "Between Generosity and Violence: Toward a Revolutionary Politics in the Philosophy of Simone de Beauvoir." In *The Philosophy of Simone de Beauvoir: Critical Essays*, edited by Margaret A. Simons, 262–75. Bloomington, IL: Indiana University Press.

Negri, Antonio. 2007. *Political Descartes: Reason, Ideology, and the Bourgeois Pro-ject*. Translated by Matteo Mandarini and Alberto Toscano. London: Verso.

Nelson, Steven. 2017. "Noam Chomsky: Antifa Is a 'Major Gift to the Right.'" *Wash-ington Examiner*, August 17, 2017. https://www.washingtonexaminer.com/noam-chomsky-antifa-is-a-major-gift-to-the-right.

Nietzsche, Friedrich. 2014. *Beyond Good and Evil/On the Genealogy of Morality*. Translated by Adrian Del Caro. Stanford, CA: Stanford University Press.

Patton, Paul. 2012. "Rancière's Utopian Politics." In *Jacques Rancière and the Contem-porary Scene: The Philosophy of Radical Equality*, edited by Jean-Philippe Deranty and Alison Ross, 129–43. London: Continuum.

Paxton, Robert O. 2004. *The Anatomy of Fascism*. New York: Vintage Books.

Rancière, Jacques. (1976) 2007. "Introduction." In *La parole ouvrière*, edited by Alain Faure and Jacques Rancière, 7–19. Paris: La fabrique.

Rancière, Jacques. (1985) 2011. "Heretical Knowledge and the Emancipation of the Poor." In *Staging the People: The Proletarian and His Double*, translated by David Fernbach, 34–56. London: Verso, 2011.

Rancière, Jacques. (1987) 1991. *The Ignorant Schoolmaster: Five Lessons in Intellectual Emancipation*. Translated by Kristin Ross. Stanford, CA: Stanford University Press.

Rancière, Jacques. (1995) 1999. *Disagreement: Politics and Philosophy*. Translated by Julie Rose. Minneapolis: University of Minnesota Press. Originally published as *La Mésentente: Politique et philosophie* (Paris: Galilée).

Rancière, Jacques. 1998a. "The Cause of the Other." *Parallax* 4 (2): 25–33.

Rancière, Jacques. (1998b) 2010. "Ten Theses on Politics." In *Dissensus: On Politics and Aesthetics*, edited by Steven Corcoran, 27–44. London: Continuum.

Rancière, Jacques. 2004. *Aux bords du politique*. Paris: Gallimard.

Rancière, Jacques. 2007a. *On the Shores of Politics*. Translated by Liz Heron. London: Verso.

Rancière, Jacques. 2007b. "Postface." In *La parole ouvrière*, edited by Alain Faure and Jacques Rancière, 332–42. Paris: La fabrique.

Rancière, Jacques. 2009. "Jacques Rancière et l'a-disciplinarité." In *Et tant pis pour les gens fatigues*, 474–89. Paris: Editions Amsterdam.

Rancière, Jacques. (2011a) 2013. *Aisthesis: Scenes from the Aesthetic Regime of Art*. Translated by Zakir Paul. London: Verso.

Rancière, Jacques. 2011b. "The Thinking of Dissensus: Politics and Aesthetics." In *Reading Rancière: Critical Dissensus*, edited by Paul Bowman and Richard Stamp, 1–17. London: Continuum.

Rancière, Jacques. (2012) 2016. *The Method of Equality*. Translated by Julie Rose. Cambridge: Polity Press.

Rancière, Jacques. 2016. "Critical Questions on the Theory of Recognition." In Honneth, Axel, and Rancière, *Recognition or Disagreement: A Critical Encounter on the Politics of Freedom, Equality, and Identity*, edited by Katia Genel and Jean-Philippe Deranty, 83–95. New York: Columbia University Press.

Robinson, Rowland "Enāēmaehkiw" Keshena. 2019. "Fascism and Anti-Fascism: A Decolonial Perspective." *Maehkōn Ahpēhtesewen*. February 11, 2017. https://onkwehonwerising.wordpress.com/2017/02/11/fascism-anti-fascism-a-decolonial-perspective.

Roediger, David R. 1999. *The Wages of Whiteness: Race and the Making of the American Working Class*. Rev. ed. London: Verso.

Ross, Alexander Reid. 2017. *Against the Fascist Creep*. Chico, CA: AK Press.

Russell, Matheson, and Andrew Montin. 2015. "The Rationality of Political Disagreement: Rancière's Critique of Habermas." *Constellations* 22 (4): 543–54.

Sakai, J. (2002) 2017. "The Shock of Recognition: Looking at Hamerquist's Fascism and Anti-Fascism." In *Confronting Fascism: Discussion Documents for a Militant Movement*, edited by Don Hamerquist, J. Sakai, Anti-Racist Action Chicago, and Mark Salotte, 95–197. 2nd ed. Montreal: Kersplebedeb.

Sakai, J. 2003. "Aryan Politics and Fighting the WTO." In *My Enemy's Enemy: Essays on Globalization, Fascism and the Struggle against Fascism*, edited by Anti-Fascist Forum 2003, 7–34. 3rd ed. Montreal: Kersplebedeb.

Santoni, Ronald E. 2003. *Sartre on Violence: Curiously Ambivalent*. University Park: Pennsylvania State University Press.

Santoni, Ronald E. 2005. "The Bad Faith of Violence: And Is Sartre in Bad Faith Regarding It?" *Sartre Studies International* 11 (1–2): 62–77.

Santoni, Ronald E. 2015. "Liberatory Violence, Bad Faith, and Moral Justification: A Reply." *Sartre Studies International* 21 (2): 74–84.
Sartre, Jean-Paul. (1943) 1956. *Being and Nothingness*. Translated by Hazel Barnes. New York: Washington Square Press.
Sartre, Jean Paul. (1946a) 1995. *Anti-Semite and Jew*. Translated by George J. Becker. New York: Schocken.
Sartre, Jean Paul. (1946b) 2007. *Existentialism Is a Humanism*. Edited by John Kulka. New Haven, CT: Yale University Press.
Sartre, Jean-Paul. (1947) 2010. "Cartesian Freedom." In *Critical Essays: Situations I*, translated by Chris Turner, 498–532. London: Seagull Books.
Sartre, Jean-Paul. (1957) 2006. "Albert Memmi's *The Colonizer and the Colonized.*" In *Colonialism and Neocolonialism*, translated by Azzedine Haddour, Steve Brewer, and Terry McWilliams, 56–62. London: Routledge.
Sartre, Jean-Paul. 1992. *Notebooks for an Ethics*. Translated by David Pellauer. Chicago: University of Chicago Press.
Sartre, Jean-Paul. 2005. "Morale et Histoire." *Les Temps Modernes*, nos. 632–634, 268–414.
Sartre, Jean-Paul. 2015. "Les racines de l'éthique." *Etudes sartriennes* 19:11–118.
Schonfeld, Zach. 2017. "Is It Okay to Punch a Nazi in the Face? Leading Ethicists Weigh In: 'No.'" *Newsweek*, January 24, 2017. http://www.newsweek.com/richard-spencer-punch-nazi-ethicists-547277.
Sewell, Jr., William H. 1980. *Work and Revolution in France: The Language of Labor from the Old Regime to 1848*. Cambridge: Cambridge University Press.
Shaw, Devin Zane. 2016a. *Egalitarian Moments: From Descartes to Rancière*. London: Bloomsbury.
Shaw, Devin Zane. 2016b. "Review of Matthew R. McLennan, *Philosophy, Sophistry, Antiphilosophy: Badiou's Dispute with Lyotard.*" *Symposium*, July 7, 2016. https://www.c-scp.org/2016/07/07/matthew-r-mclennan-philosophy-sophistry-antiphilosophy.
Shaw, Devin Zane. 2017. "Disagreement and Recognition between Rancière and Honneth," *Boundary2 Online*, March 13, 2017. https://www.boundary2.org/2017/03/devin-zane-shaw-disagreement-and-recognition-between-ranciere-and-honneth.
Shepherd, Katie. 2019a. "Portland Police Made a Dubious Claim about Protesters' Milkshakes on Twitter. What's the Evidence?" *Willamette Week*, July 2, 2019. https://www.wweek.com/news/city/2019/07/02/portland-police-made-a-dubious-claim-about-protesters-milkshakes-on-twitter-whats-the-evidence.
Shepherd, Katie. 2019b. "Texts Between Portland Police and Patriot Prayer Ringleader Joey Gibson Show Warm Exchange." *Willamette Week*, February 14, 2019. https://www.wweek.com/news/courts/2019/02/14/texts-between-portland-police-and-patriot-prayer-ringleader-joey-gibson-show-warm-exchange.
Simons, Margaret A. 1999. *Beauvoir and the Second Sex: Feminism, Race, and the Origins of Existentialism*. Lanham, MD: Rowman & Littlefield.
Simpson, Leanne Betasamosake, ed. 2008. *Lighting the Eighth Fire: The Liberation, Resurgence, and Protection of Indigenous Nations*. Winnipeg, Canada: Arbiter Ring Publishing.
Simpson, Leanne Betasamosake. 2017. *As We Have Always Done: Indigenous Freedom through Radical Resistance*. Minneapolis: University of Minnesota Press.
This Week in Fascism. 2019. "This Week in Fascism #23: Don't Let the Bridge Hit You on the Way Out." It's Going Down. August 19, 2019. https://itsgoingdown.org/this-week-in-fascism-23-dont-let-the-bridge-hit-you-on-the-way-out.
Tuck, Eve, and K. Wayne Yang. 2012. "Decolonization Is Not a Metaphor." *Decolonization: Indigeneity, Education and Society* 1 (1): 1–40.

Williams, Robert F. (1962) 1998. *Negroes with Guns*. Detroit, MI: Wayne State University Press.

Wolfe, Patrick. 2016. *Traces of History: Elementary Structures of Race*. London: Verso.

Woodford, Clare. 2015. "'Reinventing Modes of Dreaming' and Doing: Jacques Rancière and Strategies for the New Left." *Philosophy and Social Criticism* 41 (8): 811–36.

Zackodnik, Teresa. 2010. "Reaching toward a Red-Black Coalitional Feminism: Anna Julia Cooper's 'Woman versus the Indian.'" In *Indigenous Women and Feminism: Politics, Activism, Culture*, edited by Cheryl Suzack, Shari M. Huhndorf, Jeanne Perrault, and Jean Barman, 109–25. Vancouver, Canada: UBC Press.

Žižek, Slavoj. 1999. *The Ticklish Subject: The Absent Centre of Political Ontology*. London: Verso.

Žižek, Slavoj. 2002. "Afterword: Lenin's Choice." In *Revolution at the Gates: Selected Writings of Lenin from 1917*, edited by Slavoj Žižek, 167–336. London: Verso.

# INDEX

# ABOUT THE AUTHOR

**Devin Zane Shaw** teaches philosophy at Douglas College, Canada. He is author of *Egalitarian Moments: From Descartes to Rancière* (2016) and *Freedom and Nature in Schelling's Philosophy of Art* (2010). He writes about philosophy, political theory, and social movements, and co-edits the Living Existentialism book series.